Not just Porridge:
English Literati at Table

Not just Porridge:
English Literati at Table

edited by

Francesca Orestano and

Michael Vickers

Archaeopress Publishing Ltd

Summertown Pavilion
18-24 Middle Way
Oxford OX2 7LG

www.archaeopress.com

ISBN 978 1 78491 578 0
ISBN 978 1 78491 579 7 (e-Pdf)

© Archaeopress and the authors 2017

Originally published in 2015 as *Non solo porridge: letterati inglesi a tavola* by Mimesis Edizioni

Translated into English by the contributors

Cover image; https://commons.wikimedia.org/wiki/File:A_skeletal_figure_surveying_three_doctors_around_a_cauldron,_Wellcome_L0001225.jpg

All rights reserved. No part of this book may be reproduced, or transmitted, in any form or by any means, electronic, mechanical, photocopying or otherwise, without the prior written permission of the copyright owners.

This book is available direct from Archaeopress or from our website www.archaeopress.com

Contents

Francesca Orestano
Introduction. Food tasted and described: a kind of literary history iii

Cristina Paravano
Roger of Ware: a medieval masterchef in Chaucer's *Canterbury Tales* 1

Margaret Rose
Caliban's dinner 13

Giovanni Iamartino
At table with Dr Johnson: food for the body, nourishment for the mind 17

Chiara Biscella
Jane Austen: appetite and sensibility 35

Anna Rudelli
Romantic food at Dove Cottage: Dorothy Wordsworth's cookery and kitchen garden 43

Marco Canani
Percy Bysshe Shelley, a vegetarian poet 57

Beatrice Moja
Mrs Beeton: cooking, science, and innovations in the Victorian kitchen 69

Claudia Cremonesi
Charles Dickens from street food to the restaurant 81

Elena Ogliari
Henry James goes on a diet: a chronicle of a private drama 93

Karin Mosca
Bennett, Strachey and the preparation of the omelette 107

Maria Cristina Mancini
Leopold Bloom's grilled mutton kidneys 117

Francesca Orestano
Virginia Woolf and the cooking range 125

Francesca Gorini
A. A. Milne: Tea (and lots of honey) in the Hundred Acre Wood 135

Angela Anna Iuliucci
Roald Dahl's revolting food fantasies 145

Ilaria Parini
Bridget Jones and the temptations of *junk food* *153*

Dalila Forni
Coraline: frozen food vs a warm-hearted family? 165

Notes on the authors 177

Francesca Orestano

Introduction

Food tasted and described: a kind of literary history

This book was concocted during the meetings and debates held in the attic cells of the former convent near the church of St Alexander, today part of the Department of Foreign Languages, in Milan. A group of young English literature scholars (a couple a bit less young) used to meet there and discuss literature and food, prompted by the theme that EXPO was ubiquitously advertising – 'Food for the planet, energy for life'. Gradually, unexpectedly, the first ideas kept growing into a common project, overflowing across the centuries, involving more authors, books, recipes. Now that the task is completed, offering a survey that embraces medieval culinary adventures as well as today's predicament with junk food and exotic frozen substances, one may suggest that it does not just offer a map of cookery in England across the centuries, but that in its very idiosyncratic and humble way it also provides a kind of literary history, albeit told from a gastronomic perspective.

It is a literary canon *sui generis*: having been established by analysing the food preferences and discourses of famous men and women of letters, by poets and novelists. Our book lingers on the threshold of the kitchen rather than in the classroom: closer to the cooking range than to library shelves and their precious tomes. But the material from which these essays are made is also, undeniably, the ingredient – the crumbs, the leftovers? – of whatever exists in texts of a more elevated literary genre and authoritative reputation.

The first essay by Cristina Paravano focuses, in a light but scholarly way, on Roger of Ware, and offers a portrait of a late fourteenth century masterchef. He is not a secondary character in the group of pilgrims described by Geoffrey Chaucer, the 'father' of English literature. On the road between London and Canterbury the cook often has his say and the journey is enriched by aromas and ingredients of recipes that announce a local food culture, but also keen to mix local products with spices imported from distant countries, creating unusual combinations. This adventurous attitude towards the exotic in matters of food is even more clear in the contribution of Margaret 'Maggie' Rose. Caliban's dinner on the one hand reminds the reader that in the sixteenth century in England poor people went foraging, and foraging in the fields and open country provided them with a variety of edible vegetables. Their meat diet was very limited. On the other hand, the island colonised by Prospero suggests that there are new and exotic types of food, such as ground nuts – potatoes already? – that Caliban digs from the earth, plus berries, monkeys to be roasted, and strange scamels. This is the age of Shakespeare, with its division into the King and the poor, slaves and masters, domestic and exotic: the island contains and reveals those social and cultural tensions that will flare up in the conflict between King and Parliament, and in the war that will mark the central decades of the 17th century.

But these problems do not seem to affect Izaak Walton, who composes his fishing manual, *The Compleat Angler* (1653), in the heat of the war. Walton strolls along his placid stream, thinking about pike and trout, devices for angling, hooks and bait: and then he gives us a wonderful recipe for carp. Take the carp, scour him clean, open the fish and place inside some small bundles of Marjoram, Thyme, Parsley, a sprig of Rosemary, some Onions, a few pickled Oysters and three Anchovies.

> Then pour upon your Carp as much claret wine as will onely [*sic*] cover him; and season your claret well with salt, Cloves and Mace, and the rinds of Oranges and Lemons, cover your pot and set it on a quick fire, till it be sufficiently boiled; then take out the Carp and lay it with the broth into the dish, and pour upon it a quarter of a pound of fresh butter melted and beaten, with half a dozen spoonfuls of the broth, the yolks of two or three eggs, and some of the herbs shred, garnish your dish with Lemons and so serve it up.

Everything is fresh and local: but the French claret wine, cloves and mace, and the rinds of oranges and lemons, altogether suggest that frequent exchanges and imported products shape the English taste. Increasingly, commerce becomes the factor that places England at the centre of the world. Thus Joseph Addison in the *Spectator* (1711, n. 69) can describe London as 'this metropolis a kind of emporium for the whole earth'. And he explains to the readers of one of the first European periodicals, that while nature spreads her products everywhere, England is the place where they are enjoyed, owing to its intense commerce with distant countries:

> The food often grows in one country, and the sauce in another. The fruits of Portugal are corrected by the products of Barbadoes: the infusion of a China plant sweetened with the pith of an Indian cane. The Philippick Islands give a flavour to our European bowls.

Tea, spices, cane sugar. Even though English weather does not help, and local berries are very sour, exotic delights like peaches, figs, apricots and melons come to the island, the centre indeed of a global market.

> Natural historians tell us, that no fruit grows originally among us, besides hips, and haws, acorns and pig-nuts, with other delicates of the like nature; that our climate of itself, and without the assistances of art, can make no further advances towards a plum than to a sloe, and carries an apple to no greater a perfection than a crab: that our melons, our peaches, our figs, our apricots, and cherries, are strangers among us, imported in different ages, and naturalised in our English gardens; and that they would all degenerate and fall away into the trash of our own country, if they were wholly neglected by the planter, and left to the mercy of our sun and soil.

Merchants, natural historians, scholars in botanical science, geographers channel towards England an unceasing flux of information, specimens of seeds and plants:

> Our ships are laden with the harvest of every climate; our tables are stored with spices, and oils, and wines: [...]. My friend Sir Andrew calls the vineyards of France our gardens: the spice-islands our hot-beds; [...]. Nature indeed furnishes us with the bare necessaries of life, but traffick gives us greater variety of what is useful, and at the same time supplies us with everything that is convenient and ornamental. Nor is it the least part of this our happiness, that whilst we enjoy the remotest products of the north and south, we are free from those extremities of weather which give them birth; that our eyes are refreshed with the green fields of Britain, at the same time that our palates are feasted with fruits that rise between the tropicks.

All over the 'green fields of Britain' there are gardens and intensive cultivations: hot greenhouses enable delicate vegetables from faraway lands to be grown, for the tables of the wealthy. Alexander Pope describes the ceremony of coffee-making in *The Rape of the Lock*: a hot, scented and aromatic drink is sipped in China cups, by dainty bejewelled ladies, between card games and other amusements typical of Queen Anne's day. Our poet could well describe the fashionable liquor, being himself a gourmet, and, as the legend goes, meeting his death through an excess of potted lampreys.

Giovanni Iamartino shows that from the limited perspective of food it is possible to paint a fresco of a whole century. This happens when the subject of the investigation is Samuel Johnson, the man of letters who 'is' the eighteenth century, as our Johnson scholar reminds us at the opening of his essay. Not only does Johnson appear as the genial editor of the *Dictionary*, where the entries devoted to food abound, but he also offers his biographers – Iamartino culls rich material from four biographies – a remarkable amount of reflections on food, and on mankind. With typical philosophical shrewdness and culinary wit, acknowledging his preferences but keeping his appetite under control, Dr Johnson provides the features of a detailed cultural landscape. The context is London, already a modern, swinging city where he often dines out, invited by friends, or at a restaurant; where it is possible to buy food already cooked, take-away food indeed, and where dining out means to share conversation as well as food, so that a serious subject can be debated while tasting the best lamb or veal – and avoiding porridge and vegetables.

Poised between appetite and sensibility, Chiara Biscella draws a portrait of Jane Austen, the writer who even today enjoys an unceasing dialogue with her fans, in the many blogs devoted to her works. In her novels Austen cleverly orchestrates dinners and tea ceremonies, where, together with the movements of teapots and trays of sweets, we can follow the development of social relationships – not always marked by sweetness. Above steaming cups of tea, glances, words, whispers and reticent silences are observed. The formal sequence of the necessary actions required for the preparation and consumption of a cup of tea – actions belonging to a ritual that even today denotes Englishness (despite the replacement of cups with mugs, and of tea leaves, once religiously kept in the tea caddy, with practical tea bags) – allows Austen's heroines to hide cautiously in the background, but without missing for an instant the drama that is unfolding on the drawing room public stage. Far from these mundane contexts, the Romantics enjoy their rural pleasures.

Anna Rudelli knowledgeably describes the environment and the typical day of the Wordsworth siblings at Dove Cottage, in the Lake District. As one suspected, the sister of the poet is responsible for the domestic ménage. In the kitchen garden Dorothy grows beans, peas and various vegetables, picks gooseberries; at home, she makes bread, savoury pies and sweet biscuits, and she cooks the pike and bream that William occasionally catches in the lake. The romantic group around the Wordsworths often enjoys excursions among the picturesque Cumberland hills, lakes and waterfalls: on such occasions Dorothy prepares sandwiches, filled with cold meat, using the leftovers from previous meals. Hers is a careful domestic economy, or rather ecology, where nothing goes wasted: and it will be so even when they move from the small uncomfortable Dove Cottage to the commodious and larger Rydal Mount. But not all the poets live in the quiet, rural environment of the Lakes: much more inclined to travelling, Byron and Shelley share, albeit differently, a conception of the human animal that eschews cannibalism, hence the non-consumption of animal meat. Shelley, as Marco Canani reminds us in an essay full of critical hints for further research, transposes his notion of feral instinct into a philosophy of life. The poet is wholly in favour of a vegetarian diet, followed with a strict, almost religious conviction. The description of Shelley, intent on munching pieces of bread even when he reads in the library, at the university, or converses with friends, is one that stays in our mind, together with that circle of crumbs spread on the floor, all around his armchair. Bread, oranges, dried raisins, honey and biscuits: Shelley has definitely a sweet tooth, but Canani also sets an accent on a whole period when vegetarianism and the vegetarian diet had an increasing number of votaries.

Not so for Isabella Beeton. Universally known for her *Book of Household Management*, a weighty volume of over 1000 pages published in 1861, this young writer offered a compendium for the Victorian household where the question of food is indeed central. The subject was treated by means of practical recipes, indexed, so that beside the list of ingredients and cooking method there was also to be found the cost of the preparation and the ideal season in which to obtain a successful result. Illustrations in colour completed the volume. In the pages of Mrs Beeton, introduced by Beatrice Moja in all their rich and modern complexity, we spot the Victorian way of life, and especially of those middle-class families keen on appropriating the secrets and esoteric jargon of the celebrated French chefs operating in aristocratic mansions. But the accent also fell on saving. Canned food was cheaper than fresh produce, and Mrs Beeton proposes clever imitations of costly dishes: just like Lewis Carroll who in *Alice in Wonderland* mentions a Mock Turtle that looks – and probably tasted – very much like veal. The Victorian mistress celebrates Christmas festivities with the flames of a Christmas pudding: but after this family gathering, she is also intent on cooking for the poor gallons of beneficent soup, and on feeding a special diet to invalids. A very angel in the house, a stronghold of the domestic sanctuary, according to Mrs Beeton.

Dickens instead, as we might predict from his writings, speaks at first from the streets of London. Much later in his life, and already a famous writer, he describes one of those restaurants that have sprouted like mushrooms together with the modern railway system. Introduced by Claudia Cremonesi, who has written excellent pages on the subject, a very young Boz takes pleasure in whatever is cooked in the streets, and describes with great gusto the stalls and street vendors with their enticing display of ready-cooked food. From the early morning until late evening, muffins, and steak and kidney pies inundate the busy streets of London with their tempting aromas. Many years later, a mature Dickens, dressed as the uncommercial traveller, looks for a restaurant between one train and the next. But restaurants in London seem to fall below any acceptable standard, especially those new establishments near the railway stations. Definitely for Dickens the street food tasted during his youth was inimitable. And let us not forget, in this context, the divorced wife of the great writer. Catherine Dickens, under the pseudonym of Lady Maria Clutterbuck, would produce a cookbook entitled *What Shall We Have for Dinner?* (1851). Her selection of menus would go through five editions until 1860.

In the last decades of the century, and in the following one, England becomes the home of a famous expatriate, Henry James. During his first years abroad he feels deep nostalgia for food from New England; he considers with suspicion the menus of the Continent (Italians fry too much!); but despite these shortcomings James is also tormented by a nightmare, of putting on too much weight. A meat eater, but also very keen on sweets, the American expatriate undergoes very laborious digestive processes. He likes eating practically everything, and especially the tasty condiments and rich sauces accompanying a good roast beef. In desperation, he eventually relies on a diet guru, a certain Mr Fletcher, whose method consists of imposing a very long chewing process for each morsel of food. The practical result is that James ends up by eating alone. Elena Ogliari describes with wit and gusto all these aspects, altogether offering a modern and touching portrayal of James's digestive drama. The writer will eventually abandon Fletcherism, to return, fat and joyously free, to the pleasures of conviviality and good food.

There are not two writers more different than Arnold Bennett and Lytton Strachey. Karin Mosca puts them side by side in her essay, using the omelette as a bridge between the two. Bennett, a materialist writer according to Virginia Woolf, belongs to the school of the realistic detail; Strachey seasons his biographies with doses of pungent irony, Freudian insights, pitiless stabs at the subjects he portrays. The former dines at the Savoy: the latter likes his milk and biscuits in bed. But both speak about the omelette, albeit from two very different viewpoints. Karin Mosca cleverly follows this game of mirrors, and the character of the two men of letters. Behind the positions taken by Bennett and Strachey, as far as the omelette is concerned, we may now descry the dawning of a new century, a less Victorian England, less bent on domestic rituals and willing to build up an *entente cordiale* with the seductive French cuisine.

At the same time, however, a distinct note had sounded in the work of John Ruskin. In *The Ethics of the Dust* (1866),), Ruskin had been the advocate of a healthy attitude to food, of a modern awareness of its value inseparable from the notion of waste. Matching the knowledge of past tradition to modern science, Ruskin had also traced the path to our present notions about food culture, adding to it a remarkable international note, that set English cuisine at the centre of a map made of diverse traditions, rather than enclosing it within the insularity of national recipes:

> Cookery means the knowledge [...] of all herbs and fruits and balms and spices, and all that is healing and sweet in the fields and groves and savoury in meats. It means carefulness, and inventiveness, and watchfulness, and willingness, and readiness of appliance; it means the economy of your

great-grandmothers, and the science of the modern chemists; it means much tasting, and no wasting; it means English thoroughness, and French art, and Arabian hospitality [...].

With Maria Cristina Mancini we move to James Joyce's eternal Ireland. Here Leopold Bloom, on a very special day, strolls along the streets of Dublin, allowing the reader to peep into butcher shops where delicious kidney, to be cooked in butter, is displayed; to enter restaurants of a popular kind, and restaurants for vegetarians, where people eat in haste and pints of ale are imbibed. The vagabond Bloom, in his adventurous circumnavigation, led by chance and appetite, ends up by eating a gorgonzola sandwich, with a glass of Burgundy. In pages that blend gastronomy and critical insights, we follow our modern Ulysses who closes his long day with a bedtime drink of hot chocolate.

Virginia Woolf is a different case. Born to a wealthy family of the upper middle class, the writer provides a striking example of the dramatic changes that mark twentieth century culture. In her life there won't be as many servants as in the past, and cooks sweating in the hot and dark inferno of the kitchen, in the basement: Woolf learns to cook, buys a modern cooking range, and next to her activity as a writer she can make bread, and some good dishes. Food, however, is also part of her writing: it figures as a persuasive strategy to support university education for women in *A Room of One's Own.* Here she sets a genial comparison between the lunch fare and the dinner of two colleges, in Oxbridge, one for men, the other for women. But her life is also marked by two wars, and two periods in which food has to be rationed. Virginia and Leonard celebrate the end of World War One by eating, at last, some chocolate.

Meanwhile other authors, who write for a young readership, celebrate a serene, enchanted world, peopled by funny stuffed animals. These are the protagonists of the books by A. A. Milne – escapist stories, as defined by the critic Peter Hunt – where in a reassuring wood lots of honey and malt biscuits are eaten. These books are typical of the 1920s, when England looks back with nostalgia to its ancient rural community life, trying to forget about the European waste land. Francesca Gorini deconstructs the diet of the bear Winnie-the-Pooh, in the context of what was considered healthy food for children, while the essay of Angela Anna Iuliucci is devoted to a much less reassuring author, the Roald Dahl of *Revolting Rhymes* (1982). Despite being a children's writer, Dahl directly enters the frightening area of the gothic. Iuliucci, who has already scanned that critical area, comparing visual and verbal texts, detects in Dahl's work, and especially in his *Revolting Recipes* – recipes based on worms, beetles, and similar disgusting dainties – a subtle play between irony and critique of the adult world, and its strange recipes. These are rewritten with an attitude of parody and desecration, typical of many modern children's literature texts.

Finally, the last two essays take the reader to the threshold of contemporary literature and food culture. Ilaria Parini writes on *The Diary of Bridget Jones* (1996), a modern anti-heroine who makes up for her sentimental disappointments with orgies of ready-made food – junk food indeed – and almost daily decisions to go on a diet. The passages that Parini includes in her excellent essay signal that a remarkable change has occurred in that very London where Dickens used to celebrate street food. Here and now, instead, on the shelves of a supermarket, Bridget is seduced by the coloured wrappings that represent what the consumer should find inside. But those seductive images find their counterpoint on the other side of the box, where the carbohydrates, fat and sugar of the chosen food are listed.

Dalila Forni explores with critical acumen the question of today's food from the perspective of a young girl, the protagonist of the novel *Coraline* (2002) by Neil Gaiman. How can she make the correct choice between her real mother and the 'other mother' hiding behind a magic door? How can she choose between the frozen food, warmed up by her mother in the microwave oven, and a mother who seems keen on cooking good, traditional recipes? And what about Coraline's father, bent on strange culinary experiments? The road to the correct choice, that leads to the discovery of true family values beyond the traditionally defined roles, is also the road to maturity, where fantasy is dismissed to return to reality – even if this may not always be completely satisfying. Today, microwaved food and frozen food are the customary choice for families who can share precious moments of intimacy for only a limited time in the evening. This essay is the last one in an itinerary that reflects several centuries of food culture in England, but also indirectly traces a literary history, with a formidable sequence of authors, humours and cultural contexts.

Last but not least, our literary gastronomical identity is underlined by complementing each essay with one or more recipes, culled from contemporary cooking manuals, or directly taken from the authors' biographies. These recipes (sometime with metric measurements, sometime using cups, spoons, liquid or solid ounces) may still be attempted by the curious reader who intends to give body and taste to the authors and to the aromas of the periods examined in the book.

Many thanks to Marco Modenesi, both from the authors and the editors: from the very beginning he has generously supported our project. Thanks to all the contributors, the English literature scholars but especially the young ones, who have accepted the challenge of writing essays at once light and well-informed. Thanks above all to Manana Odisheli and Michael Vickers, who have genially promoted the fortunes of this book across the Channel; to Stefano Raimondi, of Mimesis, who has granted the rights to our English publisher, David Davison, to whom our final expressions of gratitude are justly due.

This book is an immigrant. Crossing the Channel, it has received a warm welcome, and that kind of substantial and expert help that allows a foreign product to exist into a new cultural milieu, and in a different language. We are aware that best practice in operations like this requires that a text translated into English be read by a native English speaker prior to publication: Michael Vickers – again, very generously and kindly – performed this task.

Francesca Orestano
Milan, Summer 2016

Cristina Paravano

Roger of Ware: a medieval masterchef in Chaucer's *Canterbury Tales*

The last few decades have seen a steady increase in the number of food shows worldwide: from the highly competitive *Masterchef* to informative programmes on how to cook, like *Jamie's 30 Minute Meals*, and TV formats shedding light on the theatre of cooking, like *Cake Boss*. All kinds of contestants are welcomed: amateurs, famous stars, professionals, even child participants, all eager to get their chance to become the new Gordon Ramsay. The key feature of all these shows is the presence of influential and charismatic chefs as judges, such as Jamie Oliver or Buddy Valastro. Nowadays celebrity chefs stand in a preeminent position: they are the rock stars of the gastronomic world, trendsetters and culinary artists able to attain astonishing quality standards while offering dishes at exorbitantly high prices.

Not only are they experts in contemporary techniques but some of them experiment with recipes from long ago, by designing new dishes to enable their clients to savour the food of years gone by. In the American cooking series *A Taste of History*,[1] Chef Walter Staib retraces the gastronomic history of the country from its beginnings by preparing traditional recipes in famous historic locations. On the other side of the ocean, in the 2013 celebrity version of *Masterchef UK*, the audience travelled back in time. Six contestants in two teams were asked to create a medieval banquet for an army of knights in armour and cook the food in a tent outside Warwick Castle.

The Middle Ages is certainly one of the most intriguing and appealing periods in this respect. People enjoy eating at Medieval-themed restaurants, visiting fairs and festivals devoted to characters from that era, such as King Arthur or Robin Hood, and breathing its evocative atmosphere. Moreover, several websites, like 'The Old Foodie' or the award-winning 'Gode Cookery', are dedicated to food and recipes from the Middle Ages and encourage people to prepare a Medieval style meal at home.[2] The success of this period is also confirmed by the creation

---

[1] See the show website at www.atasteofhistory.org.
[2] Among the most popular websites: www.theoldfoodie.com, www.godecookery.com and www.medievalcookery.com.

Midsummer Medieval Festival, Castle of Amorosa Winery, Napa Valley, California, USA.
(Wikimedia Commons)

of the 'Society for Creative Anachronism',[3] an international organization which has celebrated the Middle Ages and the Renaissance for 50 years. Since 1966 they have been recreating Medieval events and gatherings, as in the case of a feast for the Arthurian Round Table (1993) and a Chaucerian Feast (1992)[4] hosted by the Shire of Afenegara and prepared by Chef Lord Ian Damebrigge of Wychwood. The celebration also included a tournament and a quest inspired by the story of the pilgrims heading to Canterbury. It goes without saying that all the menu items are mentioned in Geoffrey Chaucer's works.

Within the Chaucerian corpus, *The Canterbury Tales* is by far the richest in references and allusions to food and its preparation. The work offers a variety of eating habits with a strong moral and social charge; all the food mentioned in fact contributes to marking the intrinsic features of the characters and their 'diet may be used as an interpretative guideline for the health, personality or

---

[3] The organization has a frequently updated website at www.sca.org.
[4] See the webpage of the event at http://www.godecookery.com/scafeast/chafst.htm.

A woodcut from William Caxton's edition of *The Canterbury Tales* (1483).
(Wikimedia Commons)

morality of a particular consumer' (Biebel 1998: 16). The lavish table of the Franklin offers bread, wine, ale, meat pie, fish and flesh, seasonal dainties, and sharp sauces. The Summoner enjoys garlic, onions and leeks, while the supposedly frugal and austere Monk indulges in the sin of gluttony owing to his passion for the costly roast swan. For the Pardoner, this deadly vice is the cause of Man's original sin and its growing occurrence is due to the cooks:

> Thise cokes, how they stampe, and streyne, and grinde
> And turnen substaunce into accident,
> To fulfille al thy likerous talent!
> Out of the harde bones knokke they
> The mary, for they caste noght awey
> That may go thurgh the golet softe and swote.
> Of spicerie of leef, and bark, and roote
> Shal been his sauce ymaked by delit,

The Cook
(Wikimedia Commons)

To make hym yet a newer appetit.
But, certes, he that haunteth swiche delices
Is deed, whil that he lyveth in tho vices. (Chaucer 1988: 197)

The main target of Chaucer's sermon on gluttony may be one of the pilgrims, the Cook Roger, or Hodge of Ware, hired to work in a bid to counterbalance the spiritual nourishment of the pilgrimage. Pilgrims cannot be fed only with tales and devotion.

Like the Host Harry Bailey, a real-life innkeeper in Southwark at Chaucer's time, Roger is probably based on an identifiable London cook who was in a plea of debt and known as a common nightwalker who used to break curfew. What makes him even more recognizable is the allusion to an ulcerous sore on his leg; this may hint at the unhygienic conditions of his cookshop, a place that Gordon Ramsay would implacably condemn in a Medieval episode of *Kitchen Nightmares*.

However, Chaucer also provides an account of his rich repertoire of dishes and of his technical skills; his portrayal of the Cook turns out to be 'a concoction of culinary superlatives', as Donaldson puts it (1958: 891), which vividly depicts him as a masterchef *avant la lettre*:

> A COOK they hadde with hem for the nones,
> To boill the *chiknes with the marybones*,
> And *poudre-marchant tart* and *galingale*.
> Wel koude he knowe a draughte of Londoun ale;
> Maken *mortreux*, and wel bake a pye.
> But greet harm was it, as it thoughte me,
> That on his shyne a mormal hadde he.
> For *blankmanger*, that made he with the beste.
> (Chaucer 1988: 29)   [The italics are mine]

Decameron (1432)
Cooking on spit
(Wikimedia Commons)

Chaucer lists the Cook's signature dishes, which reflect both his expertise in food preparation and the main trends of Medieval cooking. The first mentioned is 'chiknes with the marybones' (chicken with the marrowbones); its recipe, included in several 15th century cookbooks, might prove inspirational for a present-day chef looking for a tasty combination:

> Cxliij. Schyconys with the bruesse. Take halfe a dosyn Chykonys, & putte hem in-to a potte; then putte ther-to a gode gobet of freysshe Beef, & lat hem boyle wyl; putte ther-to Percely, Sawge leuys, Saurey, noyt to smal hakkyd; putte ther-to Safroun y-now; then kytte thin Brewes, & skalde hem with the same brothe; Salt it wyl. (*Two Fifteenth-Century Cookbooks* 1888: 32)

According to the recipe, the chicken should be boiled with beef bones whose marrow is exquisite. Its fatty contents contribute to making the meat tastier. In the pot there is also a generous amount of parsley and savory, and a pinch of saffron; in the meantime slices of bread are drenched in the same broth to complete the dish.

In the list Chaucer includes galingale, an aromatic root of the ginger family, used both in cookery and herbal medicine (*OED* 1). The presence of this ingredient in the Cook's kitchen has several implications: on the one hand, it implies the chef's high degree of professionalism, on the other, it points at the social level of the consumers, since this root was well beyond the means of modest households. As Woolgar reminds us, galingale was used less frequently than ginger due to its cost which was half the price of saffron, the most expensive spice of the period (Woolgar 2014: 273). Spices imported from the East were extensively used in several dishes like the so-called 'poudre-marchant' tart, a spice mixture made into a tart. It is worth noting that while its exact recipe is not recorded, it is clearly stated that the food takes the form of a tart.

Medieval cooking shares with the contemporary culinary art the pleasure of the taste, the desire to produce food which was satisfying and wholesome but also pleasant to look at. Medieval feasts were all about food display. That is why many recipes are based on ground food and spices. The aim was twofold: this procedure allowed a perfect colouring and shaping of the substance, which was essential for the creation of certain dishes. On the other hand, cooks were advised to take into account the Galenic theory of the four humours before choosing a way of cooking a particular dish: as Weiss Adamson argues, combining different foodstuffs which have been crushed and ground to a fine consistency 'ensured their complete humoral mixture and influence on one another' (2012: 117).

Besides being a status symbol, spices were appreciated for their nutritional properties, their distinct taste and the vivid colours they give to a dish. Medieval cooks had a liking for brightly coloured food. The relevance of colours may be exemplified by a dish called 'blankmanger', mentioned in the prologue. Literally 'white food', it is a sort of thick white potage which consists of white ingredients. The association between its colour and purity made this dish extremely popular in Medieval times; moreover, its preparation was not limited to a particular season or period of the year, since it might likewise be made for both 'flesh days and days of abstinence', such as Lent (Woolgar 275).

> To make blaumanger gros. Tak rys & pike hem & wasch hem & stepe hem & tempere hem with good almound melk, & do it in a pot & mak it to sethe ones, & than do it doun & tak braun of hennes or of capouns, & hew it in gobetes, & cast thereto & stere it togedere, & do thereto sugre & salt & whit gres & mak it charchaunt, & dresch it in disches, & set therin fryed almoundes, & straw sugre aboue & serue it forth. (*Curye on Inglysch* 1985: 89)

Different versions of this recipe are found in the cookbooks of the period. According to the one in *Curye on Inglysh,* which dates to the 14th century, the dish contains boiled chopped poultry (capon or chicken) in chunks, almond milk, rice, crushed fried almonds – which were luxurious imports – salt and sugar. Today the dish has not lost its original colour and has been turned into a sort of rice pudding dessert, which is very popular in England but very unlike its medieval ancestor. Blankmanger is only one of the innumerable examples of coloured food. Like a painter, the cook was able to reproduce a vast array of shades: from yellow (derived from saffron and egg yolks), green (spinach and parsley) and red (sandalwood and rose petals) to blue (blackberries) and black (prunes).

The recipes cited so far show that at that time exact quantities of ingredients, temperatures and cooking time were hardly ever indicated; sometimes there were some vague instructions about the heat of the fire. This may be due to the fact that Medieval cooks did not need specific indications; many recipes were not even written but were handed down from generation to generation and the skills to prepare them passed from father to son. Therefore cooks were used to interpreting their recipes like performers, relying on their personal experience and background, imagination and instinct. In their case the geographical provenance also impacted on the preparation of a dish due to regional varieties.

The Cook in Chaucer's *Canterbury Tales* masters several cooking procedures such as frying, boiling, roasting and baking. Unlike present day cooking, Montanari notes, Medieval cuisine tended to superimpose and blend tastes rather than distinguishing and separating them. At that time they used multiple cooking techniques for the same dish in a bid to create new and original tastes (2004:77-78). Therefore the Cook's mastery of several techniques implies the possibility to produce a vast assortment of dishes and to experiment with multiple combinations of different tastes. The sophisticated Medieval cuisine was based on contrasting elements which coexisted harmonically: 'sweet-sour was the preferred taste' (Weiss Adamson 2012: 124). It regularly combined salt and sugar, since the latter, usually added to meat dishes, was treated as a spice. Actually sugar is a basic ingredient of a kind of stew called Mortreux or Mortrews according to the cookbook *Curye on Inglish*. The dish took its name from the mortar used to reduce the meat to a pulp:

> Take hennes and pork and seeth hem togyder. Take the lyres of hennes and of the pork and hewe it small, and grinde it al to doust; take brede y-grated and do therto, and temper it with the self broth, and alye it with yolkes of ayren; and cast theron powdour fort. Boile it and do therin powdour of gynger, sugur, safroun and salt, and loke that it be stondyng; and flour it with powdour gynger. (*Curye on Inglish* 1985: 107)

To begin with, chicken and pork are boiled in the same pot; then the liver of both is chopped until it is smooth. After adding grated bread and blending it with broth and egg yolks, a strong flavoured spice (presumably similar to curry) is spread on the meat which is boiled in a mixture of ginger, saffron, sugar and salt.

In the Prologue, the Cook stands out as a fully rounded figure, made of lights and shadows. Besides his shining abilities and the rich repertoire of dishes, Chaucer amusingly stigmatizes the Cook's weaknesses which he hides behind a facade of skills. We read Chaucer's praise for the Cook's profound knowledge of beer, a ubiquitous feature on any English table. While emphasizing his expertise and raising him to the level of a trained sommelier, the author's remark may also suggest an excessive attachment or addiction to beer. This finds confirmation later on when the Cook falls asleep while riding a horse, presumably due to a hangover.

When the Manciple wakes him up, the Cook feels dizzy, his sight is blurred and his breath reeking, and he falls off his horse. While the other pilgrims charitably help put the heavy, drunk Cook back on his horse, the Host, *arbiter* of the tale competition, temporarily releases him from telling a story. The scene turns out to be even more hilarious when the Manciple offers the Cook some wine and the chef, immensely pleased, drinks it.

Besides his being rather fat, asleep during the pilgrimage and drunk, the Cook is also blamed for his ulcerous sore. This skin eruption, which does not seem to be on the mend, is so distinctive and long-standing that it becomes an integral part of his identity: it may be seen, as many critics have commented, as the symbolic reflection of his immoral conduct. It may also be alluding to the recurrent plagues in London and evoke the terrible urban conditions. The association between the ulcer and the Cook ruins the public image of the chef, making his dishes unappetizing. Moreover, it makes one doubt the efficiency of his work. Is his kitchen spick-and-span? Does he follow the basic rules of hygiene for food preparation? Medieval cooks like Roger of Ware suffered from the charge of being dishonest and unclean; it is the Host Harry Bailey who gives voice to this popular belief and suspicions when he openly accuses the Cook of selling poor-quality food such as meat pies and cakes baked twice (not fresh):

> Now telle on, Roger, looke that it be good;
> For many a pastee hastow laten blood,
> And many a Jakke of Dovere hastow soold
> That hath been twies hoot and twies coold.
> Of many a pilgrym hastow Cristes curs,
> For of thy percely yet they fare the wors,
> That they han eten with thy stubbel goos;
> For in thy shoppe is many a flye loos. (Chaucer 1988: 84)

According to the Host, the way the Cook prepares his goose is sloppy so that the dish turns out to be disgusting. Probably he did not rely on the traditional recipe:

> Stubbel Goos with Percely - Goce or Capon farced. Take parcill, Swynes grece, or suet of shepe, and parboyle hem in faire water and fresssh boyling broth; And then take yolkes of eyeron hard y-sodde, and hew hem smale, with the herbes and the salte; and cast therto pouder of Ginger, Peper, Cannel, and salte, and Grapes in tyme of yere; And in other tyme, take oynons, and boile hem; and whan they ben yboiled ynowe with the herbes and with the suet, al togidre, then put all in the goos, or in the Capon; And then late him roste ynough. (*Two Fifteenth-Century Cookbooks*, 1888: 81)

A goose or a capon is to be filled with parsley, herbs, salt, ginger, pepper and cannel and alternatively, according to the time of the year, with grapes or onions, which have been all boiled together. Once it has been stuffed, it is roasted.

On the other hand, the Cook might have used bad parsley or added other ingredients to cover up the unpleasant smell of spoiled meat: ironically, the Host's words also seem to imply that his goose is stuffed not only of parsley and other herbs and spices but also of flies, the most assiduous visitors to his kitchen, often included in his menu.

Far from denying the charges, the Cook laughs at the Host's allegations. With a superior smile he promises to tell a story revolving around a host exactly like Harry in a bid to show that this category is likewise not free from blame. Nevertheless, he puts off the tale he had planned to tell and starts another that he is willing to share with the other pilgrims. Its protagonist is Perkyn Revelour, the apprentice of a master victualler more interested in dancing and wenching, as his surname suggests, than in working. His tale is located in Eastcheap, not far from the Host's own inn, an area in which cookshops were extremely numerous. The Cook's Tale stops at line 58; we may only conjecture that the conclusion has been lost or that 'it is too scabrous to be continued and is left deliberately and tantalizingly unfinished' (Pearsall 1992: 241).

Despite the incompleteness of his story, the Cook is one of the most brilliant and memorable characters for generations of readers of the *Canterbury Tales*. It might not be an exaggeration to consider Roger of Ware as a sort of masterchef. Devoid of the rigour and authority of a starred-chef, Chaucer's fat Cook indulges in drunkeness and gluttony, and is also smart at deceiving his clients. Nevertheless his intuition and talent, as well as his technical abilities, make him a real culinary artist. He embodies the principles of this unique style of cooking:

its own balance of flavours. Like his delicacies, the Cook reifies contrasting features: vice and virtue, sugar and salt, the bitter-sweet taste that make him and his recipes immortal. His dishes may be recreated today using different shapes and colours, and inspire a new wave of cooks willing to following in the footsteps of this masterchef *sui generis*.

Works cited

Austin, T. 1888. *Two Fifteenth-Century Cookery Books.* Harleian MS. 279 and Harl. MS. 4016. London, Early English Text Society, Oxford Series, No. 91.
Biebel, E. M., 1998. Pilgrims to Table: Food Consumption in Chaucer's *Canterbury Tales.* In M. Carlin and J. Rosenthal (eds) *Food and Eating in Medieval Europe*: 15-26. London and Rio Grande, The Hamledon Press.
Chaucer G. 1998. *The Riverside Chaucer*, 3. ed., F. N. Robinson (ed.), Oxford, Oxford University Press.
Donaldson, E. T. 1958. *Chaucer's Poetry: an Anthology for the Modern Reader*, New York, Ronald Press Company.
Hieatt, C. B., Butler S. 1985. *Curye on Inglysch: English Culinary Manuscripts on the Fourteenth Century*, London, Oxford University Press.
Montanari, M. 2004. *Il cibo come cultura*, Bari, Editori Laterza.
Pearsall, D. 1992. *The Life of Geoffrey Chaucer*, Oxford, Blackwell.
Weiss Adamson, M. 2012. Professional Cooking, Kitchens, and Service Work. In M. Montanari (ed.) *A Cultural History of Food in the Medieval Age*, vol. 2: 107-124. London, Berg.
Woolgar, C. M. 2014. The Cook. In S. H. Rigby (ed.) *Historians on Chaucer: The 'General Prologue' to the* Canterbury Tales: 262-276. Oxford, Oxford University Press.

Two recipes from the Middle Ages

Chicken with the marrowbones

Cxliij. Schyconys with the bruesse. Take halfe a dosyn Chykonys, & putte hem in-to a potte; then putte ther-to a gode gobet of freysshe Beef, & lat hem boyle wyl; putte ther-to Percely, Sawge leuys, Saurey, noyt to smal hakkyd; putte ther-to Safroun y-now; then kytte thin Brewes, & skalde hem with the same brothe; Salt it wyl.

Mortreux

Take hennes and pork and seeth hem togyder. Take the lyres of hennes and of the pork and hewe it small, and grinde it al to doust; take brede y-grated and do therto, and temper it with the self broth, and alye it with yolkes of ayren; and cast theron powdour fort. Boile it and do therin powdour of gynger, sugur, safroun and salt, and loke that it be stondyng; and flour it with powdour gynger.

Margaret Rose

Caliban's dinner

Let us begin with a line spoken by Caliban in *The Tempest*. This Shakespearian comedy, or romance as critics have called it, was probably first staged by Shakespeare's company, The King's Men, at Whitehall on 1 November 1611. At the beginning of the play (Act One, scene ii) there is a violent clash between Caliban, the only native of the island and the son of a witch, and his master Prospero, the former Duke of Milan and a wizard. Prospero orders Caliban to bring some wood in to make a fire, but Caliban flatly refuses. A string of curses and insults fly between Prospero and Caliban, during which the latter makes the following statement, 'I must eat my dinner.' As owner of the island, Caliban claims his right to stop work and eat. Immediately afterwards, he goes on to remind Prospero of the peaceful, mutually profitable relationship they enjoyed before Prospero turned against him and seized his isle:

> I must eat my dinner.
> This island's mine by Sycorax my mother,
> Which thou tak'st from me. When thou cams't first,
> Thou strok'st me, and made much of me; wouldst give me
> Water with berries in 't, and teach me how
> To name the bigger light, and how the less,
> That burn by day and night: and then I lov'd thee
> And show'd thee all the qualities o' th' isle,
> The fresh springs, brine pits, barren place and fertile:
> Curs'd be I that did so!
> (Shakespeare, *The Tempest*: 2008. Act 1, ii, 333-346)

Caliban's assertion about his right to live on the island and to eat there means he refuses to perform the role of slave that Prospero has assigned to him. The Duke actually uses the term 'slave' regarding Caliban five times in this scene, while Miranda, Prospero's daughter, pronounces it once. The noun, moreover, would certainly not have gone unnoticed by a 17th century audience, including one may presume, King James I and Queen Anne when the play was first performed at Court. Even if an organized slave trade had still to come into existence in the early 17th century, already in Elizabeth's reign migrants were already in the spotlight. Some black migrants had already arrived in the capital. In two official documents addressed to the Lord Mayor of London, in 1596 and 1601, Elisabeth I alludes to 'those blackamoors' that some of her subjects were employing as servants. There are too many of them, she complains, and gives instructions for them to be transported. Fortunately no such action was taken. Soon after Shakespeare wrote *The Tempest*, an organized slave trade began to develop and continued until 1833 when slavery was made illegal in most parts of the British Empire, thanks to the Abolition of Slavery Act. Shakespeare, then, nearly two hundred years before the Act, created the figure of a man who is treated by his European master as a slave, and who has the nerve to defy his master and express his right and desire to eat. It is also worth remembering that Caliban uses the familiar, and now archaic 'thou' form, as he stands up to Prospero, underlining that he considers Prospero his equal and not his superior. He also chooses an uncompromising 'must' rather than a more courteous linguistic construction. He might have said, 'I'd like to eat my dinner', or 'Please may I eat my dinner'. Unfortunately, from our perspective today, Prospero's magic art means he comes out on top and Caliban is forced to toe the line. As the exchange draws to a close, we hear Caliban saying:

> I must obey: his art is of such pow'r,
> It would control my dam's god, Setebos,
> And make a vassal of him. (I.ii.434).

What exactly did the term 'dinner' mean in the early 17th century? Today in British English 'dinner' alludes to the meal that middle and upper class people eat in an evening from about 6 PM to 8 PM, while for the working class it often implies their midday meal. For Shakespeare and his contemporaries, dinner was the most important meal of the day, eaten between noon and 3 PM, the exact time varying according to a person's social class. The wealthy ate a great variety of meat and fish, accompanied by a few seasonal vegetables. By contrast, at the opposite end of the scale, the poor folk, who possessed neither land nor property, would eat very little meat and fish, but an abundance (if they were lucky) of seasonal vegetables and fruit (see Abala; Fitzpatrick). Tenantless people, at times of famine, would go foraging in the open countryside, in search of herbs, edible flowers, greens, fruit and root vegetables. It is worth remembering that at the time most people were familiar not just with the nutritional value of plants and herbs, but also with their medicinal properties.

Even if Caliban does not mention a precise menu when he alludes to his dinner, he does point to several kinds of food and drink in his exchange with Stephano and Trinculo, the Butler and Clown in the service of the King of Naples (Act 2, scene ii). In order to win over the two Neapolitans and convince them to join his scheme to overthrow Prospero, Caliban offers to take them on a trip around the island. In the following passage he anticipates the sort of food and drink they will see and find as they take their walk. In the following verses, Caliban's repeated use of the first person pronoun and the fast rhythm reveal his enthusiasm and excitement. This state of mind might be motivated by the fact that Caliban, as owner of the island, is keen to show the place to his friends. He is, moreover, probably already anticipating gathering some berries and wood and fishing, activities that guarantee his survival as well as that of the newcomers:

> I'll show thee every fertile inch o' th' island; and
> I will kiss thy foot: I prithee, be my god
> [...]
> I'll show thee the best springs: I'll pluck thee
> berries; I'll fish for thee, and get thee wood enough.
> (Act II.ii.148-149; 160-164)

A short while later, Caliban actually imagines himself already at work, as he talks about extracting pignuts from the rocks and hunting for marmoset.

> I prithee, let me bring thee where crabs grow;
> And I with my long nails will dig thee pig-nuts; show
> thee a jay's nest, and instruct thee how to snare the
> nimble marmoset; I'll bring thee to clustering filberts,
> and sometimes I'll get thee young scamels from the
> rock. Wilt thou go with me?
> (Act II. ii, 167-172)

In such passages Caliban shows his familiarity with the foodstuffs and water supply on the island. His behavior is that of a forager, who knows exactly where he can find crab apples, nuts, berries and jays' nests. He is also a hunter of scamels (probably a sort of goat) and marmosets (a kind of small monkey) and he is perhaps a fisherman.

Such multitasking distinguishes Caliban from the other characters in the play, including Prospero and Miranda, and the King of Naples and his entourage. The Neapolitans, members of one of the most opulent courts in seventeenth-century Europe, wander aimlessly around the island after the shipwreck. When in Act 3, scene iii, Alonso and his courtiers finally come upon the banquet that Prospero has prepared for them, they are starving and thirsty. But, just like Caliban, they are not allowed to eat. Following Prospero's instructions, his spirit Ariel makes the banquet disappear in a flash before their very eyes.

In conclusion I should like to imagine Caliban's dinner on the basis of the food and drink mentioned in the play, by Caliban, but also by Prospero and Trinculo. Let us suppose that the Duke decides to give his servant/slave a few hours off from his hard labour. The result might be that this native of the isle has time to rustle up a tasty meal. Seeing that for Caliban this is a meal of a lifetime, I have invented a rather lavish one.

Caliban's Dinner
Two roast marmosets, with a purée of crab apple
Stuffed Jay decorated with chopped nuts
Goat's milk cheese
Root vegetables
Caliban's special apple pie
Fresh spring water flavoured with berries (the berries might be blackcurrants or blackberries)
A bottle of red wine, which Trinculo and Stephano have given Caliban from the Royal cellar.
A King of wines, of course.

How would the Elizabethan dietaries have considered this menu? Seeing that it contains a lot of meat and only a few vegetables, they would have viewed it favourably. Too many vegetables were considered unhealthy because they were grown in the earth and contained a lot of water. Thus the dietaries of Andrew Boorde, Thomas Elyot and Thomas Moulton. According to the Galenic system of medicine, too many vegetables would cause an imbalance of the humours, and subsequently the diner would fall ill. Caliban's dinner, however, lacking as it is in spices, would not have pleased wealthy Elizabethans, who indulged their love of spicy foods by buying expensive produce imported along the Spice Routes. Nor are there any herbs or flowers on the menu, ingredients that were used liberally in cooking and in medicine for their therapeutic properties. One item on the menu would undoubtedly have surprised Elizabethans as exotic, strange, or even revolting, namely the roast marmosets or small monkeys. Today many people buy organic produce, if possible locally grown and in season. They love going to Indian, Thai, Nepalese restaurants, keeping an eye open for new restaurants serving food they have never eaten before. So maybe to a greater degree than the Elizabethans and Jacobeans we can appreciate Caliban's dinner, even its more bizarre ingredients.

Works cited

Abala, K. 2002. *Eating Right in the Renaissance*, Berkeley, University of California Press.
Boorde, A. 1542. *Dietary of Health*.
Elyot, T. 1539. 'Castle of Helth'.
Fitzpatrick, J. (ed.), 2007. *Renaissance Food from Rabelais to Shakespeare*, Farnham, Ashgate.
Moulton, T. 1531. 'This is the Mirror or Glass of Health'.
Shakespeare, W. 2008. *The Tempest*, edited by Jonathan Bate and Eric Rasmussen, RSC, London, Macmillan.
Vaughan A. T. and Mason Vaughan, V. 1991. *Shakespeare's Caliban. A Cultural History*, Cambridge, Cambridge University Press.

Giovanni Iamartino

At table with Dr Johnson:
food for the body, nourishment for the mind

Johnson's life and Johnson's 'Lives'

Samuel Johnson epitomises the spirit of the eighteenth century in England. His life (1709-1784) spans three quarters of the century; his literary and critical output both embodies and shapes the taste of the day, connecting himself and his readers to other great names of the English and European literary traditions. His famous *Dictionary of the English Language* (Johnson 1755) provides evidence of both the linguistic usage of his world and the literary and scientific culture which lay at the heart of that world. Extraordinary as a writer, therefore; but also unique as a man, both for his personality and the events of his life, and for the fact that a number of differing accounts of this personality and these events were compiled and published from soon after Johnson's death in 1784. Most outstanding and best known is James Boswell's *The Life of Samuel Johnson, LL.D.*, first published in 1791; but we must not forget that this work was preceded, and also followed, by many other versions of the life of the man who was already recognised as exceptional by his contemporaries.

I will use the *Life* (Boswell [1791] 1980) and three other early biographies – those by Hester Lynch Piozzi (1786), John Hawkins (1787) and Arthur Murphy (1792) – to take a 'gastronomic journey' through the world of eighteenth-century England, well aware that, despite his uniqueness, Samuel Johnson is the figure who, perhaps paradoxically, best represents this world. Why draw upon several biographies and not just Boswell's *Life* alone? Because every biography reveals, but at the same time conceals – so it would seem expedient to integrate the different perspectives and interpretations present in each one, especially here, where the intention is not to contemplate Johnson the writer, seated at his desk, but Johnson the man, seated at the dining tables of his affluent friends or in the tavern. Boswell, a Scot, had already developed an extraordinary admiration for Johnson long before he knew him personally and, once they had met, he consciously and intentionally became his biographer. Hester Lynch, on the other hand, knew Johnson through being married to Henry Thrale, a wealthy beer magnate who often welcomed Johnson into his home and who sought his company at the seaside (at Brighton, then known as Brighthelmstone) and on pleasure trips to Wales and Paris. Hester's vision of Johnson was more personal and feminine; she was a brilliant, cultured woman, who cooked – or rather had someone else cook – meals for the great man and did her best to keep up with him in conversation. Sadly, the relationship came to an end after Thrale's death, when Hester married her social inferior, the Italian maestro Gabriele Piozzi. In a sense, John Hawkins and Arthur Murphy – both of them men of letters – complement each other quite well. Hawkins had known Johnson since the beginning of his writing career and was a founding member of the *Literary Club* in 1764; however, a quarrel with Edmund Burke – the famous politician and writer, a friend of Johnson's and a member of the club – led to Hawkins's resignation and his estrangement from Johnson. The Irish comedy writer Arthur Murphy, who had introduced Johnson to the Thrales, enjoyed a lifelong friendship with Johnson, marked by mutual admiration.

Smiling with the wise, and feeding with the rich

To introduce my story, I quote two episodes from Boswell. In the first, Johnson is commenting on the line 'I'd smile with the simple, and feed with the poor' from *Florizel and Perdita*, the adaptation of Shakespeare's *Winter's Tale* by Johnson's friend, David Garrick:

> Poor David! Smile with the simple! What folly is that! And who would feed with the poor that can help it! No, no: let me smile with the wise, and feed with the rich. (Boswell 1980: 408)

In the second, as a dinner guest at the home of Edward Dilly, the bookseller:

> Before dinner Dr. Johnson seized upon Mr. Charles Sheridan's *Account of the late Revolution in Sweden,* and seemed to read it ravenously, as if he devoured it, which was to all appearance his method of studying. 'He knows how to read better than any one (said Mrs. Knowles;) he gets at the substance of a book directly; he tears out the heart of it.' He kept it wrapt up in the table-cloth in his lap during the time of dinner, from an avidity to have one entertainment in readiness when he should have finished another; resembling (if I may use so coarse a simile) a dog who holds a bone in his paws in reserve, while he eats something else which has been thrown to him. (Boswell 1980: 942)

This is Johnson in a nutshell: the 'rational' Johnson, who rejects commonplaces and poetic posturing; Johnson the man of the world and Johnson the man of letters; and, most importantly for my story, the Johnson who drew nourishment from both books and food, with the same insatiable appetite. This last image, and its implications, are confirmed by Boswell when he describes the lifestyle of his idol:

> His general mode of life, during my acquaintance, seemed to be pretty uniform. About twelve o'clock I commonly visited him, and frequently found him in bed, or declaiming over his tea, which he drank very plentifully. He generally had a levee of morning visitors, chiefly men of letters [...] He seemed to me to be considered as a kind of public oracle, whom every body thought they had a right to visit and consult; and doubtless they were well rewarded. I never could discover how he found time for his compositions. He declaimed all the morning, then went to dinner at a tavern, where he commonly staid late, and then drank his tea at some friend's house, over which he loitered a great while, but seldom took supper. I fancy he must have read and wrote chiefly in the night, for I can scarcely recollect that he ever refused going with me to a tavern, and he often went to Ranelagh, which he deemed a place of innocent recreation. (Boswell 1980: 437)

It is striking that this uniformity in Johnson's 'general mode of life' should be so irregular: still in bed at midday, sometimes till two in the afternoon (Murphy 1792: 88), Johnson dines at an hour that we would consider very late, has tea at a friend's house, and generally skips supper. Then he works – reading and writing – at night. Indeed, it was very noticeable to his friends that his wigs were often singed on the side of his good eye by being too near to the candle he used for reading. Johnson's habits were undoubtedly odd and he maintained them even when staying with the Thrales, provoking remonstrations from the lady of the house, who was obliged to serve him breakfast when everyone else was expecting to hear the dinner bell (Lynch Piozzi 1786: 292). But perhaps this was not so very strange: in those days, mealtimes were not so strictly regulated as they are today and, furthermore, they tended to vary considerably from one social class to another, each with its own requirements and economic possibilities (Drummond and Wilbraham 1958: 206-231). For the affluent middle classes with whom Johnson associated, it was normal to have breakfast between 10 and 11 in the morning; dinner was at 5 or 6 in the afternoon and supper would be served at 10 PM or even later. It was only towards the end of the eighteenth century that dinner was moved to around 2 PM and supper to 8 PM. It was also during this period that the typical English custom of five o'clock tea started to spread. One need only glance through the pages of Johnson's *Dictionary* for confirmation of all this: MEAL is defined as 'the act of eating at a certain time', without specifying the exact hour; BREAKFAST is 'the first meal in the day', DINNER 'the chief meal; the meal eaten about the middle of the day'; and SUPPER 'the last meal of the day; the evening repast' (Johnson 1755). All that can be said for certain is that the midday meal was the main meal of the day, defined as *dinner*. Nowadays this is also referred to as *lunch*, a word which in Johnson's day meant 'as much food as one's hand can hold' (Johnson 1755). For Italians it usually suggests a sandwich, often hastily consumed while standing up in a bar in the middle of the working day!

Turning again to the *Dictionary*, according to a recent study which analyses both editions, Johnson lists and defines 223 words relating to food (Pinnavaia 2006: 153n). The most famous of these definitions is certainly the one for oats – OATS: 'A grain, which in England is given to horses, but in Scotland supports the people' – which Johnson must have written with tongue in cheek, given that nearly all his assistants for compiling the dictionary were Scots. On the whole, the definitions for foodstuffs are simple and effective (PIE: 'Any crust baked with something in it'; SWEETMEAT: 'delicacies made of fruits preserved with sugar'), some are vaguely scientific (BUTTER: 'An unctuous substance made by agitating the cream of milk, till the oil separates from the whey'). And it is easy to glean from the *Dictionary* that Johnson liked plums and pears better than peaches: for the definitions of such words, and many more botanical terms, Johnson relied on Philip Miller's *Gardener's Dictionary* (1731), but whereas the definition of *peach* is only five lines long, for *plum* the citation from Miller lists 32 different varieties and for *pear* 84, taking up 60 lines!

At table with Dr Johnson: food

In order to discover Samuel Johnson's tastes and habits with regard to food and culinary matters, we should return to his biographers. I have already mentioned his preference for a 'late and tedious breakfast' (Boswell 1980: 172), often consisting of 'tea and cross-buns' (510) or 'tea and rolls and butter' (636). But when staying with the Thrales he would consume 'seven or eight large peaches of a morning before breakfast' (Lynch Piozzi 1786: 102-103). Only on Good Friday did he restrain himself at breakfast time: 'I observed that he fasted so very strictly, that he did not even taste bread, and took no milk with his tea; I suppose because it is a kind of animal food', though in later years, even on that day of fasting, Boswell saw him 'drinking tea without milk, and eating a cross-bun to prevent faintness' (Boswell 1980: 619, 1221).

Regarding breakfast, the episode that Boswell recounts with most pleasure is undoubtedly the time when he accompanied Johnson to Lichfield, the writer's hometown:

> I saw here, for the first time, *oat ale*; and oat cakes not hard as in Scotland, but soft like a Yorkshire cake, were served at breakfast. It was pleasant to me to find, that *Oats*, the *food of horses*, were so much used as the *food of the people* in Dr. Johnson's own town. (Boswell 1980: 707)

Browsing through the pages of these early biographies one can find several brief references to the food consumed by Johnson and his fellow diners. Boswell mentions *sausages* (the ones from Bologna are 'the best in the world'!), *meat pye*, *larks*, *beef-steak*, *oysters*, *plumb-pudding* [sic], *muffins* and *jelly* (Boswell 1980: 495, 511,

1332, 1211, 1216, 417, 1018, 616); in Piozzi's anecdotes we can also find – and add to my list – *goose*, *omelet*, and *roast beef* accompanied by *truffles* and *mushrooms* (Lynch Piozzi 1786: 103, 122, 120). Two extracts are particularly worthy of comment:

> Johnson's own notions about eating however were nothing less than delicate; a leg of pork boiled till it dropped from the bone, a veal-pye with plums and sugar, or the outside cut of a salt buttock of beef, were his favourite dainties. (Lynch Piozzi 1786: 102)

> To my great surprise he asked me to dine with him on Easter-day. I never supposed that he had a dinner at his house; for I had not then heard of any one of his friends having been entertained at his table. He told me, 'I generally have a meat pye on Sunday: it is baked at a publick oven, which is very properly allowed, because one man can attend it; and thus the advantage is obtained of not keeping servants from church to dress dinners.' [...] As a dinner here was considered a singular phenomenon, and as I was frequently interrogated on the subject, my readers may perhaps be desirous to know our bill of fare. Foote, I remember, in allusion to Francis, the *negro*, was willing to suppose that our repast was *black broth*. But the fact was, that we had a very good soup, a boiled leg of lamb and spinach, a veal pye, and a rice pudding. (Boswell 1980: 511-12)

These two passages not only provide us with the menus of Johnson's favourite meals but they also give us an interesting insight into his world. First of all, especially in London people who were not well-to-do (and Johnson undoubtedly was not) often lacked the facilities to cook at home. It was more economical to buy food ready cooked and take it home. There was a well-known street in London, lined with shops selling cheap, ready-to-eat food, called *Porridge Island*, which Lynch Piozzi refers to in her *Anecdotes* (1786: 103-104; see also Picard 2001: 64). The 'publick oven' mentioned by Johnson is evidently a baker's oven because bread was not baked on Sundays, so it was possible to use the ovens for other purposes.

The fact that Johnson hardly ever invited people to dinner, or rather, that it was his habit (and not only his) to eat out, is a point I will come back to below. Here, I would like to mention another moment in Johnson's domestic life when, late one evening, Boswell dropped by and found Johnson in the company of Mrs Williams – an impoverished blind woman who had for many years been a permanent guest at Johnson's home – and a son (Boswell specifies 'a natural son') of the second Lord Southwell:

> The table had a singular appearance, being covered with a heterogeneous assemblage of oysters and porter for his company, and tea for himself. (Boswell 1980: 1015)

As we now know, Johnson did not usually partake of supper, contenting himself with vast quantities of tea. The cold supper for his guests consisted of oysters and beer, for, strange though it may seem, this was poor man's fare, because at the time oysters were plentiful and cheap – it should not surprise us that Johnson used to buy oysters to feed his cat, Hodge (Boswell 1980: 1216).

Boswell sums up Johnson's eating and drinking habits in his account of a conversation between Johnson and Mr Edwards, once a fellow student at Pembroke College, Oxford, at a chance encounter forty years later:

> EDWARDS. 'How do you live, Sir? For my part, I must have my regular meals, and a glass of good wine. I find I require it.' JOHNSON. 'I now drink no wine, Sir. Early in life I drank wine: for many years I drank none. I then for some years drank a great deal.' EDWARDS. 'Some hogsheads, I warrant you.' JOHNSON. 'I then had a severe illness, and left it off, and I have never begun it again. I never felt any difference upon myself from eating one thing rather than another, nor from one kind of weather rather than another. There are people, I believe, who feel a difference; but I am not one of them. And as to regular meals, I have fasted from the Sunday's dinner to the Tuesday's dinner, without any inconvenience. I believe it is best to eat just as one is hungry: but a man who is in business, or a man who has a family, must have stated meals. I am a straggler. I may leave this town and go to Grand Cairo, without being missed here or observed there.' EDWARDS. 'Don't you eat supper, Sir?' JOHNSON. 'No, Sir.' EDWARDS. 'For my part, now, I consider supper as a turnpike through which one must pass, in order to get to bed'. (Boswell 1980: 957-58)

Through Boswell, Johnson also airs his views on different eating habits in other places. During his journey through France with the Thrales, he takes exception to the local *cuisine* – 'Their meals are gross' – and on a visit to a Benedictine monastery on a fasting day, he is less than enthusiastic about the menu: 'soup meagre, herrings, eels, both with sauce; fried fish; lentils, tasteless in themselves' (Boswell 1980: 1015, 656). Clearly, Samuel Johnson was no fan of legumes; in this case the lentils are insipid, while in Wales, again while travelling with the Thrales, he is disparaging about young peas:

> When we went into Wales together, and spent some time at Sir Robert Cotton's at Lleweny, one day at dinner I meant to please Mr. Johnson particularly with a dish of very young peas. Are not they charming? said I to him, while he was eating them. – 'Perhaps (said he) they would be so – to a pig'. (Lynch Piozzi 1786: 63)

Further away from his beloved England – if only in his imagination – Johnson has occasion to discuss the eating habits of Tahiti: there they eat dogs and subsist on the fruit of the bread tree. On the first point, his friend Goldsmith observes that the same custom is practised in China but then the matter is dropped and there are no further comments from Johnson. On the second point, Johnson is unequivocal: 'No, Sir, (holding up a slice of a good loaf,) this is better than the bread tree' (Boswell 1980: 525, 538).

In a passage already cited above, Hester Lynch points out that 'Johnson's own notions about eating however were nothing less than delicate'. Boswell confirms this: 'No man ate more heartily than Johnson, or loved better what was nice and delicate' (Boswell 1980: 768). In short, we are dealing with a gourmet, who is able to philosophise about food and who, on a practical level, does not hesitate to take his wife to task when the meal is not to his liking:

> Johnson loved his dinner exceedingly, and has often said in my hearing, perhaps for my edification, 'that wherever the dinner is ill got there is poverty, or there is avarice, or there is stupidity; in short, the family is somehow grossly wrong: for (continued he) a man seldom thinks with more earnestness of any thing than he does of his dinner; and if he cannot get that well dressed, he should be suspected of inaccuracy in other things.' One day when he was speaking upon the subject, I asked him, if he ever huffed his wife about his dinner? 'So often (replied he), that at last she called to me, and said, Nay, hold Mr. Johnson, and do not make a farce of thanking God for a dinner which in a few minutes you will protest not eatable'. (Lynch Piozzi 1786: 149-150)

And it is not difficult to imagine the mortification of the waiter at an inn who, after serving roast mutton to Johnson and Boswell during one of their journeys, received the following reprimand: 'It is as bad as can be: it is ill-fed, ill-killed, ill-kept, and ill-drest' (Boswell 1980: 1285). The following episodes from the *Life* provide further insight into Johnson's approach to food and deserve quoting at length:

> At supper this night he talked of good eating with uncommon satisfaction. 'Some people (said he,) have a foolish way of not minding, or pretending not to mind, what they eat. For my part, I mind my belly very studiously, and very carefully; for I look upon it, that he who does not mind his belly will hardly mind anything else.' He now appeared to me *Jean Bull philosophe*, and he was, for the moment, not only serious but vehement. Yet I have heard him, upon other occasions, talk with great contempt of people who were anxious to gratify their palates; and the 206th number of his *Rambler* is a masterly essay against gulosity. His practice, indeed, I must acknowledge, may be considered as casting the balance of his different opinions upon this subject; for I never knew any man who relished good eating more than he did. When at table, he was totally absorbed in the business of the moment; his looks seemed rivetted to his plate; nor would he, unless when in very

high company, say one word, or even pay the least attention to what was said by others, till he had satisfied his appetite, which was so fierce, and indulged with such intenseness, that while in the act of eating, the veins of his forehead swelled, and generally a strong perspiration was visible. To those whose sensations were delicate, this could not but be disgusting; and it was doubtless not very suitable to the character of a philosopher, who should be distinguished by self-command. But it must be owned, that Johnson, though he could be rigidly *abstemious*, was not a *temperate* man either in eating or drinking. He could refrain, but he could not use moderately. He told me, that he had fasted two days without inconvenience, and that he had never been hungry but once. They who beheld with wonder how much he eat upon all occasions when his dinner was to his taste, could not easily conceive what he must have meant by hunger; and not only was he remarkable for the extraordinary quantity which he eat, but he was, or affected to be, a man of very nice discernment in the science of cookery. He used to descant critically on the dishes which had been at table where he had dined or supped, and to recollect very minutely what he had liked. [...] and he then proceeded to alarm a lady at whose house he was to sup, by the following manifesto of his skill: 'I, Madam, who live at a variety of good tables, am a much better judge of cookery, than any person who has a very tolerable cook, but lives much at home; for his palate is gradually adapted to the taste of his cook; whereas, Madam, in trying by a wider range, I can more exquisitely judge.' When invited to dine, even with an intimate friend, he was not pleased if something better than a plain dinner was not prepared for him. I have heard him say on such an occasion, 'This was a good dinner enough, to be sure; but it was not a dinner to *ask* a man to.' On the other hand, he was wont to express, with great glee, his satisfaction when he had been entertained quite to his mind. One day when he had dined with his neighbour and landlord in Bolt-court, Mr. Allen, the printer, whose old housekeeper had studied his taste in every thing, he pronounced this eulogy: 'Sir, we could not have had a better dinner had there been a *Synod of Cooks*. (Boswell 1980: 331-332)

Not only does this confirm Johnson's interest in food but it also describes his way of eating – voracious, perhaps even coarse, but always intense – reflecting, if you think about it, the way he lived. Later in the *Life*, when referring again to Johnson's lack of moderation in eating and drinking (it was all or nothing, just enough was unacceptable), Boswell makes this shrewd observation:

[Mr. Thrale] told me I might now have the pleasure to see Dr. Johnson drink wine again, for he had lately returned to it. When I mentioned this to Johnson, he said, 'I drink it now sometimes, but not socially.' The first evening that I was with him at Thrale's, I observed he poured a quantity of it in a large glass, and swallowed it greedily. Every thing about his character and manners was forcible and violent; there never was any moderation; many a day did he fast, many a year did he refrain from wine; but when he did eat, it was voraciously; when he did drink wine, it was copiously. He could practice abstinence, but not temperance. (Boswell 1980: 1121)

And, just as he did for all life's experiences, in the case of food, too, Johnson was quick to reflect and theorise:

> he said, 'I could write a better book of cookery than has ever yet been written; it should be a book upon philosophical principles. Pharmacy is now made much more simple. Cookery may be made so too. A prescription which is now compounded of five ingredients, had formerly fifty in it. So in cookery, if the nature of the ingredients be well known, much fewer will do. Then as you cannot make bad meat good, I would tell what is the best butcher's meat, the best beef, the best pieces; how to choose young fowls; the proper seasons of different vegetables; and then how to roast and boil, and compound. [...] But you shall see what a Book of Cookery I shall make! I shall agree with Mr. Dilly for the copyright.' Miss Seward. 'That would be Hercules with the distaff indeed.' Johnson. 'No, Madam. Women can spin very well; but they cannot make a good book of Cookery'. (Boswell 1980: 942-943)

At table with Dr Johnson: drink

Moving on from food to drink, it is immediately apparent that the picture is much less complex, though Johnson's attitude remains unchanged: excess is practised but it is restrained by reason, while intemperance can be defeated only by abstinence; and, as in the case of food, the social dimension, the link with conversation and human interaction are fundamental to drinking, too. Boswell tells us that, as a young university student, Johnson was not averse to port, but he preferred to drink alone, to avoid being seen drunk:

> Talking of drinking wine, he said, 'I did not leave off wine because I could not bear it; I have drunk three bottles of port without being the worse for it. University College has witnessed this.' BOSWELL: 'Why then, Sir, did you leave it off?' JOHNSON: 'Why, Sir, because it is so much better for a man to be sure that he is never to be intoxicated, never to lose the power over himself. I shall not begin to drink wine again, till I grow old, and want it'. (Boswell 1980: 911)

> When I drank wine, I scorned to drink it when in company. I have drunk many a bottle by myself; in the first place, because I had need of it to raise my spirits; in the second place, because I would have nobody to witness its effects upon me. (Boswell 1980: 747)

These words refer to the period 1776-1778, long after Johnson had given up alcohol. Even though later in life he did start to drink wine again for a while, his attitude is clear: drinking to excess deprives a man of his reasoning powers and his self-control – it is a sin against God and against humanity, a sin which Johnson did not wish to risk committing:

> Sir, I have no objection to a man's drinking wine, if he can do it in moderation. I found myself apt to go to excess in it, and therefore, after having been for some time without it, on account of illness, I thought it better not to return to it. Every man is to judge for himself, according to the effects which he experiences. (Boswell 1980: 687)

> BOSWELL. 'I think, Sir, you once said to me, that not to drink wine was a great deduction from life.' JOHNSON. 'It is a diminution of pleasure, to be sure; but I do not say a diminution of happiness. There is more happiness in being rational.' (911)

> I now no more think of drinking wine, than a horse does. The wine upon the table is no more for me, than for the dog that is under the table. (915)

> Johnson harangued against drinking wine. 'A man (said he,) may choose whether he will have abstemiousness and knowledge, or claret and ignorance'. (981)

> A gentleman having to some of the usual arguments for drinking added this: 'You know, Sir, drinking drives away care, and makes us forget whatever is disagreeable. Would not you allow a man to drink for that reason?' JOHNSON. 'Yes, Sir, if he sat next *you*.' (493)

Other pages in the *Life* are devoted to discussions on the pros and cons of drinking wine, and Lynch Piozzi also recounts several episodes on the same topic (1786: 119, 261). In one famous episode,

> Johnson harangued upon the qualities of different liquors; and spoke with great contempt of claret, as so weak, that 'a man would be drowned by it before it made him drunk.' He was persuaded to drink one glass of it, that he might judge, not from recollection, which might be dim, but from immediate sensation. He shook his head, and said, 'Poor stuff! No, Sir, claret is the liquor for boys; port, for men; but he who aspires to be a hero (smiling) must drink brandy. In the first place, brandy is most grateful to the palate; and then brandy will do soonest for a man what drinking *can* do for him. There are, indeed, few who are able to drink brandy. That is a power rather to be wished for than attained. (Boswell 1980: 1016)

There are references to other types of wine and liqueurs in the biographies: for example, as a young man Johnson was partial to *Bishop*, a sort of sangria containing wine, oranges and sugar; other beverages referred to include port, madeira and, of course, punch (Boswell 1980: 176, 291, 294,707). Surprisingly perhaps, Johnson is scornful of Tuscan wine:

> Florence wine I think the worst; it is wine only to the eye; it is wine neither while you are drinking it, nor after you have drunk it; it neither pleases the taste, nor exhilarates the spirits. (1016)

Beer, the drink of the people, hardly gets a mention in the *Life*, with the exception of Lichfield Ale, which gave Boswell, Joshua Reynolds and Dr Burney the chance to drink Johnson's health, Lichfield being his native city (1139-1140).

When it comes to hot beverages, tea takes pride of place:

> Tea was his favourite beverage; and, when the late Jonas Hanway pronounced his anathema against the use of tea, Johnson rose in defence of his habitual practice, declaring himself 'in that article a hardened sinner, who had for years diluted his meals with the infusion of that fascinating plant; whose tea-kettle had no time to cool; who with tea solaced the midnight hour, and with tea welcomed the morning. (Murphy 1792: 89)

All of this would appear to be true if, as rumour has it, on a single occasion Johnson gulped down sixteen or seventeen cups of his favourite infusion. Boswell speaks of 'His defence of tea against Mr. Jonas Hanway's violent attack upon that elegant and popular beverage' (Boswell 1980: 222), and Lynch Piozzi recalls that

> he made his company exceedingly entertaining when he had once forced one, by his vehement lamentations and piercing reproofs, not to quit the room, but to sit quietly and make tea for him, as I often did in London till four o'clock in the morning. (1786: 124)

In the *Life*, Boswell often mentions the times when Johnson and his friends would gather round the tea table. Once, at Joshua Reynolds' house, Johnson pokes fun, albeit amicably, at the over-simplicity of the popular ballads collected in the *Reliques of Ancient English Poetry* by Bishop Percy, improvising one of his own on the theme of tea, which was being served at the time:

> I pray thee, gentle Renny dear,
>   That thou wilt give to me,
> With cream and sugar temper'd well,
>   Another dish of tea.

> Not fear that I, my gentle maid,
>   Shall long detain the cup,
> When once unto the bottom I
>   Have drank the liquor up.
>
> Yet hear, at last, this mournful truth,
>   Nor hear it with a frown,
> Thou can'st not make the tea so fast,
>   As I can gulp it down.   (Hawkins 1787: 389-90)

But the most singular episode relating to the 'tea ceremony' occurred at the residence of the great man himself:

> We went home to his house for tea. Mrs. Williams made it with sufficient dexterity, notwithstanding her blindness, though her manner of satisfying herself that the cups were full enough appeared to me a little aukward; for I fancied she put her finger down a certain way, till she felt the tea touch it. (Boswell 1980: 420)

Whether out of delicacy or kindness, at this point Boswell adds a note saying that he was probably wrong: perhaps poor Mrs Williams' fingers felt the heat of the tea from the outside of the cup.... Coffee and chocolate are an alternative quite frequently mentioned by Boswell. I quote only from Lynch Piozzi (1786: 102) when she says that in order to compensate for his abstinence from wine, Johnson 'took his chocolate liberally, pouring in large quantities of cream, or even melted butter'.

Consuming food as a social activity

While all of this documents Johnson's very personal relationship with eating and drinking, in the context of eighteenth-century England it is impossible to ignore one aspect that has been largely overlooked in the passages quoted so far, namely, the eminently 'social' nature of the consumption of food and beverages at that time. Eating and drinking out had become commonplace, clubs were proliferating, and – especially for Johnson – the art of conversation was seen as nourishment of the mind, complemented by the nourishment of the body. Let us therefore examine these points more closely.

From the early days of Johnson's life in London, as he himself would tell Boswell several years later, dining meant dining out, eating well and in good company:

> He had a little money when he came to town, and he knew how he could live in the cheapest manner. [...] 'I dined (said he) very well for eightpence, with very good company, at the Pine Apple in New-street, just by. Several of them had travelled. They expected to meet every day; but did

not know one another's names. It used to cost the rest a shilling, for they drank wine; but I had a cut of meat for six-pence, and bread for a penny, and gave the waiter a penny; so that I was quite well served, nay, better than the rest, for they gave the waiter nothing'. (Boswell 1980: 75)

Even when his economic situation improved, Johnson did not have his meals cooked at home; and when one of his friends, Bennet Langton, gave him some game, he in his turn passed it on to others, keeping for himself only what was already cooked (Boswell 1980: 232). Another time, when Boswell invited him out to lunch,

> Before coming out, and leaving her [Mrs Williams] to dine alone, he gave her choice of a chicken, a sweetbread, or any other little nice thing, which was carefully sent to her from the tavern, ready-drest. (Boswell 1980: 986)

So the take-away is not just a recent invention! But rather than take food home, Johnson loved to eat out, in a public eating-house or as a guest at the home of one of his wealthy friends. There are many references in the *Life* to Johnson's habitual eating places: 'Clifton's eating-house, in Butcher-row' (283), the 'Mitre' (284, 295, 299, 302 and *passim*), the 'Turk's Head coffee-house, in the Strand' (315, 328), the 'Crown and Anchor tavern, in the Strand' (397, 489, 493, 746), the 'British Coffee-house' (495), the 'Somerset Coffee-house, in the Strand' (688). Here are Johnson's words on the subject, as reported in an interesting passage from John Hawkins's biography:

> In contradiction to those, who, having a wife and children, prefer domestic enjoyments to those which a tavern affords, I have heard him assert, that a tavern-chair was the throne of human felicity. – 'As soon,' said he, 'as I enter the door of a tavern, I experience an oblivion of care, and a freedom from solicitude: when I am seated, I find the master courteous, and the servants obsequious to my call; anxious to know and ready to supply my wants: wine there exhilarates my spirits, and prompts me to free conversation and an interchange of discourse with those whom I most love: I dogmatise and am contradicted, and in this conflict of opinion and sentiments I find delight'. (Hawkins 1787: 87)

This passage by Hawkins is taken up again in a note by Boswell, who says more or less the same things, adding, however, that dining at a tavern is even more enjoyable than dining at the home of friends or acquaintances because

> The master of the house is anxious to entertain his guests; the guests are anxious to be agreeable to him: and no man, but a very impudent dog indeed, can as freely command what is in another man's house, as if it were his own. Whereas, at a tavern, there is a general freedom from

anxiety. You are sure you are welcome: and the more noise you make, the more trouble you give, the more good things you call for, the welcomer you are. No servants will attend you with the alacrity which waiters do, who are excited by the prospect of an immediate reward in proportion as they please. No, Sir; there is nothing which has yet been contrived by man, by which so much happiness is produced as by a good tavern or inn'. (Boswell 1980: 697)

Be that as it may, while the names of the taverns, inns and coffee-houses where Johnson dined with his friends abound in the *Life*, even more frequent are mentions of the invitations he received, which often included Boswell. Phrases such as 'One day dining at old Mr. Langton's' (305), 'being at dinner at Mr. Thomas Davies's the bookseller' (580), 'Next day I dined with Johnson at Mr. Thrale's' (600) come up again and again in the *Life*.

But all of this was evidently not enough for Johnson. Thus, following a trend that had begun in the previous century, over the years he himself promoted the formation of more than one club – a club being, according to the definition in his *Dictionary*, 'An assembly of good fellows, meeting under certain conditions' (Johnson 1755 s.v. CLUB 4; see also Picard 2001: 198 and Clark 2012). After informally setting up a club for weekly meetings on Tuesday evenings at the King's Head, a tavern near St Paul's Cathedral, famous for its steaks (Hawkins 1787: 219-220), in the winter of 1748-1749 he founded the Ivy Lane Club, which took its name from the street in which it was located, perhaps to escape from the 'drudgery of defining' and perhaps to get away from his wife, Tetty, who spent much of her time in bed drinking and reading love stories, but certainly 'with a view to enjoy literary discussion, and amuse his evening hours' (Boswell 1980: 137). In February 1764, Reynolds suggested to Johnson that they should form a literary club, to be called the *Turk's Head Club* – after the tavern in Gerrard Street, Soho, where the members would meet. Later on it became known as *The Literary Club* or simply *The Club* (because, as Boswell tells us, the venue was subsequently changed). Initially the members met on Mondays for dinner; then, from 1772, every fortnight for lunch. Lastly, in December 1783, a year before his death, Johnson founded the *Essex Head Club* with his friend Dr Brocklesby; the members met three times a week at the Essex Head Tavern, which was run by a former servant of the Thrales' in Essex Street off the Strand, close to Johnson's home.

What was the purpose of these clubs and who joined them, with their secret ballots and their exclusiveness (anyone who was 'black-balled' by even one of the members was refused admission)? More importantly, why were they created? In Johnson's case, the main attraction was the idea of a group of friends meeting regularly – over lunch or dinner, certainly – but also, and above all, to nourish the mind and the spirit through conversation: conversation as a cure for the melancholy of solitude, conversation as an enrichment of the mind, conversation as a rational instrument for investigating reality, conversation as an arena for the free exchange of differing ideas. It would be interesting to pursue this topic, taking into account the context of eighteenth-century England and focusing on Johnson in particular (see, for example, Burke 1992 and Rogers 2012). Here, anyway, I would just like to underline that for Johnson conversation was 'a trial of intellectual vigour and skill' (Boswell 1980: 1150) and that a distinction has to be made between conversation and talk:

> Though his usual phrase for conversation was *talk*, yet he made a distinction; for when he once told me that he dined the day before at a friend's house, with 'a very pretty company;' and I asked him if there was good conversation, he answered, 'No, Sir; we had *talk* enough, but no *conversation*; there was nothing discussed'. (Boswell 1980: 1210)

> When I complained of having dined at a splendid table without hearing one sentence of conversation worthy of being remembered, he said, 'Sir, there seldom is any such conversation.' BOSWELL. 'Why then meet at table?' JOHNSON. 'Why, to eat and drink together, and to promote kindness; and, Sir, this is better done when there is no solid conversation; for when there is, people differ in opinion, and get into bad humour, or some of the company who are not capable of such conversation, are left out, and feel themselves uneasy. It was for this reason, Sir Robert Walpole said, he always talked bawdy at his table, because in that all could join'. (Boswell 1980: 756)

This is probably the reason why, despite the pleasure of dining in the homes of his wealthy friends and in the company of the select few, Johnson also loved going to taverns and taking part in the meetings of the clubs he belonged to. Anyway, in either case, the connection between enjoyment of food and the social and intellectual pleasures of contact with others – at certain moments, 'a very high intellectual feast' (Boswell 1980: 617) – is fundamental.

An Englishman's taste

To conclude this overview of the role of eating and drinking in the life and thought of Samuel Johnson, I would like to quote some passages showing how food and drink are used by Boswell and Johnson as metaphors to define people and things. First, it is Boswell who compares the styles of Joseph Addison and Samuel Johnson through the image of wine: 'Addison's style, like a light wine, pleases everybody from the first. Johnson's, like a liquor of more body, seems too strong at first, but, by degrees, is highly relished' (Boswell 1980: 161). One may wonder whether Boswell, in using this image, might have been inspired by the words of Johnson on Richard Steele, Addison's friend and fellow journalist:

> When we talked of Steele's Essays, 'They are too thin (says our Critic) for an Englishman's taste; mere superficial observations on life and manners, without erudition enough to make them keep, like the light French wines, which turn sour with standing a while for want of *body*, as we call it'. (Lynch Piozzi 1786: 59-60)

Still more telling is the simile used by Johnson to define the two cardinal values of his thought and life, namely, judgement and friendship:

> I [Boswell] still insisted that admiration was more pleasing than judgement, as love is more pleasing than friendship. The feeling of friendship is like that of being comfortably filled with roast beef; love, like being enlivened with champagne. JOHNSON. 'No, Sir; admiration and love are like being intoxicated with champagne; judgement and friendship like being enlivened. (Boswell 1980: 624)

Finally, to round off this imaginary meal at table with Dr Johnson, I wish to repeat the words – symbolically linking food and conversation – that this giant of eighteenth-century England used to describe his close friend David Garrick's way of conversing:

> Garrick's conversation is gay and grotesque. It is a dish of all sorts, but all good things. There is no solid meat in it: there is a want of sentiment in it. Not but that he has sentiment sometimes, and sentiment, too, very powerful and very pleasing: but it has not its full proportion in his conversation. (Boswell 1980: 708)

'Solid meat' is what Johnson – in his works and with his words, as handed down to us by his biographers – has left to future generations for the nourishment of their hearts and minds.

Works cited

Boswell, J. 1980. *Life of Johnson*, R.W. Chapman, Introduction by P. Rogers, Oxford, Oxford University Press.

Burke, J. J., Jr. 1992. Talk, Dialogue, Conversation, and Other Kinds of Speech Acts in Boswell's Life of Samuel Johnson. In K. L. Cope (ed.), *Compendious Conversations: The Method of Dialogue in the Early Enlightenment*: 65-79. Frankfurt, Peter Lang.

Clark, P. 2012. Clubs. In J. Lynch (ed.), *Samuel Johnson in Context*: 143-150. Cambridge, Cambridge University Press.

Drummond, J.C. and Wilbraham, A. 1958[2.] *The Englishman's Food. A History of Five Centuries of English Diet*. London, Jonathan Cape.
Hawkins, J. 1787. *The Life of Samuel Johnson, LL.D.*, London, J. Buckland *et al.*
Johnson, S. 1755. *A Dictionary of the English Language*, London, J. & P. Knapton *et al.*
Lynch Piozzi, H. 1786. *Anecdotes of the Late Samuel Johnson, LL.D., during the Last Twenty Years of His Life*, London, T. Cadell.
Murphy, A. 1792. *An Essay on the Life and Genius of Samuel Johnson, LL.D.*. London, T. Longman *et al.*
Picard, L. 2001. *Dr. Johnson's London*, London, Phoenix Press.
Pinnavaia, L. 2006. Idiomatic Expressions regarding Food and Drink in Johnson's *Dictionary of the English Language* (1755 and 1773). *Textus. English Studies in Italy* 29 (1): 151-165.
Rogers, P. 2012. Conversation. In J. Lynch (ed.), *Samuel Johnson in Context*: 151-156. Cambridge, Cambridge University Press.

Eighteenth-century drink receipts

These drink receipts were graciously provided by a very fine gentleman of our acquaintance Mr. Mike Williams.

To make a punch in the manner of P. Dunning, Esq.
Take five to eight ounces of Dark Rum or Brandy, as you wish, and put it to 24 ounces of fresh cool water, add to it the juice of ½ lemon and two or three tablespoons of the best refined sugar. (If you are close to the West Indies, Muscavado or Havana brown sugar can be used) If you please, grate in some nutmeg. This makes about a quart of a most delicate, fine, pleasant & wholesome liquor.

The Fish House Punch

Take one cup packed brown sugar and mix in a pan with four cups of water and boil 5 minutes. Squeeze the juice from 9 lemons and pour into the hot syrup. Add the lemon rinds. Cool the syrup and chill overnight so that the flavours blend. Just before you serve the punch, remove the rinds. Mix in 2 cups of the juice of pineapples, 1 fifth of Dark Rum, ½ of a fifth of Cognac and 4 tablespoons of peach brandy. Mix well. Pack a large punch bowl with crushed ice and then pour the punch over the ice and serve.

Second Horse Punch

½ pint light-bodied rum from the West Indies
½ pint peach Brandy, as made in South Carolina
½ pint juice of the lemon

5 tablespoons of bitters
4 tablespoons brown sugar
Stir thoroughly. If ice can be had, pour the mixture over a large block of ice. Add two to three pints of effervescent mineral water and serve at once.

Chiara Biscella

Jane Austen: appetite and sensibility

Introduction: food and society

It is a truth universally acknowledged that a cup of tea, in possession of pastries and biscuits, has the power to carry us away in time and space, in that typically English atmosphere that Jane Austen's novels embody to perfection. Indeed, those who will recall any work of the writer or one of the many film or television adaptations, will be reminded of scenes of elegant balls with sweets and cakes, conversations at the breakfast table or around a picnic blanket, invitations to dinner or to afternoon tea. These are occasions that Jane Austen uses to reveal how relationships are slowly woven among characters, to portray their social class or again to give more information about some specific circumstance; moreover, allowing us in the 21st century to take a closer look at the social and food habits of her times.

Thus the author, who does not usually insist on the description of courses and dishes, instead offers the reader in one of the last chapters of *Pride and Prejudice*, through Mrs Bennet's words, a brief account of what Mr Bingley and Mr Darcy are given for dinner when invited at Longbourn:

> The dinner was as well dressed as any I ever saw. The venison was roasted to a turn – and everybody said, they never saw so fat a haunch. The soup was fifty times better than what we had at the Lucas's last week; and even Mr. Darcy acknowledged that the partridges were remarkably well done; and I suppose he has two or three French cooks at least. (Austen 1996: 418)

Soup, venison, partridges: a rich supper is especially organized to tempt Mr Bingley into an engagement with Jane; a supper that moreover shows that the choice and preparation of food could become the symbol of a precise position in society. As Pen Vogler (2013) notes, partridges could in fact only be offered by those whose estates were extensive enough to support the shooting of game, while the disdainful reference to French cooks suggests an inclination towards local dishes rather than capricious aristocratic French recipes. The passage also provides a clear allusion to Mr Darcy's supposed pride.

As a side dish to this kind of event based on good food, however, are the feelings that inspire such a moment; sentiments that are revealed through overt or implied gestures and on which Jane Austen lingers with unique mastery. In the hands of the writer, a dinner is easily transformed into an occasion that directs the movements of every single character, as if each of them was a pawn on a chessboard.

> When they repaired to the dining-room, Elizabeth eagerly watched to see whether Bingley would take the place which, in all their former parties, had belonged to him, by her sister. Her prudent mother, occupied by the same ideas, forbore to invite him to sit by herself. On entering the room he seemed to hesitate; but Jane happened to look round, and happened to smile: it was decided -- he placed himself by her. [...] His behaviour to her sister was such, during dinner-time, as shewed an admiration of her, which, though more guarded than formerly, persuaded Elizabeth that, if left wholly to himself, Jane's happiness, and his own, would be speedily secured. Though she dared not depend upon the consequence, she yet received pleasure from observing his behaviour. It gave her all the animation that her spirits could boast; for she was in no cheerful humour. Mr. Darcy was almost as far from her as the table could divide them. He was on one side of her mother. She knew how little such a situation would give pleasure to either, or make either appear to advantage. She was not near enough to hear any of their discourse; but she could see how seldom they spoke to each other, and how formal and cold was their manner whenever they did. Her mother's ungraciousness made the sense of what they owed him more painful to Elizabeth's mind; and she would, at times, have given anything to be privileged to tell him that his kindness was neither unknown nor unfelt by the whole of the family. (Austen 1996: 417)

In this case, the attention of the reader is not caught by the delicacy and sophistication of what is being served, but rather by the unfolding of emotions at the dining table. The smiles and attentions on the part of Mr Bingley towards Jane act as a clear signal of their renewed love; similarly, if the choice of their seat at table is for Jane and Bingley the best possible one, this same choice becomes a real instrument of torture for poor Elizabeth: not only is she far from her beloved Mr Darcy – whose love for her, she is now inclined to think, has totally disappeared – but she even has to suffer from the humiliation of seeing him sitting next to her mum. Mrs Bennett indeed barely speaks to him or else merely converses in a cold manner, devoid of both grace and wisdom.

Food in Austen's novels is clearly regarded on the one hand as ostentation, and on the other as a social occasion. The ironic gaze of the writer does not hesitate to depict the trends of the moment or to subtly mock the affectation of the British upper classes. For example, invitations to dinner or to afternoon tea at

Lady Catherine de Bourgh's are considered a great honour by Maria Lucas, to the point of being actually counted – nine dinners and two teas (Austen 1996: 348); dinner at the Grants' in *Mansfield Park* is described as 'elegant and plentiful' and Jane Austen sarcastically outlines its 'wide table, the number of dishes, [...] the passing of servants' (Austen 1996: 583-4); again, dinner parties given by Mrs Elton are real style lessons for those who, living in the countryside, are not aware of the latest fashion trends in Bath:

> She was a little shocked at the want of two drawing rooms, at the poor attempt at rout-cakes, and there being no ice in the Highbury card parties. Mrs. Bates, Mrs. Perry, Mrs. Goddard and others, were a good deal behind hand in knowledge of the world, but she would soon shew them how every thing ought to be arranged. In the course of the spring she must return their civilities by one very superior party; in which her card tables should be set out with their separate candles and unbroken packs in the true style, and more waiters engaged for the evening than their own establishment could furnish, to carry round the refreshments at exactly the proper hour, and in the proper order. (Austen 1996: 887-8)

And let us not forget that picnics, lunches and dinners are very often the way for Austen to sketch invisible exchanges of glances, reveal intimate conversations, disclose the eccentricities and quirks of the characters, thus allowing the reader to know them better. In the novel *Emma*, for example, it is only too easy to realize that there are frequent occasions where food serves the purpose of unveiling thoughts and feelings. Mr Woodhouse is thus portrayed from the very beginning as an incorrigible hypochondriac terrified by wedding cakes and other devilish foodstuffs (Austen 1996: 731); dinner after Miss Taylor's wedding ceremony seems tasteless because of the absence of the beloved governess (Austen 1996: 724) and a recounting of the steps that led to Mr Elton's engagement with his future wife is briefly but significantly enriched by references to parties and dinners, gazes and smiles:

> [...] the history which he had to give Mrs. Cole of the rise and progress of the affair was so glorious -- the steps so quick, from the accidental rencontre, to the dinner at Mr. Green's, and the party at Mrs. Brown's -- smiles and blushes rising in importance -- with consciousness and agitation richly scattered -- the lady had been so easily impressed -- so sweetly disposed -- had in short, to use a most intelligible phrase, been so very ready to have him, that vanity and prudence were equally contented. (Austen 1996:834-5)

The tea ceremony

As seen so far, it is indisputable that Jane Austen prefers to put greater emphasis on the social context in which food and beverages are consumed, rather than engaging in long, accurate descriptions of dishes. Nevertheless, references to food and meals abound in her novels, and her private letters disclose the importance for her of eating well. This is what she writes to her sister Cassandra:

> My mother desires me to tell you that I am a very good housekeeper, which I have no reluctance in doing, because I really think it my peculiar excellence, and for this reason – I always take care to provide such things as please my own appetite, which I consider as the chief merit in housekeeping. I have had some ragout veal, and I mean to have some haricot mutton to-morrow. We are to kill a pig soon.[1]

Austen likes taking care of her own appetite, so no doubt that she is also interested in that of the characters she pens. And which is, then, the most frequently mentioned foodstuff in Austen's works? It is, sure enough, tea, with 58 occurrences in her six major novels: not a real food, but a drink that in the collective imagery has represented for centuries the entire British nation and that in our writer's novels is given a symbolic and metaphoric value on the one hand, while on the other it contributes to illustrating the habits of society.

Tea is a ritual, a ceremony, a 'solemn procession' (Austen 1996: 644) as Austen herself defines it, but also a much more intimate moment if compared to lunch or dinner: alone with a cup of tea, characters manage to have a private conversation far from eavesdroppers. For example, one could quote the dialogue between Colonel Brandon and Elinor, in which Mr Willoughby's engagement to Miss Gray, and its consequences for Marianne, are discussed (Austen 1996: 118); or one might recall the difficult, worrisome conversation between Elizabeth and her father after Lydia's flight (Austen 1996: 393); or again one could mention the first, enjoyable exchange between Catherine and Mr Tilney:

> There was little leisure for speaking while they danced; but when they were seated at tea, she found him as agreeable as she had already given him credit for being. He talked with fluency and spirit — and there was an archness and pleasantry in his manner which interested, though it was hardly understood by her. After chatting some time on such matters as naturally arose from the objects around them, he suddenly addressed her with — 'I have hitherto been very remiss, madam, in the proper attentions of a partner here; I have not yet asked you how long you have been in Bath; whether you were ever here before; whether you have been at the Upper Rooms, the theatre, and the concert; and how you like the place altogether. I have been very negligent — but are you now at leisure to satisfy me in these particulars? If you are I will begin directly. (Austen 1996: 1012)

---

[1] Letter of 17th November 1798, digitalized by www.Pemberley.com

Tea is also associated with a different quality, that of being a 'necessary of life' (Mayson 2000), in the words of Mrs Beeton; so the character of old Mrs Bates in *Emma* is said to be 'almost past everything but tea and quadrille' (Austen 1996: 732), a description that emphasizes the power of tea over everyone and at every age. Most of all, however, tea is described as a beverage capable of restoring both body and mind: thus Elinor, who had never left her sister's bedside during her illness, indulges at last in a cup of tea after the doctor's announcement that Marianne is out of danger (Austen 1996: 184); and thus in *Mansfield Park* Mrs Price cannot think about anything else but a good, refreshing cup of tea to offer to her own children, finally home after a long journey (Austen 1996: 664). Such an episode has moreover a strong metaphorical value, showing the striking contrast between the disorder of William and Fanny's birthplace and the refined elegance of life at Mansfield Park. Indeed, at Mrs Price's place, even something as simple as brewing tea seems to generate confusion, with a consequent waste of time and words; conversely, at Mansfield Park, tea time is a stylish event marked by a definite rhythm: it is an unchanging ritual whose rules must be obeyed by every participant. It is in the constant repetition and the stability of such a formal tea ceremony that Fanny Price draws the strength to keep calm after Henry Crawford's unwelcome wedding proposal:

> Fanny could hardly have kept her seat any longer, or have refrained from at least trying to get away in spite of all the too public opposition she foresaw to it, had it not been for the sound of approaching relief, the very sound which she had been long watching for, and long thinking strangely delayed. The solemn procession, headed by Baddeley, of tea-board, urn, and cake-bearers, made its appearance, and delivered her from a grievous imprisonment of body and mind. Mr. Crawford was obliged to move. She was at liberty, she was busy, she was protected. (Austen 1996: 644)

The solemn procession of trays, teapots and cakes brings comfort to Fanny, freeing her from Mr Crawford's oppressive presence and allowing her to get rid of the embarrassment of not knowing what to do or what to say.

Finally, tea in Jane Austen's works gives us a chance to peep into the domestic economy and, more generally, into the habits and customs of the later 18th century: how and where was tea kept? Who prepared it and served it? How and at which time of day was it usually drunk? Indications in this regard are indirectly conveyed by the writer herself, who very often depicts the heroines of her novels – or their mothers – in the act of brewing tea. As Kim Wilson writes:

> In Jane Austen's time, servants almost never prepared the tea, [...] because tea was too expensive to be entrusted to them. In an era when

the family maid might be selling even used tea leaves out the back door, her employers certainly didn't want to trust her with new tea. (Wilson 2011: 94)

Tea was thus prepared by the lady of the house or by one of her elder daughters. It was kept under lock and key in the drawing room in an elaborate tea caddy. Tea was usually served on two occasions: in the case of an informal tea party, family and friends would get together for tea one or two hours after lunch; in the case of a formal event, tea was offered when the gentlemen, who had spent the moments after dinner alone, would join the ladies in the sitting room. This was the right occasion to introduce children to guests: during tea time children did not intrude much; in fact, they were easily kept under control thanks to the biscuits and sweets usually offered as an accompaniment to a cup of tea (Comodini 2012: 25).

Conclusions: the legacy of Jane Austen

The paramount importance of tea in Jane Austen's novels is undeniable, as even our contemporary mass culture seems to suggest. Indeed, by merely Googling keywords such as 'Jane Austen and tea' or more generic expressions as 'Jane Austen and food', one is easily catapulted into a cyber-reality of online literary salons, more or less serious blogs, and television programmes. One might even find a diverting e-shop of tea bags, evocatively named *Bingley's Teas Limited*, where we might purchase the most interesting varieties of teas with the most intriguing names: 'Compassion for Mrs Bennet's Nerves', 'The Patience of Miss Price', 'Mr Darcy's Pride', or 'Marianne's Wild Abandon' are just a few examples. Yet, it is precisely these ramifications in contemporary culture, at once cultural and playful, that contribute to the making of Jane Austen as a great author, whose literary and culinary talent will never cease to surprise us.

Works cited

Austen, J. 1996. *The Complete Novels*. London, Penguin.
Austen, J. *Letters. Brabourne Edition*. Digitalized by Pemberley.com
Angelici, R. *I menu di Jane Austen*, published online, April 6th, 2013, in www.jasit.it
Black, M., Le Faye, D., 1995. *The Jane Austen Cookbook*. Chicago, Chicago Review Press.
Comodini, E. 2012. 'Jane Austen e il cibo: contesto e significazione in *Sense and Sensibility*, *Mansfield Park*, ed *Emma*'. MA Dissertation, Università degli Studi della Tuscia.

Sutherland, E. 1990. 'Dining at the Great House: Food and Drink in the Time of Jane Austen.' *Persuasions*, 12: 88-98.
Mayson, I. M. 2000. *Mrs Beeton's Book of Household Management.* Oxford, Oxford University Press.
Duquette, N. A. 2008. 'Laughter over Tea: Jane Austen and Culinary Pedagogy.' *Persuasions on line*, V. 29, 1, http://www.jasna.org/persuasions/on-line/.
Vogler, P. 2013. 'Pride and partridges: Jane Austen and food.' *The Guardian*, 21 November 2013.
Wilson, K. 2011. *Tea with Jane Austen.* London, Francis Lincoln.

Bath buns

From Mrs Raffald's *The Experienced English Housekeeper*, 1769. Mrs Raffald tells us to 'send them in hot for breakfast', which sounds rather indigestible for these rich, buttery buns, and may have been why, when Jane was staying with a rather mean aunt, she joked to Cassandra that she would make herself an inexpensive guest by 'disordering my stomach with Bath buns'.

Makes 12 cakes

1 lb/450g all-purpose (plain) flour
1 tsp salt (optional — not in original, but we find yeast buns very bland without it)
⅔ cup/150g butter
¼ oz/7g sachet active dried yeast
2 tbsp sugar
1 tbsp caraway seeds
1 cup/225ml milk

For the glaze

2 tbsp superfine (caster) sugar
1 tbsp milk
Sugar nibs, or a few sugar cubes, roughly crushed and mixed with a few caraway seeds. These are in place of the caraway comfits — sugar-coated caraway seeds — that Mrs Raffald would have used.

Add the salt to the flour, if using, and rub the butter in until it is like coarse bread crumbs; sprinkle in the yeast, sugar, and caraway seeds, and mix it together well. Warm the milk, and stir it into the dry ingredients to give a soft dough; add a little milk if necessary.

Give it a good knead for about ten minutes on a floured surface until it is smooth and pliable; return to the bowl, cover with a cloth, and let it rise in a warm place until double in size; it may take a good two or three hours because the butter in the dough impedes the rising action of the yeast.

Punch the air out of the dough and make up 12 cakes, put onto greased baking sheets, cover with a damp tea towel or plastic wrap (cling film) and leave to rise again for up to 1 hour.

Preheat the oven to 375°F/190°C/Gas Mark 5.

Bake for 12–15 minutes until they are golden brown.

Heat together the milk and sugar for the glaze, and brush it over the hot buns, then strew the crushed sugar cubes and caraway seeds over the top.

Anna Rudelli

Romantic food at Dove Cottage:
Dorothy Wordsworth's cookery and kitchen garden

Natives of Cockermouth, some 30 miles north of Grasmere, the Wordsworth offspring – Richard, William, Dorothy, John and Christopher – lost their parents at a very early age and were thus obliged to spend their youth apart: Dorothy stayed with her maternal grandparents in Penrith while John studied at Hawskhead Grammar School, and William and Christopher were at Cambridge. Richard, the eldest brother, was employed as a law clerk. They only met during the summer holidays. As a consequence of their forced separation, the Wordworths – and especially William and Dorothy – felt very attached to one another, to the point that the two decided that they would go and live together whenever possible. After their 1794 trip to the Lake District, during which they visited Keswick, Grasmere, Windermere and Borrowdale, William and Dorothy understood that this was the region where they wanted to settle. Even so, it was five years before they succeeded in moving to Grasmere, arriving there on 20 December 1799.

Originally, Dove Cottage was an inn called 'The Dove and Olive Bough'. When William and Dorothy moved there, the chimney in one room did not draw properly and the house was cold and humid. Still, such trivia did not affect Dorothy. She 'is much pleased with house and appurtenances, the orchard especially; in imagination she has already built a seat with a summer shed on the highest platform in this our little domestic slip of mountain' (Clark 1960: 17). There was a lot of work to do to fix a house in such a condition, considering that the walls had to be painted, the doors needed mending 'and heaven knows what' (Clark 1960: 19). Yet Dorothy immediately showed her ability as mistress of the house and busied herself in making the cottage comfortable.

The building is two storeys high. On the ground floor there are the kitchen and the parlour, a low-ceilinged room, wainscoted with oak and with diamond-paned windows; it is the main room of the lower floor. Behind the kitchen there are the scullery – which served as cellar and laundry – and a bedroom (Dorothy's). Upstairs there are the main bedroom (William's), a sitting room and 'a tiny annex hardly bigger than a cupboard' (De Selincourt 1933: 111) which Dorothy wallpapered with newspapers in order to isolate it from

Dove Cottage. Vegetable garden.
Copyright Anna Rudelli

Dove Cottage. Back garden.
Copyright Anna Rudelli.

humidity and cold, and which would later become the nursery for William's offspring. Once the house was ready, both Dorothy and William could devote themselves to their own tasks: he wrote while she looked after house and garden. In between chores and walks in the neighbourhood, Dorothy also kept a journal and – from time to time – composed poetry. Chores were interspersed with literary activities. One morning, for instance, Dorothy was very busy copying out her brother's poems, then she stopped for a while to gather peas for lunch. Later on in the afternoon Coleridge came to bring her a book, the *Annual Anthology*, containing works by Robert Southey and Coleridge himself, among other poets.

Living at Dove Cottage

An ordinary day at Dove Cottage entailed a little bit of working in the kitchen garden – in May it means hoeing peas, beans and radishes – then Dorothy had to cook, iron and mend clothes. In the afternoon, sometimes accompanied by William, Dorothy usually took a walk in the woods to gather flowers and plants to transplant in the garden; she also went to gather the mail at Ambleside or Rydal, the neighbouring towns. More often than not the Wordsworths took an afternoon nap. Tea time was usually spent with neighbours and friends: very seldom did they have tea or dinner by themselves. Evening, instead, was generally the time for reading and writing – William wrote poetry, Dorothy kept her journal, wrote letters and composed poetry as well.

People thought that the Wordsworths were rich because their garden was full of flowers, plants and vegetables. But in fact they were not wealthy in the Dove Cottage years. The profusion of greenery was due to the fact that whenever she went for a walk, Dorothy came back home with some herbs, shrubs and mosses to plant in the three yards between the front door of the cottage and the Town End road, enclosed by a dry stone fence built by William.

Usually Dorothy worked in the garden in the morning. However, she did not work there alone: Molly, the neighbour who helped to look after the house, was usually the one who weeded and cleared the garden, but sometimes her neighbour Aggy Ashburner also helped. John, Dorothy's brother, helped sticking the peas and sodding the ground. As a rule, the hard work fell on William: he cut down the winter cherry tree they had in the orchard, prepared pea sticks, spread manure on the soil, raked, dug a well at the very back of the garden and built a path that led to the upper end of the garden where he built a summer house. Other friends and neighbours helped in the garden: we read about 'John Fisher, T[homas]A[shburner], S[ally]A[shburner] and Molly working in the garden' (Wordsworth 1991: 27).

On 21 May 1802 William and Mr Simpson, a neighbour, went fishing after sunset, because evening in the Wordsworth household was as busy a moment of the day as any other. One cannot forget the passage in Dorothy's journal in which she records her going out on a solitary, twilight evening ramble, her picking shrubs and flowers and her planting them by moonlight, immediately after getting back home.

> In the Evening I was watering plants when Mr & Mrs Simpson called—I accompanied them home—& we went to the waterfall at the head of the valley—it was very interesting in the Twilight. I brought home lemon thyme & several other plants, & planted them by moonlight. (Wordsworth 1991: 7-8)

It was not unusual for Dorothy to work in the garden after the sun had set, during the summer: evening was the chosen moment to water plants, weed, stick peas and plant broccoli, sow kidney beans and spinach – even though it might be a cold evening – and to plant honeysuckle around the yew tree.

Even though in her book *Becoming Wordsworthian: a Performative Aesthetics* Elizabeth Fay writes that Dorothy's botanical interest was 'purely aesthetic and not housewifery' (Fay 1995: 104), Dorothy and William actually had a very thriving kitchen garden and orchard whose produce they consumed and cooked in a variety of ways, and also exploited for medicinal purposes.

In the kitchen garden they grew peas, radishes, onions, carrots, turnips, strawberries, lemon thyme, wild thyme, French beans, broccoli, kidney-beans, spinach, scarlet beans and potatoes, side by side with flowers, mostly gathered around Rydal Lake and its woods: lilies, periwinkle, London Pride, daisies, brooms, wild columbine, honeysuckle, foxgloves, mulleins, pansies and sunflowers.

Life at Dove Cottage and in the neighbourhood was pretty liberal and informal: visits to and from friends were often unannounced and might last long: Coleridge came over frequently, and more than once he stayed at Dove Cottage for longer periods, especially when he was too tired to ride back home, some twelve miles from the cottage. The easy-going lifestyle of the Wordsworths included also returning home to supper at 10 PM, which happened more than once, or taking an evening walk to eat gooseberries.

Dorothy's journal opens with a remark about food. At the time of writing – 14 May 1800 – William and John were leaving for Gallow Hill, near Scarborough, to visit their friends, the Hutchinsons. They set off with cold pork sandwiches in their pockets, lovingly prepared by their sister. It happened very often that the Wordsworths did not dine at home, for a variety of reasons: because they suddenly decided to go hiking in the mountains or to tramp to Keswick to visit Coleridge. In these cases, they either brought food from home – prepared by Dorothy, as usual – or they ate at some farmhouse or inn that they found on their way. When they took mountain walks, after a rich and strengthening breakfast – the broth William had every morning was substituted with something more inviting – William and Dorothy usually ate sandwiches made with leftovers and stored in a tin box, and apples picked in their orchard. Other times they bought bread and cheese or dined on ham, bread and milk at a farm on their way back to Grasmere. During their rambles they did not carry water with them, so they had to rely on the streams they found along the paths. Once they were leaving Thirsk on foot and were overpowered by thirst, thankfully quenched from a nearby brook. At the end of the ramble, when they arrived in Rievaulx, they both were very hungry and found a farmhouse, where they feasted on boiled milk and bread. On their way to Keswick, when they did not eat potted beef and some sweets, William and Dorothy often stopped at John Stanley's, landlord of the King's Head at Thirlspot, at the head of Thirlmere Lake, where they usually ate bread and drank beer or tea. On one occasion, shortly after Christmas Day, the Wordsworths went to John Stanley and preferred to eat roasted apples and Christmas pie rather than the cold mutton sandwiches that they were carrying in their pockets.

The summer diet at Dove Cottage

Eating out did not mean stopping by at farmhouses and inns alone, or eating sandwiches during mountain rambles. Eating out also entailed dining in the heart of nature just for the sake of it, which during the summer happened very often, especially considering that William and John would go fishing with their neighbours on a daily basis. Sometimes Dorothy accompanied them and caught some fish as well. Usually they fished in Grasmere Lake, where they could find bass and pike. Most of the times they spent the whole day there, and Dorothy brought them food and drinks on the lakeshore, where they dined together.

Usually they were lucky: after setting pike floats – Dorothy helped William in this task – on the morning of a cold June Wednesday, William and John went back to Dove Cottage in the afternoon with two pikes. On a successful fishing afternoon, Dorothy came home after tea with a 7 ½ lbs pike. The waters of the English Lakes abounded in fish: on a very fruitful fishing afternoon on Grasmere Lake, Dorothy, Mr and Miss Simpson, Miss Falcon and Mr Gells caught 13 bass. Luck was not always on their side however: after a whole fishing day, it might happen they went back home with just two small pikes.

Dove Cottage. The Summer House.
Copyright Anna Rudelli

Even though by now it seems clear that the summer diet at Dove Cottage consisted mostly of fish and the produce of the vegetable garden, we do not find detailed references in Dorothy's journal about how it was cooked. We only know that sometimes pikes were boiled and roasted, while at other times they were stuffed. We can assume that the herbs and vegetables that grew in the kitchen garden, such as wild and lemon thyme for instance, which Dorothy planted in June, were used to season the dishes.

On a Sunday in August 1802, the Wordsworths ate roast fish for lunch, then took an afternoon nap followed by a visit to Mr Simpson, where they ate black cherries. Dinner consisted of a pea dish. Once again, no recipe for the peas dish is indicated, but on scanning *The English Art of Cookery* – a 1788 cookbook compiled by Richard Briggs, a London chef – one finds various directions on how to cook them. There are two recipes for pea soup, one for veal and peas, another for stewed peas and lettuces, peas *à la Française* (which required the use of a Spanish onion – or English onion if the Spanish variety was not available – side by side with nutmeg, butter, flour and ketchup! [*sic*]), and the recipe for an omelette made with green peas. Considering that a few days before cooking this mysterious dish Dorothy had received a basket of lettuces as a gift, it is quite possible that she prepared the stewed peas and lettuces.

Cooking and baking

As a rule, one cannot find detailed recipes in the journal or indications on how to prepare food. There are always however references to the act of cooking and baking. In nearly every entry we may read that Dorothy baked bread, pies and tarts on a daily basis. When her brother married Mary Hutchinson, she helped Dorothy with the household management, cooking included. The interesting fact about baking is that every time Dorothy baked, she recorded it in her journal, even though nothing else specific happened, as the entries for Friday, 19 September 1801 and Tuesday, 2 November 1802 testify. In the former case, the only word written for the day is 'Baking.' (Wordsworth 1991: 35), whereas in the latter we read a slightly longer sentence, preceded by the phrase 'Baking Day' (Wordsworth 1991: 134) in capital letters.

On a hot Sunday morning in August, at six, Dorothy prepared pies, stuffed a pike and baked a loaf. We can assume that she did not eat all this food at once, since she was at home alone and on these occasions she preferred a frugal, 'hasty' dinner, as we can read every now and again. On one of these occasions – 19 May 1800 to be precise – perhaps because it was a Sunday, perhaps just because she felt like it, Dorothy treated herself with a hasty pudding, presumably some kind of porridge made of corn flour mixed with milk. Here is the recipe according to Richard Briggs:

> Take a quart of milk, put in four bay leaves, and set it on the fire to boil; beat up the yolks of two eggs with a little cold milk and salt, stir them into the milk, take out the bay leaves, then with a wooden spoon in one hand, and flour in the other, stir it in till it is of a good thickness, but not too thick, keep it stirring, and let it boil; then pour it into a deep dish, and put pieces of butter here and there on it. You may put a piece of butter in the milk instead of the eggs if you like it best. (Briggs 1788: 389-390)

Sometimes Dorothy prepared small loaves of bread instead of the usual large loaf, while the pies, depending on the season, included gooseberry or giblet as ingredients. It is interesting to note that Dorothy usually wrote no comments about the outcome of a dish. In the journals one can read only two remarks on this point: one is negative and the other is somewhat self-praising. 'The night before we had had broiled the gizzard and some mutton and made a nice piece of cookery for Wm's supper' is clearly the positive one, whereas 'Baking bread apple pies, and giblet pie--a bad giblet pie' shows dissatisfaction with the preparation of a dish.

One evening, after a walk to Ambleside to gather the mail – 'No letters! - only one newspaper' (Wordsworth 1991: 2) – Dorothy eats pudding. William is still away in Yorkshire with their brother John, so she is home alone. Once again there is not a more detailed reference to what kind of pudding it was, whether it was sweet or savoury: the Oxford English Dictionary reports that in modern use 'pudding' refers almost exclusively to sweet dishes, with the exception of a few savoury. During one of the frequent visits to her neighbours the Simpsons, Dorothy gathers gooseberries with them, and later on prepares a gooseberry pudding. Tommy, the Simpsons's son, enjoys it a lot at teatime.

On another occasion, Dorothy brings a basketful of gooseberries home to make preserve. In this case, she wrote down the recipe: 'Boiled gooseberries--N.B. 2 lbs of sugar in the first panfull, 3 quarts all good measure--3 lbs in the 2nd 4 quarts--2 ½ lbs in the 3rd' (Wordsworth 1991: 16). In any case, what we have just read looks more like an annotation for personal use rather than an actual recipe, as the 'N.B.' comment further suggests. We should also remember that Peter Brears, in his *Cooking and Dining with the Wordsworths*, notes that these annotations are in fact a sign of Dorothy's inexperience in making preserve, considering that she has to adjust the amount of sugar three times: Brears maintains that she doesn't have the 'elementary knowledge' (2011: 23) that people with some cooking skills have. The Simpsons also brought to the Wordsworths cream, potatoes, plums, pork and seed cake, the recipe of which is reported in Brigg's *The English Art of Cookery* (see Appendix). In exchange, Dorothy gave them peas and French beans, which abounded at Dove Cottage. They were not the only friends and neighbours with whom the Wordsworths exchanged food: they sent bread to the Coleridges, who lived at Greta Hall in Keswick and sent gooseberries in return. Gooseberries also came from Peggy Hodgson, a neighbour. The fact that Dorothy made preserve thus does not come as a surprise. Mrs Olliff, from Grasmere, brought some yeast, whereas Peggy Ashburner, after receiving a gift of goose from the Wordsworths sent back some honey, '--with a thousand thanks' (Wordsworth 1991: 41). On a Sunday lunch in January the Wordsworths feasted on turkey sent by Mrs Clarkson, Dorothy's most intimate friend who lived in Eusemere.

We must not forget that hardly a day passed without poor people and beggars knocking at the door of Dove Cottage, and asking for help, usually monetary. Dorothy prefers to feed them, instead of giving them money. So one day, when 'a very tall woman, tall much beyond the measure of tall women, called at the door' (Wordsworth 1991: 10), Dorothy gave her some bread. In her journal there are many and often lengthy descriptions of poor sailors, soldiers and beggars who stop by at the cottage to ask for money or some bread. A soldier, for instance, is given a penny and a slice of bacon.

The winter diet at Dove Cottage – and Christmas

The Wordsworths, especially during the summer months, caught fish in the nearby lakes and could rely on the produce of their vegetable garden for their sustenance. As a consequence, there was always fresh and home-grown food on the table. Considering the fact that during winter the kitchen garden did not give any produce, the diet was way less varied, even though fruits and vegetables were still part of the sustenance at Dove Cottage, as many journal entries demonstrate. It is interesting to note that Dorothy does not often refer to the purchase of food, except for some occasions when she reports buying bacon, fresh cream and mustard. In autumn and winter the Wordsworths ate potatoes, plums and apples, with which Dorothy prepared bread apple pie, tarts, and which were also roasted. Just as fish was consumed frequently during the summer, so meat was eaten in winter: giblet pie, pork, turkey, roast goose, roast or broiled mutton, broiled gizzard and boiled eggs were the core of the winter diet at Dove Cottage. When meat was roasted, it was done in large quantities, so that it could be eaten cold and used to prepare sandwiches to eat during outdoor rambles.

Around Christmas time, the Wordsworths enjoyed eating Christmas Pie even though they did not prepare it themselves: they would rather eat it at John Stanley's inn. Considering the number of ingredients necessary for its preparation and their cost, it is not surprising that Dorothy and Mary did not prepare a Christmas Pie at home (see recipe in Appendix) – we never have to forget that the Wordsworths were very careful in the management of their money during the Dove Cottage years. The size of the dish would actually have been the last of their concerns, if we keep in mind the numerous friends who visited the Wordsworths daily. Moreover, had they decided to cook it, they could have eaten leftovers for a long time: the preservation of food at the cottage was quite easy, because beneath the scullery floor there ran a stream, and the room was rather cold the whole year round. What they did bake around Christmas time was gingerbread: in the last entry of the *Grasmere Journals* we read about William's fancy for some gingerbread, and about his caring sister who immediately put on her spencer and cloak and walked to Matthew Newton's – a 'bread merchant' as William Green refers to him in his *Guide to the Lakes* (Green 1819: 392) – to buy six pennyworth to satisfy her brother's wish. The next morning they baked it themselves.

It is important not to confuse gingerbread with parkin cake, which also contained ginger and whose preparation Dorothy records in her journal. Unfortunately, there is no reference to the recipe in Dorothy's journal, nor in Brigg's cookery book, probably because it is a regional dish typical of Lancashire and West Yorkshire, where it is usually prepared on Guy Fawkes Night. The main difference lies in the ingredients: parkin cake is basically prepared with oatmeal, flour, black treacle, fat and ginger whereas to make gingerbread one needs butter, flour, sugar, ginger, nutmeg, treacle and cream.

Drinks and beverages (with and without alcohol)

Tea was an ever-present drink at Dove Cottage. There are days in which it seems that the Wordsworths consumed nothing except for tea. Tea was bought once a year from the well-known tea firm Twinings, founded in London in 1706. Tea was expensive (at around 7 shillings per pound). While they were at Dove Cottage the Wordsworths usually ordered 20lbs per year, as well as some coffee. Later on, when their savings allowed it, they would buy as much as 75lbs of Souchong, 30lbs of Congou and 6lbs of West India coffee.

Tea was not the only drink that one could find in the Wordsworth household however, for there were also alcoholic beverages such as rum and brandy, usually taken warm and with water. And even though in his poem 'The Waggoner' William defines himself 'a simple water-drinking Bard', he enjoyed spirits as well. As a matter of fact, William, together with his sister, bottled rum at home and once needed to borrow some bottles from Mr Simpson because he didn't have enough. A few days after bottling, Mr Simpson called in at Dove Cottage to drink a glass of it, followed by Charles Lloyd, another neighbour. During a mountain ramble with William and Coleridge, Dorothy 'drank a little Brandy and water and was in Heaven' (Wordsworth 1991: 95). In his foreword to *Wordsworth's Gardens*, Peter Elkington suggests that in their vegetable garden at Dove Cottage the Wordsworths grew a plant that was a remedy for hangovers, namely thyme. 'An infusion of the leaves removes the headach ocasioned [*sic*] by the debauch of the preceding evening' (Buchanan 2001 xii).

After three years of life at Dove Cottage the Wordsworths were forced to move away because the family was growing: by the end of 1803 Mary and William had been married for one year and she had already given birth to two children; her sister Sara had come to live at Town End as well, to be of help. The cottage with its two bedrooms was becoming too small for a growing family, to the point that Dorothy slept in the parlour downstairs, on a camp bed. They moved first to Allan Bank, then to the Grasmere Rectory and finally to Rydal Mount, on the shores of Rydal Water. Even though Rydal Mount was a much bigger house and their finances were more stable, the Wordsworths continued the lifestyle they had established in the Dove Cottage years, keeping a kitchen garden – a much larger one, considering that the grounds around Rydal Mount were seven or eight times more extensive than those at Dove Cottage – an orchard, a Summer House and all the love of poetry, nature and mountain rambles that they had inaugurated during the Dove Cottage years.

Works cited

Brears, P. 2011. *Cooking and Dining with the Wordsworths*, Ludlow, Excellent Press.

Briggs, R. 1788. *The English Art of Cookery, According to the Present Practice: Being a Complete Guide to All Housekeepers, on a Plan Entirely New; Consisting of Thirty-Eight Chapters*, London, G. G. J. and J. Robinson.

Buchanan, C. 2001. *Wordsworth's Gardens*, Lubbock, Texas Tech University Press.

Green, W. 1819. *The Tourist's New Guide, containing a Description of the Lakes, Mountains and Scenery, in Cumberland, Westmorland, and Lancashire*, 2 vols., Kendal.

Clark, C. (ed.) 1960. *Home at Grasmere. Extracts from the Journal of Dorothy Wordsworth and the Poems of William Wordsworth*. London, Penguin.

Cochrane, M. and R. 2001. *Housekeeping with Dorothy Wordsworth at Dove Cottage*, Beverley, Highgate of Beverley.

De Selincourt, E. 1933. *Dorothy Wordsworth*. Oxford, Oxford University Press.

Fay, E. A. 1995. *Becoming Wordsworthian: a Performative Aesthetics*, Amherst, University of Massachusetts Press.

Gittings, R. and Manton, J. 1988. *Dorothy Wordsworth*, Oxford, Oxford University Press.

Southey, R. (ed.) 1800. *The Annual Anthology 1799-1800*, 2 vols., London, T.N. Longman and O. Rees.

Wordsworth, D. 1971. *Journals of Dorothy Wordsworth*, Mary Moorman ed., Oxford, Oxford University Press.

Wordsworth. D. 1991. *The Grasmere Journals*, ed. Pamela Woof. Oxford, Oxford University Press.

Recipes. Sweet ...

Gooseberry pie

Lay a thin paste round the rim of your dish, put a little sugar at the bottom, pick your gooseberries, and if it is rainy weather, or they are dusty, wash them, and lay them in, put sugar over them, put a little water in the dish, put a nice puff paste over them, and bake them in a moderate oven; let the pie be cold before you send it to table; or if you like it, you may cream it the same as a green coddling pie. (Briggs 1788 429)

Parkin cake

Take half a peck of flour, a pound and a half of fresh butter, put the butter into a saucepan, with a pint of new milk, and set it on the fire; take a pound of sugar pounded, half an ounce of all-spice pounded, and mix them with the flour; when the butter is melted pour the milk and butter in the middle of the flour, and work it up like paste; pour in with the milk and butter half a pint of good ale yeast, set it before the fire to rise before it goes to the oven; put in two ounces of carraway-seeds, put it into a hoop, and bake it in a quick oven. (Briggs 1788 528)

... and savoury

Giblet pie

Take two pair of young goose giblets, scalded and washed clean, and cut them in pieces the same as for stewing or soup; lay a thin paste round the rim of your dish, put in your giblets, season them with pepper and salt, put a little butter on them, and put in a gill of water; put a puff-paste half an inch thick over them, close it, rub it over with the yolk of an egg, ornament the top, and bake it two hours in a good oven; when it is taken out put some good gravy in, and send it up hot.

When your giblets begin to get hard put them in a sauce-pan, cover them with water, stew them till they are tender, and let them stand till they are cold before you put them in the pie. Some put a thin beef-steak at the bottom, and some thin lamb-chops, but in that case you may do as you think proper (Briggs 1788: 413).

Yorkshire Christmas Pie

Take a fine large turkey, a goose, a large fowl, a partridge, and a pigeon, and bone them all nicely; beat half an ounce of mace, half an ounce of nutmegs, a quarter of an ounce cloves, half an ounce of white pepper ground, and two large spoonsful of salt, all mixed together; open all the fowls down the back, lay the turkey on the dresser, season it in the inside, lay the goose breast downwards in the turkey, then season the goose, put in the fowl the same way, then the partridge, then the pigeon, close them together, to make them look like a whole turkey, as well as you can; case and bone a hare, and cut it in pieces, with six woodcocks, moor game, or small wild fowl all boned; make a bushel of flour with ten pounds of butter into a paste, as directed, make the bottom and sides very thick, and raise it as high as you can, put in some seasoning, then lay in the turkey, &c. breast uppermost, lay the hare on one side, and the woodcocks, moor game, or wild fowl, on the other side, sprinkle seasoning over all, put four pounds of butter on the top, lay on a thick lid, ornament the sides and top, but first rub it over with the yolk of an egg, put paper over it, and bake it in a hot oven for six hours; let it stand till it is cold before you cut it. It will keep a good while (Briggs 1788: 410).

Marco Canani

Percy Bysshe Shelley, a vegetarian poet

Vegetarian and vegan eating habits have gained increasing popularity over the last few years. The need to reduce the impact of man on the environment, the development of ecological and ecocentric feelings, and the desire to reduce the intake of animal fats and proteins are just some of the reasons that account for this change. In 2014, a study published by the Heinrich Böll Foundation – an organisation working in the field of human rights and environmental sustainability – revealed that about 375 million people worldwide are vegetarian (Chemnitz and Becheva 2014: 67). This research, however, suggests interesting differences among the continents, but also from the viewpoint of gender. Such evidence confirms the idea that eating habits are not only determined by rational principles by which human beings satisfy their biological needs. They are, in fact, cultural practices through which people affirm their individual, social and religious identity (see Kittler, Sucher and Nelms 2012).

From a historical perspective, vegetarianism finds its origin in the Western classical tradition. The Greek philosopher Pythagoras was probably the first to ban butchered meat from the table, condemning its consumption almost as a taboo. Sensitive as he was to Egyptian, Babylonian and Oriental influences, Pythagoras believed in metempsychosis, the idea of the perpetual re-embodiment of the human soul in various forms of life. From this perspective, eating meat was not different from cannibalism, and as such it was considered as a crime that corrupts the individual (Spencer 1995: 38-46; Stuart 2006: 39-42).

Inspired by these classical examples, English culture reveals a long and serious reflection on the adoption of the 'Pythagorean' or 'natural' diet. In 1837, the disciples of the English merchant James Pierrepont Greaves established at Alcott House, in Surrey, the so-called 'Concordium', a community of people who considered themselves as 'united individuals […] desirous, under industrial and progressive education, with simplicity in diet, dress and lodging, etc., to retain the means for the harmonic developement [sic] of their physical, intellectual and moral natures' (Gregory 2007: 22). The members of the 'Concordium' – which also had two official magazines, *The Healthian* and *The New Age* – followed a diet strictly based on porridge, cereals, bread with raisins, and fresh fruit. In addition, the community could meet their needs by growing their own vegetables.

The early Victorian age witnessed the apex of the English reflection on what would be vegetarianism. In 1847, William Oldham – one of the members of Alcott House – published a call for 'a Physiological Conference' from the pages of William Horsell's *Truth-Tester*. The conference took place the following September at Northwood Villa – a hydropathic institute run by Horsell in Ramsgate, Kent, – and resulted in the creation of the Vegetarian Society, which was crucial in institutionalising food and cultural practices that were already well established in England (Spencer 1995: 252).

Vegetarianism in England between the 18th and the 19th century

In the Augustan Age, Alexander Pope had harshly criticised human tyranny over the other animal species. Like Pythagoras, Pope did not claim that men should give up meat for health reasons. Instead, he had denounced the barbarous slaughter of both domestic animals and wildlife, paving the way for the eighteenth-century reflection on human cruelty that is powerfully shown by William Hogarth's 1751 series of engravings *The Four Stages of Human Cruelty*.

The natural diet was especially popular during the Romantic Age. At that time, as Morton notes, vegetarianism was often the expression of various feelings and trends, from a 'cutting edge of bourgeois consumer style' to 'a thread of continuity from the religious radicalism of the seventeenth century' and 'a logical extension of Enlightenment discourse on the rights of women and men' (Morton 2006: 52). It is therefore not surprising that one of the strongest advocates of vegetarianism was Percy Bysshe Shelley. His poetry notably reflects his revolutionary and utopian beliefs, blending his desire of radical reform with Neoplatonic idealism. Shelley's defence of the vegetarian diet shapes his life as well as his works, and although it stems from idealistic and ethical principles, it is sustained by his knowledge of late eighteenth and early nineteenth century anatomy. In Shelley's thought, Ancient Greek culture and mythology forestalled and illustrated what contemporary anatomy would prove.

Shelley's vegetarianism, between theory and practice

Shelley most likely became interested in vegetarianism while at Oxford, when his refusal of aristocratic and bourgeois values resulted in his expulsion from University College in 1811. Since the late eighteenth century, eating habits in England had become different on the basis of social status. These changes were the result of more intensive animal breeding practices and new and more accurate fodder production techniques. The increase in the supply of meat had therefore sparked what the sociologist Thorstein Veblen would label as a 'trickle-down effect'. In the early 1800s the emerging middle class welcomed

THE VEGETARIAN SOCIETY,

75, PRINCESS STREET, MANCHESTER.

ESTABLISHED A.D. 1847.

President—The Rev. Professor John E. B. Mayor, M.A., Senior Fellow of St. John's Cambridge.

Treasurer—Edwin Collier, Esq., Manchester.

Vice-Presidents:—

W. E. A. Axon, Esq., F.R.S.L., Manchester.	Rev. John Higgins, Melbourne
Edmund J. Baillie, Esq., F.L.S., Chester.	A. F. Hills, Esq., London.
Miss Brotherton, Seedley, Manchester.	A. O. Hume, Esq., C.B., Simla.
The Hon. F. J. Bruce, Arbroath, N.B.	T. C. Lowe, Esq., B.A., Hamstead Hill School, Birmingham.
The Rev. James Clark, Salford.	Edward Maitland, Esq., B.A., London.
The Rev. H. S. Clubb, Philadelphia.	John Malcolm, Esq., F.R.C.S. Eng.
Edwin Collier, Esq., Manchester.	The Rev. W. J. Monk, M.A., Dodington Vicarage
General J. M. Earle, London.	James Parrott, Esq., Salford.
Peter Foxcroft, Esq., Glazebrook	Isaac Pitman, Esq., Bath.
J. W. Goddard, Esq., Leicester.	H. Rickards, Esq., Douglas, Isle-of-Man.
D. Gostling, Esq., Bombay.	H. S. Salt, Esq., London.
T. Anderson Hanson, Esq., London.	Mrs. John Smith, Glasgow.
Edward Hare, Esq., C.S.I., Bath	J. J. Willis, Esq., Austwick.
William Harrison, Esq., Manchester.	

Foreign and Colonial Representatives.

AMERICA: Rev. W. P. Alcott, Boxford, Mass., U.S.A. Elder F. W. Evans, Shaker Settlement, Mount Lebanon, New York, U.S.A.

Executive Committee:—

Mr. Ernest Axon.	Mr. Robert Gibbon.	Mr. W. Huntington.	Mr. A. C. Warren
Mr. James Booth.	Mr. J. J. Greenhalgh.	Mrs. Joseph Knight.	Mr T. J. Wood.
Mr. A. W. Duncan, F.C.S.	Mrs. W. Harrison.	Mr. Joseph Roberts.	

Honorary Auditor—Mr. Alfred Tongue, F.C.A. Seedley, Manchester.

Honorary Librarian—Mr. Ernest Axon. | *Honorary Secretary*—Mr. William E. A. Axon,
Secretary—Mr. Joseph Knight.

NOTE.— All Communications to be directed, not to individuals, but to **THE VEGETARIAN SOCIETY, 75, PRINCESS STREET, MANCHESTER.**

AIMS.—To induce habits of abstinence from the Flesh of Animals (Fish, Flesh, Fowl) as Food, and to promote the use of fruits, pulse, cereals, and other products of the Vegetable Kingdom.

SUBSCRIPTIONS.—The Society is supported by (a) Members, (b) Associates, and (c) Subscribers, to each of whom the Society's Magazine *(The Vegetarian Messenger)* is posted monthly. Supporters of each class contribute a minimum subscription of half-a-crown a year. Minimum subscription for West Indies, etc., 3s.; India, China, etc., 3s. 6d.; Australasia, South Africa, etc., 4s. Remittances are requested in Cheques (payable to Edwin Collier), or Postal Orders. If stamps are sent, halfpenny postages are preferred.

CONSTITUTION.—The Society is constituted of a President, Vice-Presidents, Treasurer, an Executive Committee, a Secretary, and an unlimited number of Members and Associates, who have subscribed to the Declaration of the Society. The Forms of Declaration may be obtained on application

DEFINITIONS.—(a) A "Member" agrees to *adopt* the Vegetarian system of Diet (*i.e.*, abstinence from Fish, Flesh, and Fowl as Food), may *vote* at the Society's meetings, and is eligible for election to any office of the Society. (b) An "Associate" agrees to *promote* the Vegetarian system, and may *attend* the Society's meetings. (c) A "Subscriber" may *attend* the Society's meetings.

Notice of the Vegetarian Society, 1890.
(Wikimedia Commons)

meat consumption, which had long been a privilege of the aristocracy, while the lower classes still followed a diet that was largely based on milk, porridge, potatoes and vegetables (Perkins 2003: 118).

The first literary instance of Shelley's defence of vegetarianism is included in his 1813 *Queen Mab: A Philosophical Poem*. However, Thomas Jefferson Hogg records in his biography that even at Oxford the poet would privilege a 'plain and simple' diet, mostly based on bread:

> [Shelley] could have lived on bread alone without repining. [...] [H]is pockets were generally well-stored with bread. A circle upon the carpet, clearly defined by an ample verge of crumbs, often marked the place where he had long sat at his studies, his face nearly in contact with his book, greedily devouring bread at intervals amidst his profound abstractions. For the most part he took no condiments; sometimes, however, he ate with his bread the common raisins which are used in making puddings, and these he would buy at little mean shops. (Hogg 1904: 112-13)

Shelley was especially fond of bread with raisins, which he would devour while studying at the library. After about 1810, Shelley condemned meat consumption believing in the equality of every living being in nature. His diet was thus largely based on carbohydrates, fibres and vitamins coming from fruit and vegetables. In addition, the poet was fond of sugary food. Along with his beloved bread with raisins, Shelley also had a passion for honey and fruit preserves:

> The common fruit of stalls, and oranges and apples were always welcome to Shelley; he would crunch the latter as heartily as a schoolboy. Vegetables, and especially salads, and pies and puddings were acceptable. [...] Like all persons of simple tastes, he retained his sweet tooth. He would greedily eat cakes, gingerbread and sugar; honey, preserved or stewed fruit with bread, were his favourite delicacies. (Hogg 1904: 113-14)

Shelley had indeed a sweet tooth, and he compensated for the absence of meat from his diet with a variety of fresh fruit and legumes. His eating regimen had evidently an ethical basis, but Shelley was also convinced of the health benefits of the natural diet:

> Flesh, fowl, fish, game, never appeared; nor eggs bodily in their individual capacity, nor butter in the gross: the two latter articles were admitted into cookery, it is true, but as sparingly as possible, and their presence was provisional, interlocutory, under protest, as culinary aids not approved of and soon to be dispensed with. The injunction extended to shell-fish. [...] We had soups in great variety, that seemed the more delicate from the absence of meat. There were vegetables of every kind,

> [...] either plainly or stewed, and otherwise artfully and scientifically arranged and disguised. Puddings, tarts, confections, sweets, abounded. Cheese was under the ban –, anathematized, excommunicate. Milk and cream might not be taken unreservedly; however, they were allowed to form ingredients in puddings, and to be poured sparingly in tea, as an indulgence to the weakness of neophytes, tender plants. (Hogg 1858 II: 419-20)

During his short stay at Oxford, Shelley took on those eating habits he would strongly defend and promote in the following years. At that time, though, his abstinence from meat seems not to have been absolute. While staying in Dublin with the poet in March 1812, Harriet Westbrook wrote a letter to Elizabeth Hitchener which suggests a more hard-and-fast vegetarian diet in spite of the scarcity of fresh produce:

> You do not know that we have forsworn meat & adopted the Pithagorean [*sic*] system; about a fortnight has elapsed since the change and we do not find ourselves any the worse for it. What do you think of it? many say it is a very bad plan but as facts go before argument we shall see whether the general opinion is true or false – we are delighted with it & think it the best thing in the world; as yet there is but little change of vegetable, but the time of year is coming on when there will no deficiency. (Jones 1964 I: 274-75)

In 1813, Shelley's reflection on vegetarianism begins to shape his poetry. In that year, he published his first long poem, *Queen Mab*, which reveals his plea for political and social reform. Influenced by Rousseau's *Emile*, William Godwin's ideas, and the ideals of the libertarian revolutions of the late eighteenth century, Shelley harshly criticises institutions for corrupting human nature and hopes for a future steered by the redeeming force of love. *Queen Mab* also discloses Shelley's pantheistic view, according to which every creature occupies a specific place in the harmonious design of nature. Thus, towards the end of Canto VIII, the faery Mab foresees a utopian future in which man will be reconciled with nature. Terror and suffering will disappear from the world, and so will butchering and meat consumption:

> [...] no longer now
> [man] slays the lamb that looks him in the face,
> And horribly devours his mangled flesh,
> Which, still avenging Nature's broken law,
> Kindled all putrid humours in his frame,
> All evil passions and all vain belief,
> Hatred, despair and loathing in his mind,
> The germs of misery, death, disease and crime. (Shelley 1977: 63)

The ecocentric aspect embedded in Shelley's thought, and his plea for animal protection, are the result of his pantheistic conception of nature, but they paradoxically develop an anthropocentric view. Embracing a vegetarian diet is a way not only to re-establish the equality between man and animal, but also between fellow human beings. Moreover, the 'natural' diet could help to eliminate the differences between social classes while ensuring the purification of the soul. Thus, in the Appendix to *Queen Mab*, Shelley included a detailed note in which he first introduced the principles he would expound in the pamphlets 'A Vindication of Natural Diet' (1812) and 'On the Vegetable System of Diet' (1814-15). In these essays, Shelley advocates the natural diet by combining philosophical and ethical motivations with his knowledge of early nineteenth-century science and anatomy.

Shelley's defence of the natural diet

Although the words 'vegetarian' and 'vegetarianism' were already present in English, they were not common use before the establishment of the Vegetarian Society in 1847. Shelley, in fact, used to refer to vegetarianism as the 'Pythagorean' or 'natural' diet. It should be noted, however, that by 'natural' Shelley did not simply mean a diet based on fruit, vegetables or legumes. Instead, he recommended embracing a food regimen based on products that were compatible with the metaphysical and physiological nature of the human body, and able to promote man's respectful and harmonious relationship with nature. In Shelley's opinion, the corruption of man's spirit and actions was the result of eating habits that were ill-suited for the human body:

> I hold that the depravity of the physical and moral nature of man originated in his unnatural habits of life. [...] [A]t some distant period man forsook the path of nature, and sacrificed the purity and happiness of his being to unnatural appetites. [...] The allegory of Adam and Eve eating of the tree of evil, and entailing upon the posterity the wrath of God, and the loss of everlasting life, admits of no other explanation, than the disease and crime that have flowed from unnatural diet. (Shelley 1993: 77)

Thus, natural does not simply mean 'non-animal'. A couple of years after 'A Vindication of Natural Diet,' Shelley would strongly emphasise this aspect in 'The Vegetable System of Diet'. Published posthumously in 1929, this second pamphlet is likely to have been written around 1814-1815. Linking the corruption of the human soul to food habits that he believes to be based on detrimental practices, Shelley states that '[b]y an unnatural habit is to be understood such an [sic] habit as is manifestly inconsistent with the conformation of any animal; and the inconsistency is to be esteemed a sufficient evidence of its pernicious consequences' (Shelley 1993: 150-51).

Placed at the beginning of his 'Vindication', Shelley's reference to the story of Adam and Eve establishes a clear connection to unnatural eating habits and the original sin. He believes that the consumption of meat might be the cause of violent and cruel behaviour in men, and Stuart actually suggests that in Shelley's view eating meat is an act as pernicious as the opening of Pandora's box (Stuart 2006: 386). Such a metaphor is indeed suitable, since the poet develops his argument from the myth, be it Christian or classical. In particular, the myth of Prometheus helps him to trace man's fall back to his culinary faults. One should bear in mind here that in *Prometheus Unbound* (1820) the poet would offer a highly emphatic portrait of the Titan. In Shelley's drama, Prometheus's fault is noble in that it is the result of a transgression committed to the benefit of humankind. And in his 'Vindication', Prometheus's offence does not lie in disclosing the secret of fire. The problem is its use for cooking purposes, which only seemingly make meat palatable and digestible. The human body, Shelley emphasises in his pamphlet, would not otherwise be able to process such a food:

> Comparative anatomy teaches us that man resembles frugivorous animals in every thing, and carnivorous in nothing; he has neither claws wherewith to seize his prey, nor distinct and pointed teeth to tear the living fibre. [...] It is only by softening and disguising dead flesh by culinary preparation, that it is rendered susceptible of mastication or digestion; and that the sight of its bloody juices and raw horror, does not excite intolerable loathing and disgust. (Shelley 1993: 80)

In 'The Vegetable System of Diet', Shelly would further condemn the consequences of Prometheus's sin from the point of view of human anatomy, noting that the absence of claws and fangs suggests that man is not biologically fit for the omnivorous diet. In addition, cooking as a cultural practice confirms his views. '[T]he food which is not to be eaten without the most intolerable loathing until it is altered by the action of fire and disguised by the addition of condiments,' Shelley points out, 'is not that food for which [man] is adapted by his physical construction' (Shelley 1993: 152).

Although he is primarily interested in the natural diet for ethical reasons, Shelley gives scientific grounding to his theory in the detailed bibliographical references that he adds to 'A Vindication of Natural Diet'. On the one hand, his main argument is based on two texts: Joseph Ritson's *An Essay on Abstinence from Animal Food, as a Moral Duty* (1802), and *Return to Nature, or Defence of Vegetable Regimen* (1811) by John Frank Newton, whose theories, Shelley thought, were proved by the beauty and health of his children. On the other hand, the poet drew scientific facts from George Cuvier's *Leçons d'Anatomie Comparée* (1800-1805) and dr. William Lambe's *Reports on Cancer* (1809). By referring to such studies, Shelley maintained that the absorptive surface area of the human intestine and the length of the caecum –

which is similar to that found in herbivorous species – suggest the opportunity of endorsing a vegetarian diet. Once again, scientific facts blend with cultural practices in his empirical observation that children – whom Shelley sees as individuals still untainted by society – 'evidently prefer pastry, oranges, apples and other fruits, to the flesh of animals' (Shelley 1993: 81).

Shelley's argument develops a triangulation between anatomical facts, cultural practices and food sustainability. His reception of the theories promoted by Thomas Malthus – whom he writes off as 'a eunuch and a tyrant' – is notably complex (see Morton 1994: 207-14), yet Shelley lists sustainability among the benefits of the natural diet. His concern is specifically directed to animal farming, which was developing as an industry, and Shelley reveals his debt to William Godwin's utopian rationalism in the belief that

> the spirit of the nation that should take lead in this great reform, would insensibly become agricultural; commerce, with all its vice, selfishness and corruption, would gradually decline; more natural habits would produce gentler manners, and the excessive complication of political relations would be so far simplified, that every individual might feel and understand why he loved his country, and took a personal interest in its welfare. (Shelley 1993: 85)

The connection between the individual and the social body is twofold. In addition to promoting an egalitarian diet among the different social classes, embracing a natural diet means for Shelley to strike 'at the root of the evil' (Shelley 1993: 86).

Embracing the Latin mantra *mens sana in corpore sano*, Shelley advocates the vegetarian regimen in the light of its factual benefits – from giving health and strength back to ill and weak bodies to calming mental disorders and promoting a peaceful and respectful behaviour. In the long term, the impact of meat on the human body is as negative as that of alcohol. And, Hogg records in his biography of the poet at Oxford, Shelley would equally abstain from spirituous liqueurs:

> [Shelley's] beverage consisted of copious and frequent draughts of cold water, but tea was ever grateful, cup after cup, and coffee. Wine was taken with singular moderation, commonly diluted largely with water, and for a long period he would abstain from it altogether. He avoided the use of spirits almost invariably, and even in the most minute portions. (Hogg 1904: 114)

As if he meant to further clarify and summarise the precepts of the natural diet, Shelley closes his 'Vindication' with what he must have believed to be the golden rules of healthy eating. The use of capital letters works as a reminder of the quick and simple prescriptions he leaves his readers with:

NEVER TAKE ANY SUBSTANCE INTO THE STOMACH THAT ONCE HAD LIFE.

DRINK NO LIQUID BUT WATER RESTORED TO ITS ORIGINAL PURITY BY DISTILLATION. (Shelley 1993: 89)

Although Shelley abstained completely from liqueurs, Hogg reminds us that the poet would not turn down a glass of wine when in good company. Ageing and the hereditary predisposition to diseases might not be defeated, but as a proof to his argument, Shelley closes 'A Vindication of a Natural Diet' with an Appendix – which was not originally included in the note to *Queen Mab* – that enlists thirteen vegetarians who lived to be older than 100. First and foremost is Thomas 'Old Parr', the legendary Briton who, being born in the Elizabethan Age and dead during the reign of Charles I, allegedly lived until the age of 152. If Shelley had lived that long too, he would have learnt that Old Parr would be the brand of a well-known Scotch whisky. Mass culture has associated Parr's

Drypoint by George Powle (fl. 1764–1771) after Peter Paul Rubens.
(Wikimedia Commons)

miraculous longevity with one of Shelley's taboos, and after all, in his biography, even Hogg seems to wish Shelley had taken things more lightly at times:

> I have often thought, and I have now and then even hinted, that if he could only bring himself to drink a bottle of choice port with his father, to sit sociably with him for an hour or two, and patiently to hear the old squire extol his wine and himself, they would get on much better together, and many serious difficulties and inconveniences would be avoided. (Hogg 1858 II: 415)

Literary evidence suggests that the poet continued to follow the natural diet after his elopement with Mary Wollstonecraft. Even in *Frankenstein* – whose subtitle is, quite interestingly, *or, The Modern Prometheus* – the creature refuses meat, declaring, '[m]y food is not that of man; I do not destroy the lamb and the kid to glut my appetite; acorns and berries afford me sufficient nourishment' (Shelley 2003: 118). Sunstein notes that once she got married to Shelley, Mary habitually

> laid in a store of vegetarian foods, occasionally made [Shelley] a passable pudding, without sugar, which they boycotted because it came from slave plantations. She liked her tea sandwiches cut neatly, but dinner with proper courses was a rarity unless they had company, and throughout their union friends complained about the quality of her table. (Sunstein 1989: 104)

It is difficult to establish with certainty whether Shelley followed a vegetarian diet rigorously in the decade that spans from the publication of *Queen Mab* to his death in 1822. Hogg recalls one evening in London when Shelley, despite his initial disgust, 'voraciously' devoured a plate of bacon (Hogg 1858 II: 34-35), while Wroe suggests that the poet occasionally yielded to cold meat while living in Italy (Wroe 2013: 30). In any case, fresh produce seemed not to only to satisfy the poet's bodily needs, but also his tastes. Another of Shelley's friends, the painter Benjamin Robert Haydon, recollects that the poet would gladly devour 'a bit of broccoli or cabbage on his plate, as if it had been the substantial wing of a chicken' (Morton 1994: 73). Although he might have occasionally yielded to temptation, bread, raisins, sweets, fresh fruit, legumes and vegetables formed the core of Shelley's diet even in his last years. While in Naples in 1818, the poet noted in a letter he wrote to Thomas Love Peacock that '[c]ountesses smell so of garlick that an ordinary Englishman cannot approach them' (Jones 1964 II: 58). For ethical and health reasons, Shelley renounced eating products contaminated by blood. But at the same time, he would avoid – almost like a vampire – garlic.

Works cited

Chemnitz, C. and S. Becheva (eds) 2014. *Meat Atlas. Facts and Figures about the Animals We Eat.* Berlin, Brussels, Henirich Böll Foundation and Friends of the Earth Europe.

Gregory, J. 2007. *Of Victorians and Vegetarians: The Vegetarian Movement in Victorian Britain.* London and New York, Taurus Academic Studies.

Hogg, T. J. 1858. *The Life of Percy Bysshe Shelley*, 2 vols. London, Edward Moxton.

Hogg, T. J. 1904. *Shelley at Oxford.* London, Methuen.

Jones, F. L. (ed.) 1964. *The Letters of Percy Bysshe Shelley*, 2 vols. Oxford, Clarendon Press.

Goyan Kittler, P., K. Sucher, M. Nelms. 2012. *Food and Culture.* Belmont, CA, Wadsworth Cengage Learning.

Morton, T. 1994. *Shelley and the Revolution in Taste: The Body and the Natural World.* Cambridge, Cambridge University Press.

Morton, T. 2006. Joseph Ritson, Percy Shelley and the Making of Romantic Vegetarianism. In *Romanticism*, 12, 1: 52-61.

Perkins, D. 2003. *Romanticism and Animal Rights, 1790-1830.* Cambridge, Cambridge University Press.

Shelley, M. 2003. *Frankenstein, Or, The Modern Prometheus*, ed. by S. J. Wolfson. New York, Longman.

Shelley, P. B. 1993. *The Prose Works of Percy Bysshe Shelley*, ed. by E. B. Murray. Oxford, Oxford University Press, 1993.

Shelley, P. B. 1977. *Shelley's Poetry and Prose*, selected and ed. by D. H. Reiman and S. B. Powers. New York and London, W. W. Norton & Company.

Spencer, C. 1995. *The Heretic's Feast: A History of Vegetarianism.* Hanover, NH, University Press of New England.

Stuart, T. 2006. *The Bloodless Revolution. A Cultural History of Vegetarianism from 1600 to Modern Times.* New York and London, W. W. Norton & Company.

Sunstein, E. W., 1989. *Mary Shelley, Romance and Reality.* Baltimore, The John Hopkins University Press.

Wroe, A. 2003. 'Resolutions, Destinations: Shelley's Last Year'. In *The Oxford Handbook of Percy Bysshe Shelley*: 48-64. Ed. by M. O' Neill and M. Callaghan. Oxford, Oxford University Press.

Porridge: a classic of English breakfast

Porridge should be creamy, so it is important to stir it regularly while it simmers. To make it crunchy, you may want to add some small dates or other dried fruits before serving. Sugar can be replaced with some golden syrup if you have a sweet tooth.

Ingredients (per person)
¼ cup pinhead oatmeal

¼ cup medium oatmeal
½ cup whole milk
1 cup water
a pinch of salt
sugar
dates or dried fruits

cold milk (to serve)

Heat a frying pan over a medium-high heat. Toast the oats, then put them in a saucepan with the milk and 1 cup of water. Bring slowly to the boil, stirring frequently, possibly with a wooden spoon. Simmer for about 5 minutes, and keep stirring regularly. Add a pinch of salt, and simmer for another five minutes. Cover and sit for 5 minutes before serving with some topping (like dates or other dried fruits) and some cold milk.

Beatrice Moja

Mrs Beeton: cooking, science, and innovations in the Victorian kitchen

The *Book of Household Management* by Isabella Mayson Beeton (1836-1865) is generally considered one of the most interesting works in the Victorian social and cultural context. The author's stylistic choices, the sources used, the text structure, and the comparison with similar manuals of the period altogether suggest that Mrs Beeton was able to summarise and clarify the leading concepts of nineteenth-century British *cuisine*. Indeed, domestic manuals not only describe contemporary culinary habits: they also shape reality, offering the ideal condition to be attained in the kitchen (Gray 2013: 50-52). Therefore, the series named the *Book of Household Management* published from 1861 onwards is essential to understanding how English homes and food were represented during the long reign of Queen Victoria.

The section devoted to the recipes – the largest part of the manual – was constantly updated in subsequent editions, despite the premature death of the author. Mrs Beeton's recipes, while reminding the ambitious Victorian middle class of traditional domestic values, also suggested new nutritional theories, introduced exotic culinary products, and illustrated the most fashionable ways to set the table (Humble 2000: xiv-xv).

The creative and descriptive richness that determines the success of the Beetons' manual is possible owing to the peculiar circumstances that characterised its origin and editorial history. Originally published in 1859 as a series of twenty-four monthly booklets, the material of the *Book of Household Management* was immediately re-launched on the market as a single manual, in the popular 1861 edition. Over the years, however, favoured by its success, and managed by other enterprising publishers, the text underwent many modifications that adapted it to new editions and other publishing formats; and this still happens today! The section devoted to recipes, in particular, is the part of the text most subject to continuous updating, being constantly adapted to new food tastes and eating habits developing in British culture. The long life of the *Book of Household Management*, unfortunately, does not match the brief existence of its original author: Mrs Beeton died of puerperal fever in 1865, when she was only 28. The longevity of the book, however, keeps her name alive, always mentioned in the title.

In the first edition of the *Book of Household Management*, 921 out of 1112 pages are devoted to recipes and they rely for their inspiration on a wide range of earlier cookery books. Following a widespread and well-established literary practice, in fact, Mrs Beeton copies and reworks recipes already presented by some authorities in the field (Richardson 2013: 46-47). During the Victorian age, those who worked in the kitchen were divided into two separate categories: on the one hand, great foreign chefs, mainly French, who cooked for aristocratic households, while on the other the middle class had to be satisfied with 'plain' English cooks (Hughes 2006: 190). In an attempt to coordinate these contradictory trends, Mrs Beeton renewed the tradition and chose to draw on both kinds of cookery book in order to provide her audience with a more comprehensive manual and a useful text, which reflects both convenience and a desire for social advancement.

The author of the *Book of Household Management* derives her inspiration from the British culinary tradition, paying particular attention to recipes that have always characterised local cooking. The author of the *Book of Household Management* derives her inspiration from the British culinary tradition, paying particular attention to recipes that have always characterised local cooking. Moreover, Mrs Beeton draws some interesting stylistic innovations from some simple manuals, such as the introduction of an index, taken from *The Art of Cookery Made Plain and Easy* (1746) by Hannah Glasse. She also takes from *Modern Cookery for Private Families* (1845) by Eliza Acton the graphic organisation of the recipes: apart from lists of ingredients and instructions, she also provides separate lists of cooking times and average costs, and an indication of when particular foods are in season.

However, Mrs Beeton's interest in exclusive *haute cuisine* is also noteworthy: given the extreme pragmatism shown by the author in her cookery book, the attention paid to such elite aspects seems somewhat inconsistent with her target audience. But the reason behind this attitude has a very practical goal, since Mrs Beeton wishes to mediate between her middle-class readers and the glossy, exclusive world where *haute cuisine* is appreciated (Hughes 2006: 204-5). The *haute cuisine* discourse had in fact always been characterised by a cryptic vagueness, which the recipes in manuals written by chefs were intended to be understood by only a small circle of elected connoisseurs. Mrs Beeton, on the contrary, decides to share the secrets of *haute cuisine* with the British middle class:

> IN ORDER THAT THE DUTIES of the Cook may be properly performed, and that he may be able to reproduce esteemed dishes with certainty, all terms of indecision should be banished from his art. Accordingly, what is known only to him, will, in these pages, be made known to others. In

them all those indecisive terms expressed as a bit of this, some of that, a small piece of that, and a handful of the other, shall never be made use of, but all quantities be precisely and explicitly stated. With a desire, also, that all ignorance of this most essential part of the culinary art shall disappear, and that a uniform system of weights and measures should be adopted, we give an account of the weights which answer to certain measures. (Beeton 1982: 39-40)

Thus, revealing the key-secrets of *haute cuisine*, Mrs Beeton makes it familiar, so that every woman of good will and with the right tools may learn to cook fine dishes, just like an expert French chef. In the *Book of Household Management*, this topic is introduced in the fourth chapter, 'Introduction to Cookery': a brief presentation in which Mrs Beeton explains to her readers in a practical way and simple words the exotic culinary expressions used in French cookbooks. She also adds a short glossary of the most frequent 'French terms used in modern household cookery' (Beeton 1982: 44): widespread words today, but unknown expressions at the time, such as 'bain-marie', 'menu', and 'vol-au-vent'.

Moreover, in Mrs Beeton's cookbook, traditional British cookery is contrasted against innovations proposed by two different and rather unconventional authors: William Kitchiner (1775-1827) and Jean Anthelme Brillat-Savarin (1755-1826).

William Kitchiner was an expert in science and medicine, and in his treatise *Apicius Redivivus, or the Cook's Oracle* (1817), he displayed an innovative approach to nutritional matters and the importance of healthy eating. Kitchiner often stressed the importance of seasonal food, and provided a detailed table describing when it was best to shop for groceries in order to get the freshest and cheapest produce (Hughes 2006: 360-2). *La Physiologie du Goût; ou, Méditations de Gastronomie Transcendante* (1825) by Anthelme Brillat-Savarin was the first manual to support the importance of a low-carbohydrate diet, claiming that sugar and white flour are among the main causes of obesity, and suggesting the use of protein-based ingredients as an alternative.

In agreement with these nutritional suggestions, Mrs Beeton provides her own instructions; the result, however, is not always consistent with today's scientific knowledge owing to the ignorance that prevailed on the subject at the time, as well as to the author's difficulty in interpreting the data properly. Mrs Beeton's suggestions regarding fruits, vegetables and meat offer a striking example. Although she is aware of the many nutrients provided by fruits and vegetables, she advises against the intake of these foods in the case of weak and elderly subjects, considering them too difficult to digest, even if subjected to prolonged boiling. These considerations did not apply to meat, of which Mrs Beeton recommends the consumption at every meal (Hughes 2006: 360-2).

This distorted perception of 'healthy eating' is even more evident in the anachronistic preference demonstrated by Mrs Beeton for the *service à la française* (where various dishes might be served at the same time) compared to the more elegant and wholesome *service à la russe* (where dishes were served sequentially). These two opposed ways of arranging the food on the table are an important aspect of the social and gastronomic culture of the time. In fact, in her *Book of Household Management*, Mrs Beeton states: 'MAN, it has been said, is a dining animal. Creatures of the inferior races eat and drink; man only dines. […] Dinner, being the grand solid meal of the day, is a matter of considerable importance; and a well-served table is a striking index of human ingenuity and resource' (Beeton 1982: 905). Here, the centrality of the issue is fully expressed: given the importance of dinner, the way in which it is displayed takes on a new relevance. The decorations placed on the table, the choice of certain dishes, their different cooking and presentations are all elements that the perfect 'mistress' should bear in mind when she invites guests to dinner; in fact, she must be aware that these details might jeopardise the success of the event and obscure her own gifts as a hostess.

Widespread in Europe since the Middle Ages, the French-style service was a very articulate and tidy fashion to arrange the table and to present the dishes during dinner. The table, set like a sort of modern buffet, provided different types of food in large serving plates from which all the guests could help themselves simultaneously. Sight is undoubtedly the sense that is mostly involved here: the *service à la française* is in fact a kind of stage performance in which the abundance and the opulence of the dishes presented correspond to a status symbol of wealth and power (Gray 2010: 256-7). However, between the 1830s and 1840s, the French-style service underwent a crisis due to the introduction of another manner of arranging the dinner: namely the *service à la russe*. This corresponds to today's service, where several courses are offered in succession to the diners, providing each of them with his own plate, brought to the table by a specific waiter. Whereas the French-style service was characterised by the impression and the harmonious arrangement of the food on the table, the Russian-style service changes the priorities and gives predominance to the sense of taste: food at last becomes the protagonist of the event.

In her cookery book, Mrs Beeton offers her readers several pre-set menus; only two of them however provide a Russian-style service. The author, in fact, is fully convinced that the French-style service is cheaper and simpler to arrange for the lady of the Victorian house (Gray 2010: 264). The *service à la russe* implies a greater number of waiters and of cutlery placed on the table, as well as plates – one for each diner, multiplied by the quantity of the courses. Thus, choosing the less innovative service, the 'mistress' could optimise costs and efforts.

Unfortunately, Mrs Beeton's shrewd calculations are not necessarily correct. Although the Russian-style service involves a greater number of assigned personnel, at the same time it allows an optimisation of the amount of food, thus a consequent economic advantage. The *service à la française* – with its ambition to offer a variety of food to amaze the diners rather than to be actually consumed – produces an enormous amount of waste since many courses arranged on the table are not even tasted by the guests. Furthermore, the French-style service is less healthy than the Russian style: while all the dishes are arranged on the table and all the guests observe the opulence of the dinner, the food goes hopelessly cold, becoming less and less digestible and appetising (Brown 2002: 63).

However questionable from a nutritional point of view, Mrs Beeton's choice of favouring the French-style service involves an interesting stylistic innovation in the pages of her manual. Since the emphasis in this fashion of setting the table is on the visual presentation of food, the author decided to include in her cookbook some colourful images in order to provide detailed instructions to her readers. Up to the mid-nineteenth century colour illustrations were too expensive to be included in cheap and popular editions, but the introduction of colour printing in 1835 by George Baxter reformed the market, making such costs affordable. The Beetons instantly adopted this new technology, introducing ten colour illustrations in the first edition of their *Book of Household Management*. The use of a wide variety of colours was also a cunning ploy aimed at attracting the reader's attention, intrigued by this unexpected innovation. Fully aware of the revolutionary nature of the colour plates, the author gives full rein to her enthusiasm and pride. In the 'Preface' to the *Book of Household Management*, she reminds her readers that 'The coloured plates are a novelty not without value.'

Kitchiner and Brillat-Savarin were not the only sources for the science of healthy eating employed by Mrs Beeton. In the same year that the *Book of Household Management* was published, *The Origin of Species* (1859) by Charles Darwin (1809-1882) appeared. Galvanised by the concepts presented in that work, Mrs Beeton included in her cookbook many scientific references. This is evident, for example, in the categorisation of animal species, distinguished according to the presence or absence of hooves or mammary glands, or according to their reproductive methods.

The Origin of Species also inspired Mrs Beeton's mode of describing the different staff members who served in the domestic environment. The domestic staff are divided according to a practical hierarchical system, where the roles are analysed in detail. The structure of the domestic group is not however constant and invariable: like the animal kingdom, it is characterised by a constant evolution and the need to adapt to circumstances, and the same fate awaits the internal organisation of the species inhabiting the Victorian house. Whenever the personnel are limited in number, the servants must adapt their skills, and perform the functions of the missing employees. Thus, as Hughes observes, 'the household is evolving, becoming more efficient, busily adapting to its changing circumstances' (Hughes 2006: 186).

Even the internal arrangement of the recipes in Mrs Beeton's *Book of Household Management* recalls the model proposed by Charles Darwin. The culinary matter is thus divided into specific sections according to the different macro-areas of food; and each section in turn is composed of relevant information, general observations, short historical-anthropological notes, cooking methods, and detailed recipes.

The very recipes in the *Book of Household Management* have in fact sparked much debate, in particular regarding their national origin. Although Mrs Beeton often refers to 'British cuisine', many scholars have noted that most recipes included in the manual are actually English. Only the most stereotypical recipes come from the rest of the United Kingdom (Humble 2000: xxviii). Over the many upgrades and alterations undergone over the years in successive editions of Mrs Beeton's cookbook, it is worth noting the introduction of some recipes of Imperial – or colonial – origin.

Since many British people were settling in the colonies, the most nostalgic 'mistresses' could look up the *Book of Household Management* in search of culinary tastes from the motherland to be realised with exotic ingredients. For Australia, for example, 'Mrs Beeton' – presumably dead by the time these additions were made – proposes 'Soup from Kangaroo Tails', 'Parrot Pie' and 'Roast Wallaby' (Foy 2014: 91).

The variety of ingredients proposed in Mrs Beeton's manual deserves an in-depth analysis. Although rare exotic products were beginning to appear on the Victorian tables, the food data of the time show a poor variety of ingredients, even though most of the family budget was usually spent on food (Foy 2014: 13). The pages of the *Book of Household Management* describe however a completely different situation. The manual, in fact, provides an idealized account of Victorian eating habits, instead of the conditions that actually prevailed:

> Cookbooks undeniably set up an ideal. The examples studied here often assume the presence of specific equipment, suggesting menus and table plans based on easy and consistent access to ingredients, unlimited price or location. (Gray 2013: 51)

Some recipes in the cookbook are so expensive and ambitious as to be beyond the reach of any reader: they essentially represent culinary fantasies to which the audience is drawn, while being aware that they will never cook or taste them. Mrs Beeton in fact attempts to be consistent and objective, proposing in her cookbook some recipes that are more in line with Victorian cooking habits. Unfortunately, these plain recipes are often confused with the exotic and refined instructions, creating an almost schizophrenic imbalance in the economic budget (Humble 2000: xxii-xxiv).

Mrs Beeton also displays a particular interest in hygiene and health issues. At the time, there was great ignorance on the subject: for example, many physicians thought it useless to wash their hands between one patient and another (Crow 1971: 138-9). To clarify the matter, Mrs Beeton introduced in her cookbook an entire section dedicated to invalid cookery, inspired by *Notes on Nursing* (1859) by Florence Nightingale (1820-1910). The treatment of this theme is not limited to the recipes however; in the final pages of the *Book of Household Management* the author includes, rather insistently, some admonitions on the hygienic necessities: she suggests a daily shower, and to air the rooms of the house frequently (Calder 1977: 111).

Despite the questionable originality of some parts of the text, often derived from earlier material, it is impossible to deny that Mrs Beeton's manual is an extraordinary work, open to innovative and revolutionary issues. Such a quality is still recognised today, and it once earned the cookbook the praise of Arthur Conan Doyle (1859-1930). In *A Duet, with an Occasional Chorus* (1899), Doyle dedicates an entire chapter to Mrs Beeton's manual, stating that 'this book has more wisdom to the square inch than any work of man' (Conan Doyle 1990: 116). Approval of the author is even voiced by some intellectuals who usually disapproved of Victorian precepts: Lytton Strachey (1880-1932) planned to make Mrs Beeton one of the protagonists in his *Eminent Victorians* (1918), while Wyndham Lewis (1882-1957), the Vorticist painter and writer, wrote a humorous comedy inspired by the author of *Book of Household Management*.

Works cited

Beeton, I. 1982. *Mrs Beeton's Book of Household Management* [1861]. London, Chancellor Press.
Brown, P. 2002. Dining by Design. In H. Walker (ed.), *The Meal: Proceedings of the Oxford Symposium on Food and Cookery 2001*: 58-66. Blackawton, Prospect Books.
Calder, J. 1977. *Victorian Home*. London, B. T. Batsford.
Conan Doyle, A. 1990. *A Duet, with an Occasional Chorus* [1899]. Bloomington, Gaslight Publications.
Crow, D. 1971. *Victorian Woman*. London, G. Allen & Unwin.
Foy, K. 2014. *Life in the Victorian Kitchen: Culinary Secrets and Servants' Stories*. Barnsley, Pen & Sword History.
Gray, A. 2013. 'A Practical Art': An Archaeological Perspective on the Use of Recipe Books. In M. DiMeo and S. Pennell (eds), *Reading & Writing Recipe Books 1550-1800*: 47-67. Manchester, Manchester University Press.
Gray, A. 2010. 'The Greatest Ordeal': Using Biography to Explore the Victorian Dinner. In *Post-Medieval Archaeology*, volume 44, n. 2: 255-272.
Hughes, K. 2006. *The Short Life and Long Times of Mrs Beeton*. London, Harper Perennial.
Humble, N. 2000. Introduction. In I. Beeton, *Mrs Beeton's Book of Household Management* [1861]: vii-xxx. Oxford, Oxford University Press.
Richardson, S. 2013. Useful Soup for Benevolent Purposes: the Politics of Domestic Economy. In *The Political Worlds of Women: Gender and Politics in Nineteenth Century Britain*: 39-60. New York, Routledge.

Mrs Beeton's recipes from *The Book of Household Management* (1861)

Tapioca Soup

Ingredients. 5 oz. of tapioca, 2 quarts of stock No. 105 or 106.

Mode. Put the tapioca into cold stock, and bring it gradually to a boil. Simmer gently till tender, and serve.

Time. Rather more than 1 hour.
Average cost. — 1s. or 6d. per quart.
Seasonable all the year.
Sufficient for 8 persons.
Tapioca. This excellent farinaceous food is the produce of the pith of the cassava-tree, and is made in the East Indies, and also in Brazil. It is, by washing, procured as a starch from the tree, then dried, either in the sun or on plates of hot iron, and afterwards broken into grains, in which form it is imported into this country. Its nutritive properties are large, and as a food for persons of delicate digestion, or for children, it is in great estimation. 'No amylaceous substance,' says Dr. Christison, 'is so much relished by infants about the time of

weaning; and in them it is less apt to become sour during digestion than any other farinaceous food, even arrowroot not excepted.'

Useful Soup for Benevolent Purposes

Ingredients. An ox-cheek, any pieces of trimmings of beef, which may be bought very cheaply (say 4 lbs.), a few bones, any pot-liquor the larder may furnish, ¼ peck of onions, 6 leeks, a large bunch of herbs, ½ lb. of celery (the outside pieces, or green tops, do very well); ½ lb. of carrots, ½ lb. of turnips, ½ lb. of coarse brown sugar, ½ a pint of beer, 4 lbs. of common rice, or pearl barley; ½ lb. of salt, 1 oz. of black pepper, a few raspings, 10 gallons of water.

Mode. Cut up the meat in small pieces, break the bones, put them in a copper, with the 10 gallons of water, and stew for ½ an hour. Cut up the vegetables, put them in with the sugar and beer, and boil for 4 hours. Two hours before the soup is wanted, add the rice and raspings, and keep stirring till it is well mixed in the soup, which simmer gently. If the liquor reduces too much, fill up with water.
Time. 6-½ hours.
Average cost. 1-½d. per quart.
Note. The above recipe was used in the winter of 1858 by the Editress, who made, each week, in her copper, 8 or 9 gallons of this soup, for distribution amongst about a dozen families of the village near which she lives. The cost, as will be seen, was not great; but she has reason to believe that the soup was very much liked, and gave to the members of those families, a dish of warm, comforting food, in place of the cold meat and piece of bread which form, with too many cottagers, their usual meal, when, with a little more knowledge of the 'cooking.' art, they might have, for less expense, a warm dish, every day.

Christmas plum-pudding

(Very Good.)
Ingredients. 1-½ lb. of raisins, ½ lb. of currants, ½ lb. of mixed peel, ¾ lb. of bread crumbs, ¾ lb. of suet, 8 eggs, 1 wineglassful of brandy.

Mode. Stone and cut the raisins in halves, but do not chop them; wash, pick, and dry the currants, and mince the suet finely; cut the candied peel into thin slices, and grate down the bread into fine crumbs. When all these dry ingredients are prepared, mix them well together; then moisten the mixture with the eggs, which should be well beaten, and the brandy; stir well, that everything may be very thoroughly blended, and press the pudding into a buttered mould; tie it down tightly with a floured cloth, and boil for 5 or 6 hours. It may be boiled in a cloth without a mould, and will require the same time allowed for cooking. As Christmas puddings are usually made a few days before they are required for table, when the pudding is taken out of the pot, hang it up immediately, and put a plate or saucer underneath to catch the water that may drain from it. The day it is to be eaten, plunge it into boiling water, and keep it boiling for at least 2 hours; then turn it out of the mould, and serve with brandy-sauce. On Christmas-day a sprig of holly is usually placed in the middle of the pudding, and about a wineglassful of brandy poured round it, which, at the moment of serving, is lighted, and the pudding thus brought to table encircled in flame.

Time. 5 or 6 hours the first time of boiling; 2 hours the day it is to be served.
Average cost. 4s.
Sufficient for a quart mould for 7 or 8 persons.
Seasonable on the 25th of December, and on various festive occasions till March.

Note. Five or six of these puddings should be made at one time, as they will keep good for many weeks, and in cases where unexpected guests arrive, will be found an acceptable, and, as it only requires warming through, a quickly-prepared dish. Moulds of every shape and size are manufactured for these puddings, and may be purchased of Messrs. R. & J. Slack, 336, Strand.

Lemonade for invalids

Ingredients. ½ lemon, lump sugar to taste, 1 pint of boiling water.

Mode. Pare off the rind of the lemon thinly; cut the lemon into 2 or 3 thick slices, and remove as much as possible of the white outside pith, and all the pips. Put the slices of lemon, the peel, and lump sugar into a jug; pour over the boiling water; cover it closely, and in 2 hours it will be fit to drink. It should either be strained or poured off from the sediment.
Time. 2 hours.
Average cost. 2d.
Seasonable at any time

2143.—BILL OF FARE FOR A BALL SUPPER,

Or a Cold Collation for a Summer Entertainment, or Wedding or Christening Breakfast for 70 or 80 Persons (July).

			Tongue.			
			Ribs of Lamb.		Veal-and-Ham	
	Dish of Lobster, cut up.		Two Roast Fowls.		Pie.	
3 Compôtes of Fruit.			Mayonnaise of Salmon.			20 Small Dishes of various Summer Fruits.
3 Dishes of Small Pastry.	Charlotte Russe à la Vanille.	Lobster Salad.	Epergne, with Flowers.	Lobster Salad.	Savoy Cake.	3 Cheesecakes.
4 Blancmanges, to be placed down the table.			Mayonnaise of Trout.			4 Blancmanges, to be placed down the table.
			Tongue, garnished.		Dish of	3 Fruit Tarts.
3 English Pines.	Pigeon Pie.		Boiled Fowls and Béchamel Sauce.		Lobster, cut up.	
			Collared Eel.			
			Ham.			
			Raised Pie.			
		Lobster Salad.	Two Roast Fowls.	Lobster Salad.		
			Shoulder of Lamb, stuffed.			
20 Small Dishes of various Summer Fruits.			Mayonnaise of Salmon.			3 English Pines.
3 Cheesecakes.	Dish of Lobster, cut up.	Larded Capon.	Epergne, with Flowers.	Boar's Head.	Pigeon Pie.	3 Dishes of Small Pastry.
4 Jellies, to be placed down the table.			Mayonnaise of Trout.			4 Jellies, to be placed down the table.
3 Fruit Tarts.		Lobster Salad.	Tongue.	Lobster Salad.		3 Compôtes of Fruit.
	Pigeon Pie.		Boiled Fowls and Béchamel Sauce.		Dish of Lobster, cut up.	
			Raised Pie.			
			Ham, decorated.			
			Shoulder of Lamb, stuffed.			
			Two Roast Fowls.			
			Mayonnaise of Salmon.			
	Dish of Lobster, cut up.	Savoy Cake.	Lobster Salad.	Lobster Salad.	Charlotte Russe à la Vanille.	Veal and Ham Pie.
			Epergne, with Flowers.			
			Mayonnaise of Trout.			
			Tongue, garnished.		Dish of Lobster, cut up.	
			Boiled Fowls and Béchamel Sauce.			
			Collared Eel.			

Note.—The length of the page will not admit of our giving the dishes as they should be placed on the table; they should be arranged with the large and high dishes down the centre, and the spaces filled up with the smaller dishes, fruit, and flowers, taking care that the flavours and colours contrast nicely, and that no two dishes of a sort come together. This bill of fare may be made to answer three or four purposes, placing a wedding cake or christening cake in the centre on a high stand, if required for either of these occasions. A few dishes of fowls, lobster salads, &c. &c., should be kept in reserve to replenish those that are most likely to be eaten first. A joint of cold roast and boiled beef should be placed on the buffet, as being something substantial for the gentlemen of the party to partake of. Besides the articles enumerated in the bill of fare, biscuits and wafers will be required, cream-and-water ices, tea, coffee, wines, liqueurs, soda-water, ginger-beer, and lemonade.

Claudia Cremonesi

Charles Dickens from street food to the restaurant

Charles Dickens was a lover of good food, a true 'Victorian foodie'. Dickens's passion for good food and his culinary interest may be due to the hard times when, as a child, albeit for a short time, he worked to meet the debts of his father and support his family. This traumatic experience certainly scarred the young Dickens who, from that moment on, associated food with the idea of abundance, and the symbol of a comfort he had lacked during his childhood (Ackroyd 2002: 248).

Benjamin Graves in *The Victorian Web* (1966) affirms that in Dickens's fiction food becomes a means to describe the extreme hunger that characterises some of his characters. Dickens often proposes images of 'culinary debauchery' to suggest a diet of abundance and excess which compensates for the poverty of the society he portrays. In this respect, Dickens invokes the figure of John Bull, the plump conservative character created by John Arbuthnot in 1712, the national personification of the Kingdom of Great Britain, dressed as a gentleman of the English countryside, in order to highlight the importance of nourishment and 'fullness' (Graves 1966). Indeed, food becomes a literary *leitmotif*, a *fil rouge* which ties together all his works, from the very beginning. Let us consider *Oliver Twist* (1837-38) and the passage that has become one of the most famous in Victorian literature as well as an emblematic movie scene:

> The master, in his cook's uniform, stationed himself at the copper; his pauper assistants ranged themselves behind him; the gruel was served out; and a long grace was said over the short commons. The gruel disappeared; the boys whispered each other, and winked at Oliver; while his next neighbours nudged him. Child as he was, he was desperate with hunger, and reckless with misery. He rose from the table; and advancing to the master, basin and spoon in hand, said: somewhat alarmed at his own temerity: 'Please, sir, I want some more.' (Dickens 1966: 56)

In the story and character of Oliver, we reread Dickens's personal struggle against poverty, tenaciously fought and, later, overcome thanks to his outstanding skills as a journalist and writer. The 'gruel' on which Oliver lives is a mixture of grains boiled in water or milk. Nothing appetizing, nor inviting. Nevertheless, Dickens is able to let us 'taste' it almost as if it were a delicacy, a rich and satisfying food for the stomachs of the little ravenous orphans.

It is interesting to notice that an abundance of food references had already emerged a couple of years before when Boz, in his *Pickwick Papers* (1835-36), had mentioned thirty-five breakfasts, ten lunches, thirty-two suppers, and even two hundred forty nine drinks (Ackroyd 2002: 248).

In considering Dickens's works, we see that the attention given to detailed food description is noticeable again in a passage taken from *Great Expectations* (1860-61), when the young Pip describes very accurately his sister's ritual of buttering the bread:

> My sister had a trenchant way of cutting our bread-and-butter for us that never varied. First, with her left hand she jammed the loaf hard and fast against her bib [...]. Then she took some butter (not too much) on a knife and spread it on the loaf, in an apothecary kind of way, as if she were making a plaster – using both sides of the knife with a slapping dexterity, and trimming and moulding the butter off round the crust. Then, she gave the knife a final smart wipe on the edge of the plaster, and then sawed a very thick round off the loaf: which she finally, before separating from the loaf, hewed into two halves, of which Joe got one, and I the other. (Dickens 1973: 42)

From this passage one can appreciate that the description of a simple slice of buttered bread can be something extremely elaborate and appetising for the palate of any reader and gourmet. Dickens – as is well known – also loved the holiday season. His daughter Mamie passionately recalls Christmas celebrations at the Dickenses:

> Christmas was always a time which in our home was looked forward to it with eagerness and delight, and to my father it was a time dearer than any part of the year, I think. He loved Christmas for its deep significance as well as for its joys, and this he demonstrates in every allusion in his writings to the great festival. (Dickens 1984: 79).

Christmas at the Dickenses was not just the celebration of a joyful recurrence, a moment of coming together in friendship, games and songs, but the opportunity to prepare traditional food such as roast goose and 'plum pudding', a typical Christmas pudding made with dried fruit. This was accompanied by beverages such as 'Gin Punch', or 'Smoking Bishop', a mulled wine, and finally a citrus punch enriched with Port. In *A Christmas Carol* (1843) we find this Christmas atmosphere at its most intense. Food becomes a means to redeem man's mistakes. The grouchy old Scrooge will learn the importance of values such as kindness and generosity by offering a juicy turkey to the poor Cratchit family.

> Mrs. Cratchit made the gravy (ready beforehand in a little saucepan) hissing hot; Master Peter mashed the potatoes with incredible vigour;

> Miss Belinda sweetened up the apple-sauce; Martha dusted the hot plates; Bob took Tiny Tim beside him in a tiny corner at the table; the two young Cratchits set chairs for everybody, not forgetting themselves, and mounting guard upon their posts, crammed spoons into their mouths, lest they should shriek for goose before their turn came to be helped. At last the dishes were set on, and grace was said. It was succeeded by a breathless pause, as Mrs. Cratchit, looking slowly all along the carving-knife, prepared to plunge it in the breast; but when she did, and when the long expected gush of stuffing issued forth, one murmur of delight arose all round the board, and even Tiny Tim, excited by the two young Cratchits, beat on the table with the handle of his knife, and feebly cried Hurrah! (Dickens 1988: 53-4)

The passage shows to what extent the presence of food in the works of Dickens is evidence of personal and collective pleasure in the fulfilling experience of the table. Ackroyd points out that only in the last years of his life does Dickens show less interest in good food, preferring 'other people's enjoyment of what was laid before them rather than to have any pleasure in the good things himself.' Ackroyd, moreover, reports that the writer's office boy, at that time, would define him as a 'light eater': the writer's interest was by then for 'the sentiment' evoked by food and not for 'the thing', the food itself (Ackroyd 2002: 248).

Leaving Dickens's novels aside, and getting to the point of this short culinary journey into Dickensian food writing, I intend to focus on the comparison between street food and the restaurant experience – a comparison provided by *Sketches by Boz* (1836-37) and *The Uncommercial Traveller and Other Papers* (1861).

Sketches by Boz is a work that Dickens himself considered imperfect and immature, conceived at a young age, when he was not yet Charles Dickens but the anonymous Boz, 'the man in the street; setting down in his sketches all the small events in the everyday life of common persons – bank clerks, shop assistants, omnibus drivers; laundresses, market women, and kidney-pie sellers' (Dickens 1997: vi-vii). And it is in these streets of an early Victorian London, scanned by an eye hungry for details, that we encounter street food. By contrast, descriptions of meals in restaurants will be the subject of a piece in *The Uncommercial Traveller*, a collection of memories and various topical articles gathered by a mature Dickens, evidence of an already changed culture, very different from the first decades of the century.

Thus, in *Sketches by Boz*, in 'The Streets – Morning', the eye catches scenes of a still sleeping London, in the quiet of a summer morning, until, at dawn, the streets welcome the comings and goings and the bustle of the new day which is going to start. And the food is ever-present:

Sketch by Boz Morning

[...] little deal tables, with the ordinary preparations for a street breakfast, make their appearance at the customary stations. Numbers of men and women (principally the latter), carrying upon their heads heavy baskets of fruit, toil down the park side of Piccadilly, on their way to Covent Garden, [...]. Here and there, a bricklayer's labourer, with the day's dinner tied up in a handkerchief, walks briskly to his work, [...] basket-women talking, piemen expatiating on the excellence of their pastry [...]. (Dickens 1997: 48-49)

Covent Garden market is a celebration of smells, colours and sounds. Street food is at the core of the scene, whether displayed on a table, in a basket, or wrapped in a towel. Bakeries take out the first loaves to serve a crowd of children and domestics that are waiting impatiently to buy their ration; pastry shops display in dusty trays tarts that are a little bit stale, but very appealing to the eye. Food is, therefore, the undisputed protagonist of a chaotic London summer morning. And so it is in 'The Streets – Night', a sketch vividly depicting the dark and humid winter nights, surrounded by a thick mist when in the streets the wayfarer's nostrils are inebriated by the smells of savoury steamed cooking coming from the home kitchens and invading the street. And suddenly even the muffins conquer the streets in a dynamic neighbourhood scene:

> In the suburbs, the muffin boy rings his way down the little street, [...]; for Mrs. Macklin, of No. 4, has no sooner opened her little street-door, and screamed out 'Muffins!' with all her might, than Mrs. Walker, at No. 5, puts her head out of the parlour-window, and screams 'Muffins!' too; and Mrs. Walker has scarcely got the words out of her lips, than Mrs. Peplow, over the way, lets loose Master Peplow, who darts down the street, with a velocity which nothing but buttered muffins in perspective could possibly inspire, and drags the boy back by main force, whereupon Mrs. Macklin and Mrs. Walker, just to save the boy trouble, and to say a few neighbourly words to Mrs. Peplow at the same time, run over the way and buy their muffins at Mrs. Peplow's door [...]. (Dickens 1997: 53)

After the muffins, it is the turn of the tasty kidney-pie, sold by a street stand situated near Marsh Gate and Victoria Theatre that pedestrians can hardly see in the darkness of London streets:

> The candle in the transparent lamp, manufactured with oil-paper, embellished with 'characters', has been blown out of fifty times, so the kidney-pie merchant, tired with running backwards and forwards to the next wine-vaults, to get a light, has given up the idea of illumination in despair, and the only signs of his 'whereabout,' are the bright sparks, of which a long irregular train is whirled down the street every time he opens his portable oven to hand a hot kidney-pie to a customer. (Dickens 1997: 54)

Again, in the streets of London, we meet 'flat-fish, oyster, and fruit vendors' and various pedlars committed to attract customers: a 'cheesemonger' offering 'huge piles of bright red and pale yellow cheeses, mingled with little fivepenny dabs of dingy bacon, various tubs of weekly Dorset, and cloudy rolls of best fresh' and 'the baked-potato man' (Dickens 1997: 55). Street food is ubiquitous in the *Sketches*, and its description is vivid and accurate. Only the rain, now and then thick and pouring, can clear London streets from all sorts of food. But while food abandons the streets for a moment, it enters the 'houses of refreshment' where, returning from the theatre, dozens of Londoners find pleasure and companionship while sitting at a beautifully set table where 'chops, kidneys, rabbits, oysters, stout, cigars, and 'goes' innumerable, are served amidst a noise and confusion of smoking, running, knife-clattering, and waiter-chattering, perfectly indescribable' (Dickens 1997: 56). Thus, from the lively street food we switch to closed and protected places, but still popular and rewarding.

Everything changes in *The Uncommercial Traveller*, in the essay 'Refreshments for Travellers' previously published in *All the Year Round* in March 24th 1860, and written, therefore, by a mature Dickens. Here 'indoors meals' are described very critically. It is interesting to recall that in the same year in England the 'Refreshment Houses and Wine Licences Act' was passed:

> The French idea of a 'restaurant' to refresh and restore travellers of both sexes during a journey was still foreign to British cities in 1860, but the end of March saw the second reading of Gladstone's 'Refreshment Houses and Wine Licensing Bill', which proposed: to let small retailers take out licences [...] for the sale of wine to be consumed off the premises, to let eating-house keepers take out licences for the sale of wine to be consumed on the premises, and to place all eating houses under the control of the police; the Bill became law on 1 July 1860. (Dickens 2000: 74)

Dickens's essay highlights a recurring social problem for that period, namely the difficulty to find in London a proper place to have lunch or dinner. Dickens himself maintains:

> One of the most grievous discomforts to which all visitors to London are exposed is the difficulty of finding in it either a dinner or a luncheon [...]. The want is in the deficiency of small Refreshment houses where people of moderate or even humble means may procure dinner and other necessary refreshments at a [small] cost. (Dickens 2000: 74)

'Refreshments for Travellers' opens with a negative note: Dickens, the European traveller, who has visited Italy, Switzerland and France, does not find a restaurant in England 'where I could get anything good to eat and drink in five minutes, or where, if I sought it, I was received with a welcome' (Dickens 2000: 75). Criticism is already manifest. It continues a few lines below, when the hungry customer describes his experience at a 'Refreshment station':

> I travel by railroad. I start from home at seven or eight in the morning, after breakfasting hurriedly. [...] I am hungry when I arrive at the 'Refreshment' station where I am expected. Please to observe, expected. I have said, I am hungry; perhaps I might say, with greater point and force, that I am to some

Refreshments for Travellers. Mr Grazinglands looks in at a pastry cook's window

extent exhausted, and that I need – in the expressive French sense of the word – to be restored. What is provided for my restoration? [...] I turn my disconsolate eyes on the refreshments that are to restore me. I find that I must either scald my throat by insanely ladling into it, against time and for no wager, brown hot water stiffened with flour; or I must make myself flaky and sick with Banbury cake; or, I must stuff into my delicate organisation, a currant pincushion which I know will swell into immeasurable dimensions when it has got there; or, I must extort from an iron-bound quarry, with a fork, as if I were farming an inhospitable soil, some glutinous lumps of gristle and grease, called pork-pie. While thus forlornly occupied, I find that the depressing banquet on the table is, in every phase of its profoundly unsatisfactory character, so like the banquet at the meanest and shabbiest of evening parties. (Dickens 2000: 76-7)

Unlike street food, the food found in the English 'Refreshment houses' is not inviting at all, nor satisfying. In addition to this, even the welcome and guests' reception seem to be less kind than those offered by street pedlars depicted by the young Boz. The article also reports the experience of a Mr and Mrs Grazinglands who one morning, after having arrived in London by train, had decided to put something in their stomach. They shyly gaze through the window of a pastry shop looking for a snack. What Mr Grazinglands sees is disappointing:

> He beheld nothing to eat, but butter in various forms, slightly charged with jam, and languidly frizzling over tepid water. Two ancient turtle-shells, on which was inscribed the legend, 'Soups,' decorated a glass partition within, enclosing a stuffy alcove, from which a ghastly mockery of a marriage-breakfast spread on a rickety table, warned the terrified traveller. An oblong box of stale and broken pastry at reduced prices, mounted on a stool, ornamented the doorway; and two high chairs that looked as if they were performing on stilts, embellished the counter. Over the whole, a young lady presided, whose gloomy haughtiness as she surveyed the street, announced a deep-seated grievance against society, and an implacable determination to be avenged. From a beetle-haunted kitchen below this institution, fumes arose, suggestive of a class of soup which Mr. Grazinglands knew, from painful experience, enfeebles the mind, distends the stomach, forces itself into the complexion, and tries to ooze out at the eyes. (Dickens 2000: 78)

And so the couple desist from entering the shop and look in vain for another place to take refreshment. Even the nearby bakery does not seem to offer anything good: the place is cold and dusty, cookies appear stale and the old lady has a severe frown. Finally, they decide to go to Jairing's, 'an hotel for families and gentlemen, in high repute among the midland counties' where, despite the good reputation, the experience does not seem to be satisfactory:

> Mr. Grazinglands and his charming partner waited twenty minutes for the smoke (for it never came to a fire), twenty-five minutes for the sherry, half an hour for the tablecloth, forty minutes for the knives and forks, three-quarters of an hour for the chops, and an hour for the potatoes. On settling the little bill [...] Mr. Grazinglands took heart to remonstrate against the general quality and cost of his reception. To whom the waiter replied, substantially, that Jairing's made it a merit to have accepted him on any terms. (Dickens 2000: 79)

Dickens mentions another 'case', referring directly to the reader, who should fancy himself as a traveller with twenty minutes to dine before the train departs. The Terminus of the railway station offers stale and inedible food, but 'You want your dinner, and like Dr. Johnson, Sir, you like to dine.' The alternative is a nearby hotel:

> It is a most astonishing fact that the waiter is very cold to you. [...] He is not glad to see you, he does not want you, he would much rather you hadn't

come. [...] another waiter [...] stands at a little distance, with his napkin under his arm and his hands folded, looking at you with all his might. You impress on your waiter that you have ten minutes for dinner, and he proposes that you shall begin with a bit of fish which will be ready in twenty. That proposal declined, he suggests – as a neat originality – 'a weal or mutton cutlet.' You close with either cutlet, any cutlet, anything. [...] A ventriloquial dialogue ensues, tending finally to the effect that weal only, is available on the spur of the moment. You anxiously call out, 'Veal, then!' Your waiter having settled that point, returns to array your tablecloth, with a table napkin folded cocked-hat-wise [...], a white wine-glass, a green wine-glass, a blue finger-glass, a tumbler, and a powerful field battery of fourteen casters with nothing in them; or at all events – which is enough for your purpose – with nothing in them that will come out. [...] Half your time gone, and nothing come but the jug of ale and the bread, you implore your waiter to 'see after that cutlet, waiter; pray do!' [...] when you are going away without it, [he] comes back with it. Even then, he will not take the sham silver cover off, without a pause for a flourish, and a look at the musty cutlet as if he were surprised to see it – which cannot possibly be the case, he must have seen it so often before. [...] You order the bill, but your waiter cannot bring your bill yet, because he is bringing, instead, three flinty-hearted potatoes and two grim head of broccoli, like the occasional ornaments on area railings, badly boiled. You know that you will never come to this pass, any more than to the cheese and celery, and you imperatively demand your bill; [...]. Your bill at last brought and paid, at the rate of sixpence a mouthful, your waiter reproachfully reminds you that 'attendance is not charged for a single meal,' and you have to search in all your pockets for sixpence more. (Dickens 2000: 79-82)

And even this last experience reveals itself catastrophic: unqualified waiters, slow service and questionable food. Does Dickens perhaps want to suggest that in the Victorian Age British restaurants had still much to do to achieve a satisfactory standard? Or maybe, as Boz told his readers few decades before, food should go into the street to be more appreciated and to recover its 'natural habitat'? On the one hand, a good meal in a warm, comfortable place protected from the rain and from London fog was all that every Victorian could wish for. But, on the other hand, the 'street food' described by Boz perhaps represented the true tradition – a cultural tradition to preserve, a sensory experience which should not be separated from the road and from the social experience in which food itself is made, offered, consumed. A refined palate devoted to a lavishly decked table would never agree to the 'street food' experience, but our Dickens, a gourmet and a lover of good and well-served food, would probably suggest that the colours, smells and noises of the city, the dynamism and multiplicity of the scenes experienced in the street, contribute to make meat pies, baked potatoes, muffins and tarts even more pleasant to the taste.

Works cited

Ackroyd, P. 2002. *Dickens*. London, Vintage.
Dickens, C. 1966. *Oliver Twist, or, The Parish Boy's Progress*. Ed. P. Fairclough. London, Penguin.
Dickens, C. 1973. *Great Expectations*. Ed. A. Calder. London, Penguin.
Dickens, C. 1988. *Christmas Books*. Ed. R. Glancy. Oxford, Oxford University Press.
Dickens, C. 1997. *Sketches by Boz, Illustrative of Every-Day Life and Every-Day People,*. Ed. with an Introduction by T. Holme. Oxford, Oxford University Press.
Dickens, C. 2000. Refreshments for Travellers. In *The Uncommercial Traveller and Other Papers, The Dent Uniform Edition of Dickens' Journalism* (4 Vols.). Ed. M. Slater and J. Drew. IV: 74-83. London, J. M. Dent.
Dickens, C. C. 1984. *Dining with Dickens: Being a Ramble through Dickensian Foods*. Goring-on-Thames, Elvedon Press.
Graves, B. Food in Brontë and Dickens, in *The Victorian Web* http: //www.victorianweb.org/authors/bronte/cbronte/bg5.html (accessed 31 July 2015)

Victorian street food

Muffins

Classic muffins were sweet buns born in the Anglo-Saxon world (and judging by the recipe, unlike the 'English muffins' introduced from the USA comparatively recently, muffins having ceased to be a popular item in England at the time of WW1). The origin of the name 'muffin' is still uncertain. Some assert that the term derives from the French 'moufflet', a word used in France to describe a rather soft kind of bread. Others suppose that the term derives from the German 'muffen', a word used to describe little cakes. The term 'muffin', to indicate this tasty pastry, is used for the first time in England in 1703. At that time, however, it was written in a different way, i.e. 'moofin'.

Ingredients for 4 persons
100 g butter
2 eggs
140 g flour
110 g sugar
A pinch of yeast
Milk: 1 small cup
A pinch of salt

Preparation
First mix the butter with the sugar, then add the eggs one by one. Add the flour, the yeast, the salt and, gradually blend in the milk. When ready, carefully place

the dough in aluminium muffin cases, being careful to fill them properly. Bake in hot oven for 20-25 minutes until they are gold in colour. Allow to cool, then remove from the oven and dust with a bit of sugar.

Cornish pasty

In the late eighteenth century, the Cornish pasty became the most popular food among the boys employed in the Cornish tin mines. But, long before, this little pastry dumpling stuffed with meat and vegetables had also conquered 'the most refined' palates: it seems that Jane Seymour, the third wife of Henry VIII, was greedy for them.

Ingredients for 4 persons
For the dough (alternatively, puff pastry can be used)
450 g durum wheat flour
110 g lard
100 g butter
175 ml water
For the stuffing
250 g swede, a sliced small purple turnip (alternatively, white turnips or radishes)
200 g sliced onions
450 g minced rump beef
500 g sliced potatoes
Black pepper and salt

Preparation
In a bowl blend the flour together with a quarter of the lard; then gradually add the remaining lard, the butter and mix everything with a spoon. Pour in the water and knead until the dough is smooth and even. Place in film wrap and allow to rest in the refrigerator for 30 minutes. Then divide the dough into four parts, making four dumplings. Using a rolling pin, roll on a floured surface to make discs of ca. 22 cm in diameter. Place at the centre of each one a quarter of the sliced turnips and onions, then season. Cover with chopped raw meat, and season again. Add most of the potatoes and season yet again. Add the rest of the potatoes, but without seasoning. Dampen one side of the disc and fold over, pressing to seal. Curl the edges so that the pasty does not open. Pierce the bottom of the dough with a fork and brush with some milk. Bake for 35-40 minutes in preheated oven, checking halfway through: if the pasties tend to darken, lower the oven temperature. Once removed from the oven, cut the pasties in half to allow the steam to escape.

Steak and Kidney Pie, traditional recipe for 6 pies

For the dough (alternatively, puff pastry can be used)
200 g flour
A pinch of salt
110 g butter, or blended butter and lard
2 or 3 spoons cold water
1 beaten egg to brush the pies
For the stuffing
25 g flour
700 g beef cut in 2 cm cubes
250 g kidney cut in 1.5 cm cubes
20 g butter
1 spoon vegetable oil
2 large onions, chopped
2 carrots cut in 1.5 cm cubes
850 ml hot meat broth
Salt and pepper

Preparation
Place the flour in a large mixing bowl, season with salt and ground black pepper; add the meat cubes and blend until they are covered with flour. Heat the butter and oil in a large saucepan, and add the meat gradually, stirring for about one minute, until it browns. At this point, remove the meat, but not the gravy, and add onions and carrots, frying them over low heat for about 5 minutes. Replace the meat in the saucepan, stir and add the broth. Add salt and pepper. Cover and simmer gently over a low heat for about 2 hours, until the meat is tender or the broth reduces. Turn off the heat and cool. Make six discs with the dough using a plate of about 15 cm in diameter. Line the pie cases, and with the remaining dough make strips about 5 cm wide. Dampen the edge of the cases and place each strip around the edge, pressing well and sealing with care. Remove the excess dough with a knife, then shape the edge, using the thumb and index finger. Fill the cases with the stuffing and cover with a disc of dough, making a hole in the centre to allow steam to escape. Brush with beaten egg. Bake in oven at medium heat for 25-30 minutes, or until golden.

Elena Ogliari

Henry James goes on a diet: a chronicle of a private drama

27 January 1927. Many Londoners are reading an article in *The Evening Standard* by Arnold Bennett. Its title is 'A Candid Opinion on Henry James' and it purports to be a list of the faults affecting the prose of the American author, who had died eleven years before. According to Bennett, James's style is excessively Byzantine and his readers struggle when confronting his convoluted prose. They grope within a maze of infinite sentences – without being relieved by any happy ending that might compensate for their efforts – because James's exclusive aim seems to be to concoct abstruse metaphors, not to offer a pleasant read. Against this background, Bennett tries to delineate the personality and eating behaviour of his transatlantic colleague: pondering on the irksome Jamesian style, Bennett argues that James must have been some sort of ascetic, who, in his lifetime, never enjoyed a good pint of beer. Presumably, not even a half-pint (Bennett 1968: 134). In similar fashion E. M. Forster conceived James as a gastronomic anchorite: as he points out in the essay 'Virginia Woolf', James describes neither Lucullan banquets nor mouth-watering dishes in his works. Suffice it to say that there is nothing comparable to the juicy *Boeuf en daube* described in *To the Lighthouse* by Virginia Woolf, who often whets her readers' appetite. No, Forster comments, the dishes described by James are irremediably tasteless, for they have 'no savour whatever' (Forster 1951: 251).

The obvious question to be asked is: was Henry James in fact a gastronomic ascetic? An inspection of his private correspondence suggests an answer in the negative: in truth, James's letters to his friends and relatives show the author as a *bon vivant*, adoring beer and substantial dishes of 'roast-mutton' (James 2006-2010 I: 49, 241). In his youth, he is suspicious of those who, wanting to be excessively slim, follow a diet that is unsatisfying to the palate. In 1860, the sixteen-year-old James attends a dance school in Geneva, where the ballerinas, as skinny as sylphs, eat almost exclusively 'little glasses of syrop and 'helpings' of ice-cream about twice as large as a peach pit'. The future writer, in a letter to his friend Perry, can't help rejoicing in coming from a nation – the United States, 'our free and enlightened country' – where people are not compelled to starvation in order to be fit (James 2006-2010 I: 33).

As a true enlightened American, James – in Switzerland and Germany, two countries he visited in his adolescence – relishes huge cups of 'steaming coffee', 'sweetened wine' and 'tea,' accompanying 'boggy loaf-cake[s],' 'boiled potatoes, rolls, cold-meat and stewed cherries.' In the pension run by Mr and Mrs Stamm in Bonn, James usually enjoys a multicourse meal: he begins with 'cabbage-soup', followed by 'some boiled beef in rags and some excellent and greasy potatoes... some Westphalia smoked ham and some black beans;' and last but not least, the triumphant conclusion: 'some stewed cherries' – the speciality of the house – and some 'tarts'. James loves the cooking of Madame Humbart, the pension's cook, to the point of wanting her sent to America: not being possible to do so, he contents himself with writing down 'a lot of receipts' in his notebook to pass on to his mother. Mary Robertson James will study them, because her son expects 'a marked improvement in the cookery department' (James 2006-2010 I: 60-7).

Yet, as time passes, James's taste grows refined and Teutonic cooking sinks in his personal hierarchy of the world's best cooking. Germany strikes the thirty-year-old James as 'a ponderous land of sodden veal and odorous cabbage' where gastronomic 'luxuries' – 'salmon & peas, corn & tomatoes, melons & ice-cream' – remain unknown. The writer was then making a Grand Tour of Europe and his itinerary includes a long stay in Italy. He first sets foot in the Bel Paese in 1869. Visiting the villages overlooking Lago Maggiore he is comforted by the sight of fields and orchards; but, suffering from chronic constipation and digestive problems, he hopes that Italian fruits and vegetables may be a remedy. He hoped in vain. Italians – as James relates in his letters – are used to frying every vegetable in lard: finding some vegetables not soaked in fat is utterly impossible. In addition, wine is of low quality, oil difficult to digest... Complaints about food are James's favourite topic in the letters to his brother William. His Italian experience is incidentally marked by 'a moving intestinal drama' which forces the novelist to make frequent pilgrimages to several doctors' sanctuaries and to have hot chocolate – a low-fat hot chocolate made with water, not milk – and beefsteaks for breakfast. Rather than eating fried vegetables, he resorts to beefsteaks for breakfast like Ishmael and Queequeg in the fifth chapter of *Moby Dick*. Yet, James was not obliged to work on a whaler.

In Florence, James's bowels have a rest for a while, because he dines at the Café Anglais, where cooking – as the name of the café suggests – is not Italian. But in Rome, the next stop in his itinerary, his drama worsens to the point of contemplating a sudden escape from Italy. Unfortunately, a departure from Italy would deprive him of a more pleasant cultural intoxication. James visits Italy to swallow and assimilate as much culture and beauty as he can (Herford 2010: 57). In his letters from Italy, food metaphors and words recur to define his role as artist-tourist looking for spiritual satiety. In November, he writes:

'in the morning I have regularly gone to the Vatican, & in the afternoon have strolled about at hazard, seeking what I might devour, & devouring (frequently with something of the languor of fatigue) whatever I have found'. However, the appropriation of another culture is a complex process. Musing over his own digestive problems, James tells William he finds it difficult to assimilate and digest what he has being seen in Italy: 'this Italian tone of things [...] lies richly on my soul & gathers increasing weight, but it lies as a cold & foreign mass – never to be absorbed & appropriated' (James 2006-2010 II: 173, 113). Besides these troubles, beauty and culture are not a panacea for all evils: in autumn, his health problems get worse, so James flees to France. Soon afterwards, he goes back to New York.

Leon Edel, James's biographer *par excellence*, argues that these disorders have psychosomatic origins: the young man is worried by financial issues – he is almost penniless – and homesick (Edel 1987: xxi). In the letter about Teutonic cooking, not only does James comment on cabbages, but also writes he would like 'to sit between you [his parents] on the sofa, holding a hand of you apiece' and 'to sit between you at dinner', thus revealing to what extent the desire to see his family is accompanied by nostalgia for American food. His 1869 letters from Italy – apart from the comments on artefacts and architectural landmarks – are a paean to his 'own happy land' where people gorge on 'boiled mutton… fresh vegetables… cracked wheat… brown bread' (James 2006-2010 II: 136).

The yearning for American cooking is triggered by relevant cherished childhood memories. These words pronounced by Miss Mumby in *The Ivory Tower* (1917) are significant: 'oh yes, food's a great tie, it's like language – you can always understand your own, whereas in Europe I had to learn about six others' (James 1917: 79). American food is natural and natal, the ability to appreciate it is not acquired by dint of education (Armstrong 1998: 42); it is the food of James's happy childhood in America and of the family microcosm.

In the autobiographical *A Small Boy and Others* (1913) James goes back to the winter of 1854, when he attended the Forest and Quackenboss School, and lingers on the memories of the waffles he devoured during the breaks. These 'oblong farinaceous compound[s]', served hot with maple syrup, were adored by all the pupils and for young Henry were 'the highest pleasure of sense' (James 2011a: 181). Yet, the best waffles were sold by John Pynsent, who had a shop next door. In the pages devoted to the farinaceous compounds, James amuses himself by presenting a mock-heroic poem to his readers: its protagonists are the Forest and Quackenboss students, appointed to assess who makes the best waffles between the school cook and Mr Pynsent. The duel is won by the latter for the 'stickiness' of his waffles, heavily sprinkled with coconut flakes. Unsurprisingly, the surname of the utmost delicacy creator was forever impressed on James's mind: indeed, many years after leaving school, the writer would use it for the humble dressmaker Miss Amanda Pynsent in *The Princess Casamassima* (1886).

In *A Small Boy and Others*, James also describes with pleasure the huge amount of fresh fruits one could buy in New York between the 1840s and 1850s. The author depicts a city untouched by immigration and industrialization: an idealized New York where any kind of peach, 'Isabella grapes' and 'Seckel pears' are at anybody's hand. In James's account, the metropolis is a 'succulent cornucopia' for its inhabitants, who enjoy the products of 'the bucolic age of the American world' (James 2011a: 61). It is an unfaithful portrayal of New York, because many of its quarters were then poverty-stricken: between 1840 and 1855, over three million European immigrants arrived in New York and a fifth of them were forced to beg for food (Collister 2011a: 6).

The description of 1840s New York in *Washington Square* (1880) is more realistic by far: James writes about Irish immigrants, rattling omnibuses and oyster saloons on Seventh Street. In a dingy oyster bar the author sets the clandestine meeting between the fortune hunter Morris Townsend and the aunt of his prey, Mrs Penniman. The affluent Mrs Penniman contents herself with a tea, whereas her plebeian interlocutor orders 'an oyster stew', a typical Irish-American dish made of oysters and milk. Today readers may be baffled by Morris's choice: how could a low-class man afford such a fine dish? However, in those days, oysters were not a luxury, but a cheap and nutritious type of street food sold at a derisory price, owing to their abundance on American shores. And while relishing his 'oyster stew', Morris lets his secret slip: his interest in Catherine Sloper – Mrs Penniman's niece – is purely economic. 'I do like the money' admits he, blurting out the novel key-word: 'money'. In *Washington Square* everything revolves around money, which is frequently alluded to throughout the narration. For instance, the oyster saloon episode ends with a reference to money: the narrator duly notes that the two dining companions decide to go Dutch.

One of the most interesting passages of *A Small Boy and Others* is a literary portrait of the writer's paternal grandmother. She lived in a large house in Albany surrounded by orchards and peach-trees: there, young Henry spent his summer playing with his siblings and cousins, and eating all the peaches he wanted. Aptly modified, this memory will resurface in *The Portrait of a Lady* (1881) as well. In the third chapter Isabel Archer – the female protagonist from Albany – fondly recalls the visits to her grandmother, which had 'a flavour of peaches', due to the many fragrant peach-trees in the house garden. Yet, the novel is not set in Albany: the protagonist first appears on the threshold of a typical English garden of 'an old English country-house' (James 1998: 19-39).

Prompted by a desire for adventure, the girl has turned her back on America to go to Europe. Curiously, her first contact with European culture takes place during a tea ceremony. The opening words of the novel are worth reading:

> Under certain circumstances there are few hours in life more agreeable than the hour dedicated to the ceremony known as afternoon tea. There are circumstances in which, whether you partake of the tea or not – some people of course never do, – the situation is in itself delightful. (James 1998: 19)

This opening is striking for its pedantic abundance – 'the ceremony known as afternoon tea', for example – does however have a point, for James is trying to reproduce British pomposity in speech. It is the mild joke of an American who has settled in England and likes making fun of his new fellow countrymen (Poirier 1960: 191-92). He does not despise the British and their customs: in fact he envies them for having old traditions, because 'it is on manners, customs, usages, habits, forms, upon all these things matured & established, that a novelist lives – they are the very stuff his work is made of' (James 1972-1984 II: 267). The five o'clock tea is one of those *paraphernalia* which constitute the novelist's working material. When James wrote the opening words of *The Portrait of a Lady*, in 1880, five years had already passed since his departure from the United States, the country he considered devoid of traditions and lacking the essential elements when compared to Europe. Indeed, in 1875, confronting the difficulty of writing about the American world, he decided to board a liner for Liverpool.

In 1875, James left the United States to settle in Europe. Initially, he resided in Paris, but after only one year, he moved to England, which was to become his permanent home. On 11 December 1876, he landed at Folkestone and set out for London. He was not a complete stranger to the bustling life of the English capital: at the very beginning of his 1869 Grand Tour he had stayed in London to have a new wardrobe made by the city tailors. Then it was cold, despite being springtime. He sojourned in a humble abode at 7 Half Moon Street. On the day of his arrival, alone in his room, he suddenly started dreading what he would see outside the lodging: London and its inhabitants could have ensnared him in a fatal trap. Recalling the beginning of *Our Mutual Friend* – the description of the corpses floating in the Thames – he claimed that he 'would rather even starve rather than sally forth into the infernal town, where the natural fate of an obscure stranger would be to be trampled to death in Piccadilly and have his carcass thrown into the Thames'. Later on, he summoned up the courage to ask the landlord about a restaurant in the surrounding area. The landlord – a man called Lazarus Fox – recommended two places: the Bath Hotel and The Albany in Piccadilly. James opted for the latter, 'a small eating-house of the very old English tradition' where he ate succulent 'joints' and 'pudding' (James 2011b: 431). James would incorporate his memories about The Albany into the tale 'A Passionate Pilgrim' (1871), which deals with the story of an American arriving in England from Italy, enthused about setting foot in so sacred a place. He wanders near Temple Bar lost in reverie, imagining Dr Johnson walking there a century before. Later on, really hungry, he heads for The Red Lion – the fictional counterpart of The Albany – where he dreams of relishing 'lamb and spinach and a rhubarb tart'. Unfortunately, he will content himself with '[sitting] down in penitence to a mutton-chop and a rice pudding.' The pilgrim's modest meal is nevertheless counterbalanced by a vision of the long-forgotten England depicted by Dickens, Smollett and Boswell (James 1978: 43). The passionate pilgrim feels the same emotions as James at The Albany: then, the writer thought of the New York and Boston restaurants, utterly inferior to that dingy 'eating-house', where he could 'see the little old English world of Dickens, [...] of Smollett and of Boswell'. In James's view, in England, even the bleakest place has its dignity, due to its being the object of attention of writers admired by him. By contrast, Boston and New York restaurants – erected in a 'desert' – lack history and tradition, thus becoming a poor imitation of their European counterparts. These comments shed further light on James's reasons for leaving the United States.

In 1876, the writer looks forward to establishing himself as a popular figure in British literary circles. Upon his arrival, he is so excited that he compares his breakfast – 'tea, eggs, bacon and the exquisite English loaf', served by the dark-faced maid Louisa – to the meal of a king (James 1972-1984 II: 82). But James is difficult to please and soon becomes dissatisfied with the monotonous meals prepared by Louisa, which usually consist of a chop and boiled potatoes accompanied by a pint of beer. Once, without apparent success, the writer attempts to persuade her to introduce a little variety in his meals or, at least, in the cooking of the potatoes. He gives an account of his failure in a letter to his sister Alice:

> H. J. (to the maid): Can't you do anything in the world with potatoes but drearily boil them?
> THE MAID: Oy dear yes, sir, certainly, we can mash them!
> H. J.: That comes to the same thing. No other way?
> THE MAID: I don't think we have heard of any other way, sir.
> H. J.: You can't fry them?
> THE MAID: I don't think we could do that, sir? Isn't that French cookery, sir? (Montgomery Hyde 1969: 8)

Luckily, James is rescued by the historian John Motley, who invites him to become a member of the Athenaeum Club, where 'the dinner is good and cheap': he thus escapes the dreadful 'London restaurants, whose badness is literally fabulous'. Had he been refused membership, he would have fled the metropolis (James 1972-1984 II: 98-99). In several letters to his family, he gives an accurate account of his evenings at the Club: for instance, the first day, he dines with the Archbishop of York, one of Lord Nelson's nephews and Richard Westmacott's son. Herbert Spencer is the most illustrious and – unfortunately – unapproachable member of the Club: the young writer seldom manages to talk with him, because Spencer is always sleeping in an armchair. On a number of occasions, James will keep him company by taking a nap next to him.

In the spring of 1877, the writer begins to enjoy his new life in London. First of all, he makes the acquaintance of Richard Monkton Milnes, a politician who often invites him to the numerous parties he organizes. On March 27th, dinner is fixed for the unusually early hour of seven o'clock to accommodate Lord Tennyson's stomach and bowels, because, as Milnes explains, 'all society has to submit to his idiosyncrasy of the poetical digestion' (Montgomery Hyde 1969: 11). Yet, in James's account of the dinner, the Laureate Poet does not seem to suffer from serious digestive disorders: the whole evening he talks about 'port wine', which is undoubtedly his favourite drink, since he is able 'to drink a whole bottle of port at a sitting with no incommodity' (James 1920: 53).

Many other dinners will take place, enabling James to extend the circle of his acquaintances. During the winter of 1878-9, which sees the publication of *Daisy Miller* and 'An International Episode', James is besieged by London hosts and hostesses. By the end of the first week of June 1879, he had dined out 107 times, a remarkable gastronomic undertaking. 'You will simply wonder what can have induced me to perpetrate such a folly, and how I have survived to tell the tale!' he sometimes jokes (James 1920: 69-70). Yet, dining out is not such a folly for a writer, because social gatherings nourish James's literary activity and an idle conversation may turn out to be the germ of an entire narrative. This is what happened in January 1895, at a nocturnal meeting with the Archbishop of Canterbury. Sipping some tea, the ecclesiastic reveals an anecdote he has recently heard: two orphan children were entrusted to the cares of the household servants, who were unfortunately evil: as a result, they corrupted the orphans, whose innocence was lost forever. Here was the seed from which sprang *The Turn of the Screw* (1898).

In the mid-1880s, however, James eschewed the ephemeral acquaintances of bourgeois *salons* to cultivate sincere and lasting literary friendships in the Republic of Letters. Day by day, he attracted an increasingly large circle of writers, including Edmund Gosse, Robert Louis Stevenson, Mrs Humphry Ward, Stephen Crane – whose partner Cora made doughnuts for James – Constance Fenimore Woolson and Edith Wharton. He freely spoke about literature with them. The following letter to Gosse, stuffed with a profusion of culinary

Henry James enjoys a doughnut from Cora Crane's kitchen, England, 1899.
(Wikimedia Commons)

metaphors, is particularly meaningful: 'could you by a miracle, if you are not afraid of a very modest dinner, come and break bread with me tonight at the primitive hour of seven? I am alone, and there is a solitary fowl. But she shall be dressed with intellectual sauce... I am famished for a little literary conversation' (Montgomery Hyde 1969: 36-41).

Friends and admirers sated his hunger for intellectual companionship, flowing constantly to Lamb House, the mansion in Rye where James settled in 1897. He welcomed the steady stream of visitors at the railway station and, in every respect, he was a generous host, even – perhaps – to excess. According to Wharton, his only fault was his fretting over the money spent to grant a pleasant stay to anybody; too much money (Wharton 1964: 244). An anecdote reported by the critic and translator Gerard Hopkins endorses Wharton's impression. When he was a boy in his early teens, Gerard spent a weekend at Lamb House. His most striking memory of this stay concerns the breakfast served the day after his arrival: 'there was an enormous, luxurious display of side dishes, and ham and eggs and scrambled eggs and kidneys and God knows what'. While little Gerard stares at the delicacies, James steals into the room, completely unheard, and looking at the large breakfast lavishly laid out in the dining-room, the writer blurts out a remarkable complaint: 'oh, what a woeful waste of wonder' (Montgomery Hyde 1969: 113).

It is no wonder that James was worried about his guests' provisions. Apart from *Daisy Miller*, his novels did not sell well: at the beginning of the 20th century, the writer sailed in deep waters. In order to recover from a difficult financial situation, he embarked on a monumental project, namely, the revision of his major works for a luxury edition with prefaces written *ad hoc*. Even so, the New York Edition was bound to be a monumental failure. While revising his work, James fervently followed a new diet fad known as Fletcherism. The regimen was named after its inventor, the American Horace Fletcher (1849-1919), who believed that one should chew every mouthful numerous times, until all the 'goodness' was extracted: then spit out the remaining fibrous material. Since a feeling of satiety was soon achieved, only small amounts of food were ingested. Fletcher quickly becomes a star in his homeland, with disciples among professors at Harvard University, where William James taught philosophy. Aware of his brother's tendency to obesity, in 1904 William sent Henry the celebrated treatise *The New Glutton or Epicure*.

The novelist had been putting on weight since his arrival in London in 1876, when his family rejoiced in his fat, considering plumpness to be a sign of good health. The writer, however, did not share their enthusiasm: 'I rejoice in your rejoicings in my fat, and would gladly cut off fifty pounds or so and send them to you as a wedding-gift' James writes in a letter to the newly-wed William (James 1972-1984 II: 180). Traces of James's annoyance at his own rotundity are even embedded in lines of *Washington Square*: Catherine Sloper, the protagonist of the novel, is said to be plain looking and unattractive to potential suitors. What does the narrator mean by plain looking? That she is overweight – Catherine is euphemistically defined as 'robust' – because she is a 'glutton' irresistibly tempted by 'cream-cakes' (James 2010: 9).

As time passes, James soon passed beyond the threshold of mere robustness: the writer became obese. Thanks to his corpulence, he was frequently compared to a well-fed *abbé* (Page 1984: xii, 122). James tried to take immediate corrective action by resorting to sport: his efforts had disastrous results. For a while, at the beginning of the 20th century, he launched himself on long bike rides across the Sussex countryside: but came back home 'in a state of deliquescence' because he was 'quite unused to any form of active exercise' and walking his dogs seemed to be the only activity he could reasonably undertake. He was not a sportsman, nor was he interested in sport. During the annual cricket weeks at Rye he usually went to the ground, but not to join in the matches: he just sat in the tent talking to the ladies with his back to the game (Page 1984: 79).

Given his lack of athleticism, becoming an adept of Fletcherism seemed to be the only way to solve his problems. He began dieting in 1904, soon after he received his copy of *The New Glutton or Epicure*: he had just finished *The Golden Bowl*. Zealously observing Fletcher's dictates, James quickly achieved his goal. Enthused, he recommended the diet to his friends and the citizens of Rye, boasting of his successes: for example, he was able to spend fifty minutes just 'over a cold partridge, a potato (three potatoes) and a baked apple'. In 1909, he rushed to Venice to have lunch with Fletcher. As he writes in a letter to Mrs Humphry Ward in 1906, James was not a mere 'adept' of The Great Masticator, but 'a fanatic'. He calls Fletcher 'the Divine Light' (James 1972-1984 IV: 415-16). Although there is a certain amount of irony in his letters about Fletcherism, James's devotion to the guru of nutrition was positive. His meals became interminable, because he spent an age munching every single morsel. A. C. Benson lunched with him at the Athenaeum in 1906: 'H. J. eats slower than I ever saw anyone eat' he records in his journal (Page 1984: 122).

Curiously, James's new eating habits had much in common with the way he reconceived the works to be included in The New York Edition. Due to rheumatic pains in his hand, he could not write the new versions of the works himself, so he dictated them to a secretary. The entire process of dictation was anything but straightforward: James would pronounce some words, then hesitate, resume his sentence, pause to meditate... his amanuensis Theodora Bosanquet coined the term 'jawbation' to describe the writer's constant chewing or rumination on what he has dictated (Bosanquet 2006: 79). James was always groping for *le mot juste* that best represented the tumults of his characters' conscience: he weighed up the words to use on his tongue; metaphorically, he fletcherized them rather as he munched his food. In the preface to *The Golden Bowl*, James deployed terms from food vocabulary in his comment on the revision process, thus making it similar to an act of literary Fletcherism: 'the 'old' matter is there, re-accepted, re-tasted, re-assimilated and re-enjoyed'. 'Re-accepted, re-tasted, re-assimilated' is a chain of verbs which The Great Masticator could have used in his works (Armstrong 1998: 46).

James's fanaticism for Fletcherism reached its climax in 1909, when the first volumes of the New York Edition proved to be a commercial disaster. This was a staggering blow. His despair at this failure prompted him to work restlessly on the remaining drafts: he went on working for many hours, deploring every interruption. Fletcherism helped him to keep guests at bay: dining with the slow eater James had become almost a torture. Moreover, the diet gave the writer a feeling of being in control, if not of the editorial market, at least of his body: it was a sort of psychological compensation. He carried Fletcherism to extremes, forcing himself to immensely long walks and even starvation (Holly 1995: 183). This extreme lifestyle had disastrous outcomes: not only did James end up detesting food, but he also sank into depression. Eventually, in January 1910, he collapsed. He blamed his sickness and attacks of depression on Fletcher. In his eyes, the guru turns from Divine Light into the '*fons et origo* of all [his] woes', a criminal who has made him teeter on the edge of death (James 1972-1984 IV: 596). Without hesitation, he abandoned the path indicated by The Great Masticator. After convalescence – when he is comforted by baskets of fruits sent by Wharton and nourishing meat broth – he is again the *bon vivant* of the past. Benson, who in 1906 had a perfect demonstration of Fletcherism, lunched with James on 21st April 1915. The writer is pale because of some cardiac problems, but his disease does not preclude cheerfulness: indeed, he is 'in a cheerful and pontifical mood'. James appreciates conviviality and relishes his meals again: 'he ate a plentiful meal of veal and pudding' is the new entry in Benson's journal (Page 1984: 124).

Works cited

Armstrong, T. 1998. *Modernism, Technology, and the Body. A Cultural Study*. Cambridge, Cambridge University Press.
Bennett, A. E. 1968. A Candid Opinion on Henry James. In S. Hynes (ed.), *The Author's Craft and Other Critical Writings*: 132-137. Lincoln, University of Nebraska Press.
Bosanquet, T. 2006. *Henry James at Work*, ed. by L. Harris Powers, Ann Arbor, University of Michigan Press.
Edel, L. (ed.) 1987. *Henry James. Selected Letter*. Cambridge, Harvard University Press.
Fletcher, H. 2008. *The New Glutton or Epicure*. Charleston, BiblioLife.
Forster, E. M. 1951. Virginia Woolf. In *Two Cheers for Democracy*: 242-258. London, Edward Arnold.
Herford, O. 2010. The Roman Lotus: Digestion and Retrospect. *The Henry James Review* 31: 54-60.
Holly, C. 1995. The Emotional Aftermath of the New York Edition. In D. McWhirter (ed.), *Henry James's New York Edition. The Construction of Authorship*: 167-184. Stanford, Stanford University Press.
Hyde, M. H. 1969. *Henry James at Home*. London, Methuen.
James, H. 1917. *The Ivory Tower*. London, W. Collins Sons & Co.

James, H. 1920. *The Letters of Henry James Vol.1*, ed. by P. Lubbock. New York, Charles Scribner's Sons.
James, H. 1972. *Essays in London and Elsewhere*. New York, Books for Libraries Press.
James, H. 1972-1984. *Letters*, IV vols. L. Edel (ed.). Cambridge MA, The Belknap Press of Harvard University Press.
James, H. 1978. A Passionate Pilgrim. In M. Aziz (ed.), *The Tales of Henry James. Volume Two: 1870-1874*: 42-101. Oxford, Clarendon Press.
James, H. 1998. *The Portrait of a Lady*, ed. with an Introduction by N. Bradbury. Oxford, Oxford University Press.
James, H. 2006-2010. *The Complete Letters of Henry James*, ed. by P. A. Walker and G. W. Zacharias. Lincoln, University of Nebraska Press.
James, H. 2010. *Washington Square*, ed. with an Introduction and Notes by A. Poole. Oxford, Oxford University Press.
James, H. 2011a. *A Small Boy and Others*, ed. by P. Collister. Charlottesville, University of Virginia Press.
James, H. 2011b. *Notes of a Son and a Brother. The Middle Years*, ed. by P.Collister. Charlottesville, University of Virginia Press.
Page, N. (ed.) 1984. *Interviews and Recollections*. London, Macmillan.
Poirier, R. 1960. *The Comic Sense of Henry James. A Study of the Early Novels*. London, Chatto and Windus.
Wharton, E. 1964. *A Backward Glance*. New York, Scribner.

Oyster stew: an Irish-American tradition

Many Irish immigrants came to the American shores even before the Great Famine, among them William James – Henry's grandfather. The vast majority were Catholic who followed religious dietary customs around holidays: for instance, they abstained from eating meat on Christmas Eve, opting for fish as their main protein. In Ireland, the Christmas Eve meal revolved around a fish called the ling, the crucial ingredient of a simple stew consisting of milk, butter and pepper to season. Irish families could not find any dried ling in the United States: instead, they found oysters, which were highly popular throughout the country. Since their taste is similar to dried ling, the original stew recipe was adapted for oysters.

Ingredients
1 pint shucked oysters in their liquid
4 tablespoons butter + extra butter (optional)
4 cups milk
2 tablespoons of white flour
1 minced celery

2 small shallot, minced
minced parsley to taste
sliced chives (optional)
salt and fresh ground black pepper to taste

Preparation
Drain the oysters, reserving their liquor: do not forget to pass the liquid through a fine strainer to remove any sand and bits of shell. In a large saucepan over medium heat, melt butter. Stir in the white flour and, after 3 or 4 minutes, the shallots and celery: sauté until they are softened and clear. Season with parsley and few pinches of salt and pepper. Cook 30 seconds. Stir in the milk and oyster liquor. Simmer very gently for 2 minutes: do not boil, keep them at a simmer. Blend in the oysters and cook them for about 2 minutes or until the edges of the oysters curl: do not overcook the oysters, since overcooking makes them tough. Remove from heat. Serve the stew right away in warm soup bowls with toasted homemade bread. Garnish each bowl with parsley, chives, or extra slivers of butter.

Karin Mosca

Bennett, Strachey and the preparation of the omelette

It is amusing that Arnold Bennett (1867-1931) and Lytton Strachey (1880-1932) may be connected by an omelette: both writers refer to this recipe in their works, even if the use they make of it is noticeably different.

In *Helen with the High Hand* (1910), Bennett devoted a whole chapter to the omelette. Helen, the young heroine of the novel, tries to make an impression on her rich and ungenerous uncle James Ollerenshaw, and with this aim she cooks a meal for him. In order to seduce and endear the old scrooge, she prepares a dish that at the beginning of the 20th century could be described as 'exotic', namely a 'kidney omelette'.

A recipe for the 'kidney omelet' was already included in the first edition of *Beeton's Book of Household Management* (1861) by Mrs Beeton (1836-1865), composed as a useful manual to teach Victorian women how to be the perfect mistresses of the house. The caption for the omelette recipe reads 'a favourite French dish' (Beeton 1982: 734). Even though kidney is a typical and popular delicacy of the English *cuisine*, the very fact of introducing it as the ingredient of a French omelette made it sound more refined and valued.

In Bennett's short novel, the long passage devoted to the making of the omelette opens with James, Helen's uncle, hearing some noises from the kitchen, and deciding to find out what his niece is doing there. What he sees leaves him a bit perplexed: Helen has broken four eggs (too many in his view, considering that just two people are going to eat them), and she is cutting some kidney. From the door, the uncle can see all the preparation of the strange recipe. In the kitchen, Helen looks like a real expert. She can keep the fire under control, to give the right degree of heat to the different ingredients that have been placed in a frying pan. The kidney, finely sliced, is slowly browning in butter, while Helen has added a pinch of salt to the eggs and is beating them with a fork. Yet, Uncle James doesn't know what she's preparing. To him her actions are mysterious, but he is enchanted while watching her pricking, turning and blending the strange concoction of eggs and meat. Helen serves the kidney omelette as a side dish for tea: 'the mystery lay on a plate in the middle of the table. In colour it resembled scrambled eggs, except that it was tinted a more brownish, or coppery, gold rather like a first Yorkshire pudding' (Bennett 1983: 41). Uncle James cannot understand – are those scrambled eggs? Is that a new recipe for a Yorkshire pudding? In the end Helen unveils the mystery and explains that the strange concoction is a kidney omelette. Uncle James is quite shocked: in his sixty years life, he has never tried an omelette, never even seen an omelette, and is quite adamant that 'omelettes form no part of the domestic cuisine in England' (Bennett 1983: 41). Even if he is annoyed because Helen has used all his supply of eggs, Uncle James decides to taste the omelette, and suddenly he experiences a revelation: he can't believe that Helen has been able to create that marvel, that dream, just by using four eggs and some kidney – ingredients not really appreciated by him until that moment. In just six minutes, Uncle James

> [...] was ravished, rapt away on the wings of paradisiacal ecstasy by a something that consisted of kidney and of a few eggs. This omelette had all the finer and nobler qualities of Yorkshire pudding and scrambled eggs combined, together with others beyond the ken of his greedy fancy. (Bennett 1983: 42)

Thanks to the exciting taste of the omelette, James starts reappraising his life, wondering how he could waste it in the monotony of the flavourless and repetitive dishes proposed by his less creative cook, Mrs Butt. And he muses: 'could it be that there existed women, light and light-handed creatures, creatures of originality and resource, who were capable of producing prodigies like this kidney omelette, on the spur of the moment?' (Bennett 1983: 42). He now looks at Helen and is fascinated by her, who has not even stained her dress while cooking: 'he might have known that so extraordinary and exotic a female person would not concoct anything so trite as a Yorkshire pudding or scrambled eggs' (Bennett 1983: 43). If Helen in just a few minutes has been able to prepare such a tasty and juicy dish, who knows how many delicacies and how many happy moments together he could have enjoyed in his life, instead of remaining a slave to his greed and rigidity.

The art of cooking is indeed the means through which Helen tries to extend her power over Uncle James. Without any doubt, she is a *new woman*: she lives by herself; she supports herself by working as a teacher; she is self-confident, even cheeky; her attitude is very far from that of a submissive angel in the house. And yet, despite her display of a free attitude, her real aim is to attract men's attention: Helen affirms that she works just to afford nice clothes and elegant accessories. Even her way of walking, sharply waving her hips, is highly seductive and a sign of her flirtatious attitude. As Clotilde De Stasio affirms, 'Helen's stylish appearance, far from being a token of independence, turns out to be only the traditional way to entice a man' (1995: 47). It all amounts to the fact that while Helen is, and claims to be, a modern girl, she does not forget her traditionally feminine characteristics and capabilities, that can conquer a man's heart. And which activity is more feminine, and represents the duty of a good wife and angel in the house, if not cooking? The girl takes advantage of her capabilities and familiarity with the culinary arts to attract Uncle James' attention. And he is enraptured by the tasty flavour of that exotic dish, especially as until that moment he had only known it from the proverb 'you can't make an omelette without breaking eggs'. Helen deserves now the place that once was Mrs Butt's. She has been able to innovate the kidney recipe, that very kidney that Mrs Butt had prepared in the same traditional fashion for three years. Helen's cooking is simple, but unusual, exotic, and with a little bit of French coquetry.

Helen's aim is not to make Uncle James fall in love with her: she has no intention of marrying her old uncle, but she wants to capture his trust; she wants to bring a bit of fresh air into the life of the old man, who, unmarried, does not know that a woman could have made his life happier. She also wants to manage his money and property. With this intention, Helen enters her uncle's house not just as a tender niece, but as a perfect housekeeper, who can cook, clean, and shop at the market ... with her uncle's money, obviously. Even when Helen spends a great part of her uncle's money to buy her much-loved accessories, the memory of the succulent omelette calms Uncle James' fury.

The omelette, in Bennett's short novel, represents the fulfilment that comes from eating something delicious and the happiness that arises from the small pleasures of life. Moreover, the omelette is the most important element of Helen's 'courting', a weapon in the hands of a woman who wants to conquer a man. Lytton Strachey by contrast would probably not have appreciated Helen's amazing cooking skills. It seems, in fact, that omelettes were a little too heavy for the eminent biographer's weak stomach.

Whilst travelling in Spain, as documented by Gerald Brenan in his *South from Granada*, Strachey suffered from the ruthless Spanish cuisine, whose dried cod, unrefined olive oil and potato omelettes (*tortillas*) were too heavy for the English writer. Strachey, who died of stomach cancer, observed a strict regimen of diet and rest throughout his entire life. In *The Bloomsbury Cookbook* (2014), Jans Ondaatje Rolls informs us that young Lytton, a pale and sickly child, was ordered to eat raw meat and porridge, and to drink Port, but he quitted this supposedly invigorating diet because of the little effect it had on his health. His favourite dishes were rice pudding (he ate at least one per day), milk and biscuits. When he grew up and left his family, the responsibility of controlling his diet rested on his house mates. His life-long partner, the painter and Bloomsbury member

Dora Carrington, in a letter addressed to Mary Hutchinson (Holroyd 1971: 747-748), gives a detailed report of Strachey's daily dietary programme: breakfast in bed, with two eggs, toast and jam without pips in it; morning break with a glass of hot milk and biscuits; lunch with rice or macaroni, vegetables, meat and milk puddings; afternoon tea; a bowl of bread and milk before going to bed; a glass of milk and biscuits, ready by his bedside in case he woke up in the night. Strachey must have been a great milk drinker! Ralph Partridge (1894-1960), the third member of the *ménage à trois* conducted with Strachey and Carrington at Mill House, had to supply the pantry: he loved cultivating his vegetable garden and taking care of the poultry.

It is not the fact that Strachey found omelettes hard to digest that relates the biographer to Arnold Bennett. In his essay 'Gibbon', contained in *Portraits in Miniature* (1931), Strachey writes:

> That the question has ever been not only asked but seriously debated, whether History was an art, is certainly one of the curiosities of human ineptitude. What else can it possibly be? It is obvious that History is not a science: it is obvious that History is not the accumulation of facts, but the relation of them. Only the pedantry of incomplete academic persons could have given birth to such a monstrous supposition. Facts relating to the past, when they are collected without art, are compilations; and compilations, no doubt, may be useful; but they are no more History than butter, eggs, salt and herbs are an omelette. (Strachey 1931: 160)

It is easy to prepare an omelette: all you have to do is simply mix together butter, eggs, salt and herbs. It is the aim of the cook to turn a simple omelette into something special to the taste. In the same way, the biographer has to recollect facts and events relating to the past, put them together and finally add his touch in the preparation of his work: in culinary terms, he has to add his secret ingredient. It is this final passage that differentiates a simple compilation of facts from biography as a work of art. In this way, the biographer can be compared to a chef, and biography to the preparation of a delicious dish.

Every recipe starts with the indication of which ingredients are needed, so the first question is, what are the 'ingredients' for the perfect biography? Strachey gives us his 'recipe' in his essay 'Macaulay', also contained in *Portraits in Miniature*: what you need are a great dose of facts (and the capacity for absorbing them), the right quantity of talent for stating them, and a pinch of point of view. Strachey was a great reader, and the British Library was his favourite place to find information about the men and women he was writing about. He did not like to live in the city, but during the period of preparation of his works it was necessary to go to the capital: we could say that he 'went shopping' in London, comparing the library to a supermarket; the books to raw food. He did not limit his research to official biographies or historical manuals: he also read memoirs, journals, articles from newspapers, letters and gossip columns. He liked to discover little curious details and anecdotes, in order to reveal, as he writes, 'the littleness underlying great events' (Strachey 1922: 31): only in this way was it possible to describe a real life, a real person, with all the human virtues and failings. Michael Holroyd, Strachey's official biographer, affirms that this preparatory phase of reading was extremely long, as it took almost twice as long as the time it took to write the biography. This was because, as a great restaurateur, Strachey had many suppliers!

The second ingredient is the capacity for stating facts. Strachey's style is very simple and linear, but at the same time his works are full of images, metaphors and repetitions that make his subjects more lively and his biographies more colourful. Even if his creation is quite simple, it creates an explosion of sublime flavours and of intense notes in the mouths of those who savour it.

Last but not least, the third ingredient is the point of view, and Strachey's perspective is surely evident in his biographies. Even if Strachey himself praises the 'divine art of impartiality' in his essay on Hume (Strachey 1931: 139), asserting that a great biographer should maintain detachment in what he is writing, the reader can detect, with no effort, whenever Strachey finds his subject congenial, and when he does not. Just as every person in the world has his or her own particular taste in matters of food, so Strachey had different opinions on his subjects.

In the preface to *Eminent Victorians* (1918), Strachey illustrates the necessary steps to follow in the preparation of a good biography. First, the biographer has to make a selection of facts, just like a great chef who has to choose the most precious ingredients to use in his creations. The biographer must simplify and clarify, select and omit, and avoid being too specific: he should not prepare a pie made of leftovers taken from the fridge, but he has to respect the natural flavours of his ingredients and combine them in the best possible way. Strachey continues his preface by stating that the wise biographer should 'attack his subject in unexpected places [...] he will shoot a sudden, revealing searchlight into obscure recesses, hitherto undivined' (Strachey 2002: 2). The biographer has to analyse an individual's life by probing even into the depths of the mind. In Strachey's works it is possible to read the most intimate thoughts of his subjects, and to discover the reasons and forces that make them adopt a certain attitude or behaviour. A good chef does not only have to know how to prepare a dish: he has to know the properties of every ingredient (calories, fats, proteins, etc.); he has to know how ingredients react when they are mixed; he has to know the time needed to cook and how these factors may altogether affect the final result. In the same way, the biographer has to dig beneath the surface, in order to obtain a deep knowledge and intimacy with his subject. However, facts are reported according to the way the biographer understands them, so once again the necessity of a point of view is confirmed.

Strachey states that a biographer should 'maintain his freedom of spirit' (Strachey 2002: 4), and for this reason he takes the liberty to talk about sex: he reacted against Victorian culture speaking freely of topics commonly considered taboo, including sexuality. Sex was like an exotic dish that no one in England had tried yet. Moreover, Strachey does not want to impart any moral lesson about ethics and religion; he does not evoke the sense of a destiny chosen by God or of a Cosmic Order, because his aim is 'to illustrate and not to explain' (Strachey 2002: 3). What he likes and what he is interested in is humanity, and he affirms that human beings cannot be treated as mere symptoms of the past, but they have an eternal value that also lasts in the present. Strachey's art of cooking is simple, just like an omelette, and sometimes this simplicity is more appreciated than a refined and elaborate dish of *nouvelle cuisine*.

We may say that Strachey's special ingredient is irony: the biographer spices his works with humour and sarcasm, imparting a new perspective, a changing light, upon the lives he is writing about. Strachey's irony is strategic, in the sense that he uses it to veil hostility and, as Richard Hutch affirms, to portray 'ambivalence in greatness' (Hutch 1988: 2). Thanks to irony, questions and doubt arise, and more opinions and perspectives are available on the same subject. The same ingredient can be cooked and seasoned in different ways, and Strachey preferred giving a spicy flavour to his works.

Arnold Bennett, therefore, chooses the omelette as the exotic and unusual dish with which Helen bewitches Uncle James and convinces him to welcome her into his house: she knows that to cook amazing dishes is the fastest way a woman can seduce a man. Strachey's omelette, by contrast, is simply a metaphor to present his idea of history and biography. Just like an omelette, his prose is simple and linear, but at the same time his talent makes his biographies pieces of art. According to Virginia Woolf, Strachey was one of the most important figures in the history of the genre, so we might dare to say that, if Strachey had been a chef with his own restaurant, he would surely have been awarded a Michelin star.

Works cited

Beeton, I. [1861] 1982. *Mrs Beeton's Book of Household Management*. London, Chancellor Press.
Bennett, A. [1910] 1983. *Helen with the High Hand*. Gloucester, Alan Sutton.
Brenan, G. 1957. *South from Granada*. London, H. Hamilton.
De Stasio, C. 1995. Arnold Bennett and Late-Victorian Woman. *Victorian Periodicals Review*, XXVIII, 1: 40-53.
Holroyd, M. 1971. *Lytton Strachey, a Biography*. London, Penguin Books.
Hutch, R. 1988. Strategic Irony and Lytton Strachey's Contribution to Biography. *Biography*, XI, 1, http://www.jstor.org/stable/23539315 (accessed June 2015).
Rolls, J. O. 2014. *The Bloomsbury Cookbook: Recipes for Life, Love and Art*. New York, Thames & Hudson.
Sanders, C. R. 1951. Lytton Strachey's Conception of Biography. *PMLA, Publications of the Modern Language Association*, LXVI, June 1951, 4: 295-315.
Sanders, C. R. 1953. Lytton Strachey's Point of View. *PMLA, Publications of the Modern Language Association*, LXVIII, 1: 75-94.
Scott-James, R. A. 1955. *Lytton Strachey*. London, Longmans, Green & Co.
Strachey, L. 2002. *Eminent Victorians: Cardinal Manning, Florence Nightingale, Dr. Arnold, General Gordon: the Definitive Edition*, P. Levy and F. Partridge (eds). London, Continuum.
Strachey, L. 1922. Mr. Creevey. In *Books and Characters: French and English*. New York, Harcourt, Brace and Company.
Strachey, L. 1931. *Portraits in Miniature*, London, Chatto & Windus.
Woolf, V. 2011. The Art of Biography. In A. McNeillie, S. N. Clarke (eds). *The Essays of Virginia Woolf*, 6 vols., VI, 1933-1941: 221-228. London, The Hogarth Press.

Omelette a la Bennet and rice pudding Strachey's style

Arnold Bennett (1867-931), English novelist, used to have lunch at the Savoy Hotel in London, where he liked to eat a special omelette stuffed with smoked haddock. The dish figures in the hotel's menu even today.

Ingredients (2 portions)
2 tablespoons butter
2 teaspoons flour
160 ml. milk
5 eggs (for one egg, separate the yolk from the white)
50 g. Parmesan, grated
black pepper
salt
170 g. smoked haddock, undyed

Preparation
Melt a teaspoon of butter in a pan over low heat; remove from the heat and add the flour, mixing all together. Return the pan over the heat and add half of the milk. When all the ingredients are combined, add the rest of the milk and half of the Parmesan. Mix and let it thicken. Add salt, pepper and the yolk of an egg. Let it cool.

Beat until stiff the white of an egg. In a mixing bowl, beat four eggs. Crumble the haddock.

Melt the rest of the butter in an omelette pan. When it is hot and foamy, but not brown, add the fish and the beaten eggs. Mix and let it cook for a minute over medium heat: the surface should remain soft, with a part of liquid egg in the centre.

After removing the pan from the heat, combine together the stiffened egg white with some Parmesan, and pour the result over the omelette. Place the dish under a grill, already hot. After half a minute, pour over the sauce you set aside and place it again under the grill, until it browns.

Slip the omelette on a plate and serve, without folding.

Rice pudding

Ingredients
300 g. rice
One lemon peel
1 l. milk
Salt
90 g. sugar
Vanilla
Cinnamon or cocoa powder

Preparation
Warm the milk over medium heat, add the vanilla seeds and the lemon peel. Add sugar and a pinch of salt. Let the milk boil, then add the rice and let it cook for 30 minutes. If necessary, add hot milk. When the rice is ready, remove the lemon peel and pour the mixture in some dessert bowls. Eat either hot or cold. Sprinkle with cinnamon or cocoa powder to taste.

Milk pudding

Ingredients
1 l. milk
8 eggs
8 teaspoons sugar

Preparation
Warm the milk over low heat. Add lemon peel or vanilla seeds to taste. Beat the eggs with the sugar, then pour into the milk. Warm the oven and fill a saucepan with water. Pour the milk mixture into some little moulds and place them in the saucepan. Cook in a bain-marie for 30 minutes, then allow them to cool. May also be served with caramel.

Maria Cristina Mancini

Leopold Bloom's grilled mutton kidneys

It is June 16th, 1904. An ordinary day, one like many other days. Leopold Bloom is a thirty-eight year old advertising agent of Jewish origin. He is an ordinary man, one like many other men, with more vices than virtues. He sets out for the streets of Dublin with a sharp and curious look towards the world that surrounds him. He retraces the steps of the hero of the *Odyssey*, wandering through the streets of a modern city. He is driven by the stimulus of curiosity, and he may even cheat on his wife Molly, a modern Penelope. Only late at night he will get back home to his wife, an opera singer who is in turn cheating on him with her manager. Leopold Bloom is the main character in James Joyce's *Ulysses* (1922), but he appears for the first time only in the fourth chapter of the novel. Joyce describes him as a man fond of 'thick giblet soup, nutty gizzards, a stuffed roast heart, liver slices fried with crust crumbs, fried hen cods' roes. Most of all he liked grilled mutton kidneys which gave to his palate a fine tang of faintly scented urine' (Joyce 2000: 65). As a character, Bloom has an uncertain identity. He is a Dubliner who completely acknowledges and takes an active part in Irish culture. At the same time, he is also a supranational person, who does not belong to any nation, a secular mind, a freethinker.

In a novel in which every word opens up further references, grilled kidneys have their own meaning. This animal part, served for breakfast, is one of the most popular dishes in the Irish and English tradition. For this reason, grilled kidneys help characterize Bloom, as well as his own culture. Moreover, kidneys, in the book, will blend with the pork, liver and onions that, with their pungent flavours and smells, go into the stream of consciousness, changing its poetics into a recognisable and immediately understandable score. *Ulysses* is a book where musicality spreads out in every direction because it was written by an aspiring tenor who had learnt to put on the page what musicians call the 'inner ear' by going beyond the objective meaning of words.

Leopold Bloom lacks the greatness and heroism of Ulysses, but like the Greek hero his curiosity is always alive. This aspect, together with a disillusioned sense of humour and a dose of ironic detachment, makes him a modern hero, and, at least in Joyce's intention, a symbol of mankind as a whole. Yet, despite this stature, he leads an ordinary life, a life lacking heroism, a dream-like life, and shaped like a long conversation with himself. Leopold Bloom is indeed an ordinary man, a man without qualities who makes Dublin the centre of his own world and changes every aspect of life, even ordinary things such as making breakfast or looking for a place to eat into a work of art. Aspects of everyday life make the focal points of Mr Bloom's wanderings through the streets of Dublin. His vagaries blend with the never-ending motion of the modern city, with the elusive words barely heard in Grafton Street shops or written on the window of a watch seller. City life also goes on with a jumble of sounds and images: pop songs, arias, and the advertisements shown on posters or worn by sandwich men.

Dublin smells of food at every hour of the day and it wraps its inhabitants with scents of several dishes, erasing the difference between breakfast, lunch and dinner. The culinary tradition of the early 20th century Dublin is made of street food, sold and directly consumed in the city thoroughfares. It is part and parcel of its material culture, which retains strong ties with the land, agriculture, climate and seasons, the environment and existing traditions. Leopold Bloom's city seems to be always hungry (perhaps as a distant legacy of the famines which occurred in Ireland in the 17th and 19th centuries). Starvation and hunger are indeed the best ingredients of what has been called 'cuisine of the poor'. The shortage of food resources, which was a permanent condition in the life of the farmer, produced what we might term the 'food lies', the tricks and clever make-believe preparations, contrived to conceal impoverished conditions. Poverty indeed gave birth to recipes lacking the main ingredient that gives them their name, thus creating an interplay of dreams and desires. The most important 'missing' ingredient used to be meat. This is why grilled kidneys seem so desirable, and whet the appetite of Leopold Bloom.

In a similar way, in England, Welsh Rarebit or Welsh Rabbit is a traditional recipe composed of a slice of toasted bread with melted cheese, while the Mock-Turtle of *Alice's Adventures in Wonderland* reminds us of the price to be paid for real turtle soup. Such recipes, conceived to find a remedy for the essential shortage of a desired foodstuff, also create a different kind of pleasure, a pleasure due to the gratification of the palate on a verbal level, a play between absence and irony, which mediates between the unconscious and reality.

Leopold's breakfast is described in the fourth chapter. Bloom prepares a cup of tea and some buttered slices of bread for his wife but his mind is so fully bent on buying kidneys that he starts talking to his green-eyed black cat. Bloom's cat thus joins the feline aristocracy of English literature together with the Black Cat in Edgar Allan Poe's eponymous short story of 1843, the Cheshire Cat of *Alice in Wonderland* (1865) and the colony of cats described by T. S. Eliot in *Old Possum's Book of Practical Cats* (1939).

Bloom goes out in the early morning: he inhales the fragrance of fresh bread, and catches 'through the open doorway [...] whiffs of ginger, teadust, biscuitmush' (Joyce 2000: 69). He goes into a butcher shop and here the modern Ulysses watches the merchandise on the counter and worries about the last kidney, which his neighbour's servant is going to buy. At the same time, he stares at woman with sensual contemplation and in this way, food acquires an erotic aspect.

With its continuous references to food, *Ulysses* becomes a celebration of a man's physical nature. Nourishment becomes as important as digestion and defecation. In Western philosophy, the sense of taste has been placed at a subordinate, lower, level when compared to the more aristocratic senses of sight and hearing, considered to be as the privileged avenues to knowledge. Compare Plato's disapproval of the taste because it is a sense linked with the 'low' pleasures of eating and drinking. In time, however, the role and status of taste would be reconsidered, so that the 18th century witnesses the full appreciation of the word 'gastronomy'. This century can be viewed as period when not only many cookery books are published, but the chef is considered both as an artist, who can compose with flavours, and as a scientist who administers chemical elements to obtain new and surprising compounds. This is perhaps why Leopold Bloom arrives at the conclusion that 'God made food, the devil the cooks' (Joyce 2000: 219). The danger of transgression is always present where the emotional sphere is affected by bodily temptation. The carnal, physical, material element, which is linked to taste and aesthetic pleasure, may also transform pleasure into sorrow, temptation and disgust.

Pleasure, which generates disgust, is referred to in the first part of the eighth chapter. After having attended a funeral, Leopold Bloom looks for a place to have lunch, but the Dubliners, who eat so fast that they gulp down food, disgust him:

> Hot mockturtle vapour and steam of newbaked jampuffes roly-poly poured out from Harrison's. The heavy noonreck tickled the top of Mr Bloom's gullet. Want to make good pastry, butter, best flour, Demerara sugar, or they'd taste it with the hot tea. Or is it from her? A barefoot arab stood over the grating, breathing in the fumes. Deaden the gnaw of hunger that way. Pleasure or pain is it? Penny dinner. Knife and fork chained to the table. (Joyce 2000: 198-99)

Leopold Bloom gets close to a vegetarian restaurant where people eat 'only weggebobbles and fruit. Don't eat a beefsteak. If you do the eyes of the cow will pursue you through eternity. They say it's healthier' (Joyce 2000: 210). In another restaurant, he notices:

> Men, men, men. Perched on high stools by the bar, hats shoved back, at the tables calling for more bread no charge, swilling, wolfing godfuls of sloopy food, their eyes bulging, wiping wetted moustaches. A pallid suetfaced young man polished his tumpler knife fork and spoon with his napkin. New set of microbes. A man with an infants' saucestained napkin roundhim shovelled gurgling soup down his gullet. (Joyce 2000: 215)

In the end, Bloom goes into Byrne's bar and he is satisfied with a cheese sandwich:

> Have you a cheese sandwich?
>
> – Yes, sir.
> – Like a few olives too if they had them. Italian I prefer. Good glass of burgundy take away that. Lubricate. A nice salad, cool as cucumber, Tom Kernan can dress. Puts gusto into it. Pure olive oil. Milly served me that cutlet with a sprig of parsley. Take one Spanish onion. God made food, the devil the cooks. Devilled crab.
> – Wife well?
> – Quite well, thanks…A cheese sandwich, then. Gorgonzola, have you?
> – Yes, sir.
> – Mustard, sir?
> – Thank you.
>
> He studded under each lifted strip yellow blobs. Their lives. I have it. It grew bigger and bigger and bigger.
>
> Mr Bloom ate his strips of sandwich, fresh clean bread, with relish of disgust, pungent mustard, the feety savour of green cheese. Sips of his wine soothed his palate. Not logwood that. Tastes fuller this weather with the chill off. (Joyce 2000: 218)

While he is eating his sandwich, he looks at the shelves and wonders about the different foods with which men feed themselves. Tasting Italian olives, gorgonzola and French wine, Bloom opens Dublin's traditional cuisine to the tastes of the world, showing himself to be a cosmopolitan eater, with eclectic tastes.

Wandering around his city, Leopold gets back home late at night and prepares a hot chocolate for himself and Stephen, who is drunk. The long day of a man and of the city he lives in symbolise everyone's day in every city of the world. The last voice the reader hears is that of Molly Bloom. Through her and her stream of consciousness concluding with a 'yes', which also symbolises her positive acceptance of life. As for Leopold Bloom, he has a dynamic vision of human events, which allows the sea of life to be agitated by hope. Perhaps his journey will remain only in his imagination like a book destined never to be written. Perhaps this little Jewish man will never leave Dublin, but while wandering for a day in his city, he has seen life and death and, like Ulysses the great, he has known the heart of men, thus giving Dublin the opportunity to become the centre of the world.

Works cited

Joyce, J. 2000. *Ulysses*. London, Penguin Books.
Maia, A. 2005. *Le Osterie di Dublino*. Turin, Il Leone Verde Edizioni.
Manferlotti, S. 2014. *Cristianesimo ed Ebraismo in Joyce*. Rome, Bulzoni Editore.
Mazzocut-Mis, M. 2015. *Dal Gusto al Disgusto. L'Estetica del Pasto*. Milan, Raffaello Corina Editore.
Terrinoni. E. 2014. *Attraverso uno specchio oscuro. Irlanda e Inghilterra nell'Ulisse di James Joyce*. Mantua, Universitas Studiorum.

Ulysses recipes

Kidney pie

Ingredients
Servings 4-6
1 tablespoon beef drippings or 1 tablespoon cooking oil
1 ½ lbs chuck steaks, cut into 1 inch cubes
½ lb ox kidney (or lamb), trimmed and diced
12 ounces puff pastry
2 onions, chopped
3 carrots, peeled and roughly diced (⅜ inch)
butter
4 large flat mushrooms, cut into thick slices
2 tablespoons flour
1 teaspoon tomato puree
1 bay leaf
1 pint veal or beef stock (or water and stock cube or granules)
Worcestershire sauce
salt and pepper
1 egg, beaten, for glazing

Method
Heat a large frying pan with a little of the dripping or oil. Season the diced beef with salt and pepper. Fry in the pan until well coloured and completely sealed. Remove meat and transfer to a large saucepan. Add a touch more oil, if necessary, to the frying pan. Season the kidneys and fry quickly to seal and colour in the hot pan. Transfer to the saucepan.

Melt a knob of butter in the pan and cook the onions and carrots for 2 - 3 minutes. Place in the saucepan with the meat. Fry the mushroom slices in a little more butter, turning in the pan for a minute or two; keep to one side.

Place the saucepan on medium heat, stirring in the flour, and allow to cook for 2 to 3 minutes. Add the tomato puree, bay leaf and mushrooms. Pour in the stock and bring to a simmer, skimming off any impurities. The meat should just be covered with the stock; if not, add more stock or water. Simmer gently, partially covered, for 1 ½ to 2 hours. Skim when necessary. After 1 ½ hours, check the meat for tenderness. If not quite soft enough, cook for an additional 30 minutes. If the meat is cooking gently, it will not need to be topped up with any additional stock or water. The sauce will have reduced, thickening in consistency and enriching the flavour. Taste for seasoning, adding a dash or two of Worcestershire sauce to the mixture. Transfer to a 2 pint pie dish and allow to cool. Preheat the oven to 220°C/425°F.

Roll the pastry ¼ -inch thick. Cut a strip of pastry to sit around the rim of the dish (this will help the top to stay in place). Brush the rim of the pie dish with some beaten egg and apply the strip. Brush again with egg. Making sure the pastry top is bigger than the dish, sit it on top. Push down around the sides, trim and crimp for a neat finish. Brush completely with egg wash and place in the preheated oven. Bake for 30 to 40 minutes until golden brown.

Irish lamb stew

Ingredients
6 tablespoons all-purpose flour, divided
1 teaspoon salt
⅛ teaspoon pepper
1-½ pounds lamb stew meat, cut into 1-inch cubes
2 tablespoons vegetable oil
3 cups water
½ teaspoon fresh dill
8 pearl onions, peeled
3 medium carrots, cut into 1-inch pieces

2 large potatoes, peeled and cubed
½ cup half-and-half cream
Hot savoury biscuits

Directions
In a large plastic bag, combine 4 tablespoons flour, salt and pepper. Add lamb; shake to coat.

In a casserole, brown lamb in oil on all sides. Add water and dill; bring to a boil. Reduce heat; cover and simmer for 1-½ hours or until meat is almost tender. Add the onions, carrots and potatoes. Cover and simmer for 30 minutes or until the meat and vegetables are tender.

In a small bowl, place remaining flour; stir in cream until smooth. Stir into stew. Bring to a boil; cook and stir for 2 minutes or until thickened. Serve with biscuits. Yield: 6 servings.

Cheese sandwich

Ingredients
2 tablespoons butter, divided
2 slices white bread
½ cup shredded extra sharp Cheddar cheese, divided

Method
Melt 1 ½ tablespoons butter in a nonstick frying pan over medium-low heat. Place bread slices in the frying pan on top of the melted butter.

Spread about ¼ cup Cheddar cheese on one slice of bread; place the other slice of bread, butter-side up, on top of the cheese. Spread about 2 tablespoons of cheese on top of the sandwich.

Melt remaining ½ tablespoon butter in the pan next to the sandwich. Flip the sandwich onto the melted butter so that the cheese-side is facing down. Spread remaining cheese on top of the sandwich. Cook sandwich until cheese on the bottom is crispy and caramelized, 3 to 4 minutes. Flip sandwich and cook until cheese is crispy and caramelized on the other side, another 3 to 4 minutes.

Francesca Orestano

Virginia Woolf and the cooking range

It's difficult to imagine Virginia Woolf standing before a cooking range, for two reasons. On the one hand, the image of the writer endorsed by much criticism is that of an intellectual, thoughtful, witty, a prey to her nerves and to depression, and possibly to anorexia: and critics dwell on her literary achievement, leaving aside the material sphere of food, apart from some biographical information (Lee 1996) or because of its symbolic value (Glenny 1999). On the other hand, how can we imagine that the woman we consider a leading figure of modern feminism might accept the humble domestic chores of cooking? – the woman who installed a printing press in her drawing room, thus sending into exile the ottoman and the whatnot, and the eternal tea table, inherited from the Victorian age?

Woolf's childhood, it is true, is spent away from the kitchen. At 22 Hyde Park Gate, where Julia and Leslie Stephen live with their own children and those born from previous marriages, the kitchen is a place severely forbidden, an off-limits zone – and invisible in any case. Situated in the basement, that scarcely lit part of the Victorian house, where the cooking range is fed with wood or coal, the Stephens' kitchen is the kingdom of Sophia Farrell, an old-fashioned cook, whose authority and power placed her above inferior servants such as serving maids and skivvies. The children play, read, write and debate well above the kitchen, go to the zoo, skate, and are sometime taken to ceremonies in which Sir Leslie is involved. The children observe, with irony and wit, the lives and moods of the adults. And they compose a domestic newspaper – *Hyde Park Gate News. The Stephen Family Newspaper* – from which we learn that Virginia likes sweets, cherries, and strawberry ice-cream. At meals, food comes to the table through a door hidden by a red baize curtain, through which the person who serves appears – and vanishes. This world and its rigid rules will also vanish in the space of a few years. Alison Light has investigated the relationship between the Stephens, Virginia Woolf especially, and their servants, the cooks especially, discovering lots of surprising material (Light 2008).

Victorian domestic culture had at its social apex, and fully visible, the mistress of the house: an angel indeed, a spiritual model; at the other end of the spectrum, material, gastronomic, digestive, concealed but not a whit less influential, the cook. They were the zenith and nadir of the domestic management. But in a 1924 essay, 'Mr Bennett and Mrs Brown', Woolf maintains that 'In or about December 1910, human character changed' (Woolf 1992b: 70). This change is going to transform all previous traditional relationships, those 'between masters and servants, husbands and wives, fathers and children'. And here Woolf chooses to describe such social transformations by summoning the figure of the cook:

> In life one can see the change, if I may use a homely illustration, in the character of one's cook. The Victorian cook lived like a leviathan in the lower depths, formidable, silent, obscure, inscrutable; the Georgian cook is a creature of sunshine and fresh air; in and out of the drawing room, now to borrow the Daily Herald, now to ask advice about a hat. Do you ask for more solemn instances of the power of the human race to change? (Woolf 1992b: 70-71)

According to Woolf, the Victorian cook – we may imagine her always busy in the ideal house of Mrs Beeton – lived like a Biblical monster in the dark depths of the house, powerful and awe-inspiring: the modern cook comes up to the first floor, to the light and air, to borrow and read the newspaper, and is no longer portrayed wearing a long white starched apron and wielding a ladle, like a sceptre of power. The modern cook wears nice clothes to go out for a stroll; her hair is cut short, and she sports funny small hats.

In addition, the Stephen siblings have left the oppressive Victorian home at 22 Hyde Park Gate, for the popular district of Bloomsbury. They live in luminous flats, decorated by Vanessa with colourful chintzes, photographs, and modern paintings. In their Bloomsbury home, the brothers' university colleagues and other intellectuals gather around the Stephen sisters. A group of artists and literati takes shape. They are lively, experimental, cosmopolitan, and bent on leaving behind the Victorian ballast, of which they write – Lytton Strachey a good instance – with a certain affection but also pungent irony, and detachment. Vanessa marries Clive Bell, Virginia Leonard Woolf. In 1914 Virginia starts attending some cooking lessons, but gives them up after having lost her wedding ring in the pudding dough.

In the Woolf household, the reign of the cook Sophia Farrell lasts from 1886 to 1912 – almost a Queen Victoria of the kitchen. Next in succession comes Nellie Boxall, in 1916, who has worked at Durbins, the modern house designed by Roger Fry. Nellie is modern, efficient, but she tends to argue with Virginia Woolf about aspects of the kitchen, and her own rights. She gives notice a hundred times, then apologizes. Nellie works for the Woolfs as a live-in servant, from 1916 to 1934. The writer's diaries are full of growing dissatisfaction and frustration: on the one hand it is difficult to manage a house without servants, and without a cook. On the other, it is difficult to endorse the roles of mistress and servant, especially when writing about female liberation. In 1925 Woolf remarks: 'And today, for the 165th time, Nelly has given notice – Won't be dictated to: must do as other girls do. This is the fruit of Bloomsbury' (Woolf 1982: 3). The Bloomsbury clique have in fact discarded much old-fashioned formality: they do not dress for dinner, and their servants do not undergo a rigid moral control. Aprons and uniforms seem a thing of the past. We find evidence of this in another family journal, *The Charleston Bulletin Supplements*, written by Virginia and illustrated by her nephew Quentin Bell between 1923 and 1927. Here we read that Mrs Bell, when a child, had swallowed the beads of a necklace with her porridge; and, to stay with our central theme, we read about the preparation of pancakes and porridge. Made by Beatrice Selwood, the Bells' cook at Charleston, known as Trisy, porridge is not so inviting, but frankly threatening:

> *Pancake day*. When in a good and merry mood, Trisy would seize a dozen eggs & a bucket of flour, coerce a cow to milk itself, & then mixing the ingredients toss them 20 times high up over the skyline, & catch them as they fell in dozens & dozens of pancakes.
>
> *Trysis porridge*. But her porridge was a very different affair. This was costive close & crusty. It dolloped out of a black pan in lumps of mortar. It stank; it stuck. (Woolf and Bell 2013: 49)

Also porridge seems a thing of the past. The new era dawns in the pages of *To the Lighthouse* (1927), the novel that contains some memories of the Stephens' summer holidays in Cornwall. A typical Victorian mistress, Mrs Ramsay, presides over her family, children and guests: albeit only at the table, because elsewhere her husband has his own way. But Mrs Ramsay offers a dinner, described in detail, where 'harmony is struck as they enjoy a Boeuf en Daube' (Woolf 1992a: xvii). Although based on a family recipe, coming from a French grandmother, this culinary masterpiece is not authored by Mrs Ramsay: her cook, Mildred, is the unseen artist.

> They were having Mildred's masterpiece – Boeuf en Daube. Everything depended upon things being served up the precise moment they were ready. The beef, the bayleaf, and the wine – all must be done to a turn. To keep it waiting was out of the question. (Woolf 1992a: 108)

And a maid is serving it:

> An exquisite scent of olives and oil and juice rose from the great brown dish as Marthe, with a little flourish, took the cover off. The cook had spent three days over that dish [...] with its shiny walls and its confusion of savoury brown and yellow meats, and its bay leaves and its wine. (Woolf 1992a: 135)

Evidently the ingredients are well-known by Woolf, and a mark of the cosmopolitan outlook of Bloomsbury; Mrs Ramsay instead represents the old generation, with its old-fashioned habits that time and the war would change.

It has been remarked that Woolf intentionally uses food as part of a strategy that operates both in the verbal domain, within descriptions, and in her own life experience.

> [...] dwelling on food was, as Woolf saw it, an act of female liberation. It was part of the process both of seeing the world through our own, female, lenses and, more actively, of righting a skewed world which had purged the sensual and elevated the rational [...]. Writing was for her a pursuit that took place within the context of domesticity, not in monastic seclusion from the activities of the kitchen. (Glenny 1999: xii)

But food also performs a cultural role, as becomes clear in the essay *A Room of One's Own* (1929) where food and its representation are used to emphasize a gender contrast, between two colleges in an imaginary educational institution called Oxbridge. In the male college a sumptuous lunch is described through a series of abundant metaphors evoking precious stones, gems, soft waves of creamy substances, buds and petals; in the female college supper is cheap, insipid, stringy, colourless, marking a lack of money ironically balanced by the generous distribution of cold water. Woolf uses food as a powerful marker of cultural identity. But she goes beyond writing about food. In 1929 a great change occurs in the Woolf household: a new and modern oil stove is installed in the kitchen, and welcomed in the diary in enthusiastic terms:

> *Wednesday 25 September*
> But what interests me is of course my oil stove. We found it here last night on coming back from Worthing. At this moment it is cooking my dinner in the glass dishes perfectly I hope, without smell, waste, or confusion: one turns handles, there is a thermometer. And so I feel myself freer, more independent – & all one's life is a struggle for freedom – able to come down here with a chop in a bag & live on my own. I go over the dishes I shall cook – The rich stews, the sauces. The adventurous strange dishes with a dash of wine in them. (Woolf 1982: 257)

Handles, a thermometer, pyrex dishes, a clean and efficient place to cook: these tools are the prelude to the preparation of rich meals, sauces, and a promise of freedom from live-in servants, cook included. As she writes to Vita Sackville-West:

> I have only one passion in life – cooking [...] I have just bought a superb oil stove. I can cook anything [...] I cooked veal cutlets and cake today. I assure you it is better than writing these more than idiotic books. (Woolf 1978: 93)

Her we discover a different Virginia, able to complement the literary use of food with her own ability as a cook. She learns to cook mushrooms, to prepare fruit for stewing, to pare cold mutton for a hotpot, to make a cottage loaf. Nellie, the affectionate tyrant, finds a new job at the Laughtons, famous movie stars. Her ability as a cook (she attended courses in French cuisine delivered by Marcel Boulestin, a famous chef at the Restaurant Français in London) is publicly acknowledged in the advertisement of a new kind of cooker, the Regulo. In a 1936 issue of the *Daily Mail* a very proud Miss Boxall can boast the perfection of her roast beef: thanks to the Regulo (Light 2008: 217).

The cooking adventure of Virginia Woolf goes on. Her confidence seems to be growing. We have a record of this in the memoirs of the last cook, Louisa Annie Everest, *alias* 'Louie'. Having earned a 'Diploma in Advanced Cooking' in 1936, Louie will work for the Woolfs from 1934 until 1969. Leonard remembers her with affection, and Louie affectionately remembers Virginia Woolf (Noble 1972).

> But there was one thing in the kitchen that Mrs Woolf was very good at doing; she could make beautiful bread. The first question she asked me when I went to Monks House was if I knew how to make it. I told her that I had made some for my family, but I was no expert at it. 'I will come into the

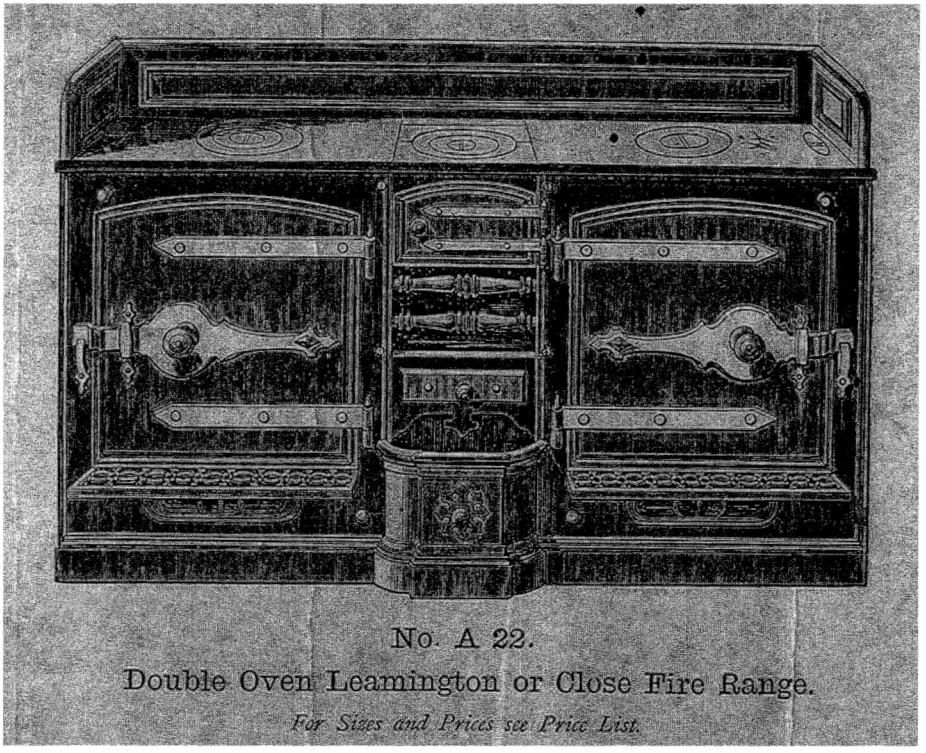

kitchen Louie' she said, 'and show you how to do it. We have always made our own bread.' I was surprised how complicated the process was and how accurately Mrs Woolf carried it out. She showed me how to make the dough with the right quantities of yeast and flour, and then how to knead it. She returned three or four times during the morning to knead it again. Finally, she made the dough into the shape of a cottage loaf and baked it at just the right temperature. (https://britishfoodhistory. wordpress.com /2014/ 07/03/virginia-woolf-bakes-bread/; Light 2008: 318)

On February 1, 2013, to mark the anniversary of Virginia Woolf's birthday, *The Guardian* published 'Virginia Woolf and Other Great Literary Cooks', by John Dugdale. Here we may find the recipe of the cottage loaf, that Virginia Woolf mastered to perfection. More recipes today are available in the recent *Bloomsbury Cookbook*, where among the many illustrations that suggest the group's creativity in the fields of painting, pottery making, house decoration, ceramics, or weaving, their ability in the kitchen is also remarkable. French food – the so-called Mediterranean diet, probably inspired by Vanessa's residence at Cassis in Provence – becomes the fashion. The already-mentioned Boulestin had published in London, for the English aspiring cooks, *Simple French Cooking for English Homes* (1923) and *A Second Helping* (1925). But side by side with the French cuisine, we should also remember that twice, in Virginia Woolf's life, war had caused food-rationing: the book a *War Time Cooking Guide* (1915) by Charles Herman Senn offered recipes for simple dishes, with just a touch of butter and sugar.

Regulo

I close these notes by quoting a Bloomsbury friend of our writer, E. M. Forster, who decides to evoke her art by choosing the critical viewpoint of food, as described in her books:

> It is always helpful, when reading her, to look out for the passages which describe eating. They are invariably good. They are a sharp reminder that here is a woman who is alert sensuously. [...] when Virginia Woolf mentions nice things they go right into our mouth, so far as the edibility of print permits. (Forster 1942: 18)

And with an explicit reference to the Boeuf en Daube in *To the Lighthouse*, Forster reminds us that thanks to this recipe all the characters around the table are happily reconciled to each other. This is Mrs Ramsay's magic, but it's not only hers:

> Such a dinner cannot be built on a statement beneath a dish-cover which the novelist is too indifferent or incompetent to remove. Real food is necessary, and this, in fiction as in her home, she knew how to provide. (Forster 1942: 19)

Such a masterpiece, he argues, could never have been described by a woman without a great passion for the art of cooking, and without long experience in the kitchen.

Works cited

Forster, E. M. 1942. *Virginia Woolf. The Rede Lecture 1941*. Cambridge, Cambridge University Press.
Glenny, A.1999. *Ravenous Identities: Eating and Eating Distress in the Lives and Works of Virginia Woolf*. New York, St. Martin's Press.
Knapp, B. L. 1988. Virginia Woolf's 'Boeuf en Daube'. In D. Bevan (ed.), *Literary Gastronomy*. Amsterdam, Rodopi, 29–36.
Lee, H. 1996. *Virginia Woolf*. London, Random House.
Light, A. 2008. *Mrs Woolf and the Servants*. London, Penguin.
Lowe, A. 'A Certain Hold on Haddock and Sausage': Dining Well in Virginia Woolf's Life and Work.' https://aliceloweblogs. wordpress. com/ published -work/a-certain-hold -on-haddock-and-sausage-dining-well-in-virginia-woolfs-life-and-work/ (access 27 march 2017)
Meigs, A. 1997. Food as a Cultural Construction. In C. Counihan and P. Van Esterik (eds), *Food and Culture: a Reader*, New York, Routledge, 95–106.
Noble, J. R. (ed.) 1972. Recollections of Virginia Woolf by Her Contemporaries. London, Peter Owen.
Ondaatje Rolls, J. 2014. *The Bloomsbury Cookbook: Recipes for Life, Love and Art*. London, Thames & Hudson.

Woolf, V. 1978. *A Reflection of the Other Person. The Letters of Virginia Woolf, 1919-1931*. Ed. N. Nicholson and J. Trautmann. London, The Hogarth Press.
Woolf, V. 1982. *The Diary of Virginia Woolf. Volume III: 1925-30*. Ed. A. Olivier Bell and A. McNeillie. London, Penguin.
Woolf, V. 1985. *Moments of Being. A Collection of Autobiographical Writing*. Ed. J. Schulkind. Orlando, Harcourt.
Woolf, V. 1992a. *To the Lighthouse*. Ed. M. Drabble. Oxford, Oxford University Press.
Woolf, V. 1992b. *A Woman's Essays. Selected Essays*. Volume One. Ed. R. Bowlby. London, Penguin.
Woolf, V., Bell, V., and Stephen, T. 2005. *Hyde Park Gate News. The Stephen Family Newspaper*. Ed. G. Lowe. London, Hesperus Press.
Woolf, V. and Bell, Q. 2013. *The Charleston Bulletin Supplements*. Ed. C. Olk. London, The British Library.

Mildred's boeuf en daube

Ingredients for 6-8 persons
1.5 kg. rump of beef
1.5 kg. skirt of beef
60 gr. bacon, lean
3 tbs flour
Salt and freshly ground pepper
250 gr. green olives, pitted
500 ml. full bodied red wine; 45 ml. cognac
3 tbs olive oil
500 ml. good beef stock
1 tbs tomato paste
1 onion, with 3 cloves stuck in it
3 tomatoes, chopped

Bouquet garni

For the marinade
Bouquet garni, parsley, thyme, celery, black pepper and nutmeg, two red onions and four carrots, finely sliced, half cup of olive oil.

Preparation
At least one day in advance, mix the marinade ingredients in a deep ceramic or glass bowl; add the meat diced into 3 cm. cubes; mix and add the wine and cognac. Cover and refrigerate, stirring now and then, for 24 hours. Next day

remove the meat from the marinade, and roll the pieces of meat in the flour. Add the diced bacon. In a large pan, with 3 tbs of olive oil, place the meat, the bacon, and brown it. Place the meat on a dish.

Over a gentle flame, put into a casserole the beef stock, a spoonful of tomato paste, a new *bouquet garni*, chopped tomatoes, olives and garlic. Stir and simmer for 20 minutes, then add the meat and the marinade. Cover the casserole with foil, then place it in the oven for about one hour; gentle heat (140°).

The *Boeuf en Daube* can be made up to 2 days in advance and refrigerated until ready to eat; to serve, remove the *bouquet garni* and reheat gently.

Francesca Gorini

A. A. Milne: Tea (and lots of honey) in the Hundred Acre Wood

A domestic fantasy

Once upon a time there was a Teddy bear whose name was Winnie-the-Pooh and who was very fond of honey. He lived in the Hundred Acre Wood with the other stuffed toys – Piglet, Eeyore, Tigger, Kanga and Roo – belonging to Christopher Robin.

Be careful, though: we are not speaking (at least at the moment) about Disney's well-known animated film *Winnie the Pooh*, but rather the delicate literary creature invented by the English writer Alan Alexander Milne in the 1920s. Pooh first appeared as a literary character in the collection of nursery rhymes *When We Were Very Young*, published in 1924. But let us proceed in an orderly fashion. At the beginning of the 20th century a bear used to live in the London zoo. Since he came from Winnipeg in Canada, he was called Winnie. Christopher Robin Milne, Alan Alexander's son, was one of this bear's most devoted little fans: he was so fond of him that he changed his own stuffed bear's name (a first birthday present) from Edward Bear to Winnie-the-Pooh.

Having worked for a few periodicals (such as the satirical *Punch*), A. A. Milne published *When We Were Very Young* when his colleague and friend Rose Fyleman, who was very happy with his first contribution to the magazine *Merry-Go-Round*, suggested he write a whole book of rhymes. In 1926 and in 1928 Milne published two prose books, *Winnie-the-Pooh* and *The House at Pooh Corner*, while in 1927 a second collection of rhymes was released with the title *Now We Are Six*. In the four Pooh books young Christopher Robin acts as the protagonist, the ideal reader and in a sense the narrator. As Milne writes in the introduction to the first Pooh book:

> You may wonder sometimes who is supposed to be saying the verses. Is it the Author, that strange but uninteresting person, or is it Christopher Robin, or some other boy or girl, or Nurse, or Hoo? (Milne 1924: viii)

If on the one hand these publications focus on a child's gradual development, eventually leading him out of the nursery room and (alas) into the world of

adults, on the other they represent one final, bright gleam of domesticity before the darkness of World War II.

The author constantly plays on the daily routine of a family with children, marked by breakfast, lunch, dinner, tea time and bath time, saying prayers, and going to bed. Milne regularly promotes traditional values and a vision of the world where the social order is not even remotely questioned. That is why the Pooh books are considered a classic example of escapist literature, whose aim was to divert the young readers' minds away from the political turbulence and uncertainties caused by the Great War, by the looming economic crisis of 1929, the rise of Nazism and World War II. The visits to the zoo, the strolls around town, life outdoors and especially the regular life of Milne's characters (it is perhaps relevant that in the same years the BBC inaugurated *Children's Hour*, a daily radio programme dedicated to the young) gave children the possibility of escaping reality and of deluding themselves that their domestic life had remained unaltered.

E. H. Shepard's delightful illustrations, the originals of which are now worth a fortune, can only contribute to this growing sense of escape from everyday reality, and the cheerful enjoyment of a simple life. Domestic life and family routine are such crucial themes in *Winnie-the-Pooh* and *The House at Pooh Corner* that the children's literature scholar Peter Hunt has classified these two prose books as typical examples of domestic fantasy in that they appropriate the fantasy genre and adapt it to a domestic context (Hunt 1992).

Nursery rhymes: butter and milk

A number of references to food and its effects on the human body are present in the collection *When We Were Very Young*, published in 1924. In the nursery rhyme

'Teddy Bear' (whose protagonist is Christopher Robin's toy Edward Bear) Milne reveals a slight preoccupation for the stuffed bear's weight:

> A bear, however hard he tries,
> Grows tubby without exercise.
> Our Teddy Bear is short and fat,
> Which is not to be wondered at;
> He gets what exercise he can
> By falling off the ottoman,
> But generally seems to lack
> The energy to clamber back. (Milne 1924: 85)

Physical exercise is part of Edward Bear's daily routine but he doesn't seem to really commit himself to it! In contrast to what Milne does in *Winnie-the-Pooh* of 1926, in *When We Were Very Young* the author does not warn his young readers against getting plump: he gets the stuffed bear to become proud of his silhouette and to accept his rotundity. The bear discovers the portrait of a French king in a book and he is only too delighted to read the caption:

> 'King Louis So and So
> Nicknamed 'The Handsome'!' There he sat,
> *And (think of it!) the man was fat!* (Milne 1924: 87)

The bear finally meets the king of France in the (very fat) flesh (it is the French monarch who calls him 'Mr Edward Bear') and he finds him so nice and pleasant that he becomes proud of being as small and tubby as he is.

The strict routine of meals is of crucial importance in every home, even in the palace of a king and queen. As Milne points out in 'The King's Breakfast', they begin their day with a royal breakfast. The social order is here seriously questioned by no less than a cow, who refuses to provide the sovereign with milk for the butter 'for the Royal slice of bread' (Milne 1924: 55). When a maid asks the animal to kindly supply some butter, the Alderney replies: 'You'd better tell / His Majesty / That many people nowadays / Like marmalade / Instead.' (Milne 1924: 56). Thanks to the Queen's mediation, the dialogue continues between the maid, the King and the cow until the animal is persuaded to provide milk and butter, to His Majesty's delight:

> The cow said,
> 'There, there!
> I didn't really
> Mean it;
> Here's milk for his porringer
> And butter for his bread'. (Milne 1924: 58)

Pooh books: honey and malt

The Pooh books' main setting is the Hundred Acre Wood, which was inspired by the park at Cotchford Farm, the Milnes' country estate. This is a secondary world where the stuffed toys' life flows slowly and is marked by strolls in the countryside, visits to friends and simple adventures. One night, for example, a new character suddenly appears in Pooh's house: this is cheeky Tigger, and Pooh's first worry is what the newcomer will have for breakfast. At first, hearing some noises in the house, Pooh fears his precious honey is in danger but he soon realises that a strange animal has arrived in the Hundred Acre Wood.

The following morning Pooh gives a sigh of relief when he discovers that Tigger doesn't like honey or Piglet's acorns (which the naïve bear calls 'haycorn'); nor does he fancy the thistles of which Eeyore the donkey is so fond. Then, in order to remind young readers that if they don't eat enough food they will not grow up properly, Pooh recites one of his much-loved rhymes:

> What shall we do about poor little Tigger?
> If he never eats nothing he'll never get bigger.
> He doesn't like honey and haycorns and thistles
> Because of the taste and because of the bristles.
> And all the good things which an animal likes
> Have the wrong sort of swallow or too many spikes. [...]
> But whatever his weight in pounds, shillings, and ounces,
> He always seems bigger because of his bounces. (Milne 1928: 29)

Piglet points out that 'shillings' should not be between 'pounds' and 'ounces' because they are not a unit of weight. But Pooh doesn't care: he innocently states that the best way to write poetry is 'letting things come' and consequently, even though the other characters say he is 'a Bear of very little brain' (or possibly just because of that) he has a very sensitive mind, which is open to emotions like the mind of a child.

Tigger finally finds his ideal food in Kanga's house: to everyone's surprise (and after Pooh has eaten all the condensed milk he finds in the kangaroo's cupboard) Tigger discovers that he is crazy about little Roo's medicine, malt extract. From that moment on, he is going to live on malt (a nourishing substance despised by everybody else) for breakfast, lunch, and dinner.

In the 1920s malt was considered a strong tonic: the syrup made of malt extract and cod-liver oil was well-known as a tonic imposed on reluctant children, who did not like it because of the disgusting flavour of the fish oil. Children were much fonder of delicious Ovomaltine, a Swiss product created in the early 20th century and introduced to Britain in 1909, as Ovaltine. This mixture originally consisted of malt, milk, eggs, and cocoa and it was to be dissolved in hot or cold milk. Because of its invigorating properties Ovaltine was advertised as food for convalescents. Though now it has been superseded by other products, Ovaltine has been very famous for a long time.

As for Winnie-the-Pooh's daily meal routine, it includes breakfast, lunch and dinner but also an afternoon tea, and a break at 11 a.m., when he usually feels 'a little eleven o'clockish' (Milne 1928: 31). His meals generally consist of lots of honey but Pooh also likes to add to his diet 'a simple meal of marmalade spread

Ovaltine advertisement (1909)

lightly over a honeycomb or two' (Milne 1926: 99), a few sandwiches (Milne 1928: 65), some condensed milk and everything he can find in a cupboard, as previously mentioned.

Pooh's daily routine also includes some morning exercise, to prevent him from becoming too plump. The reader may in this case read between the lines and find a useful piece of advice for children: do not eat too many sweets and food or you will be tubby and something unpleasant may happen to you. Just as in Pooh's misadventure: one morning, after completing his physical exercise, the bear pays a visit to Rabbit. He can hardly enter the animal's burrow and once in, he can't get out! Luckily the forest's deus ex machina, that's to say Christopher Robin, intervenes. The child is the heroic figure in this domestic fantasy in that he always finds the right solution while Pooh represents the messy, thoughtless anti-hero:

> 'Then there's only one thing to be done,' [Christopher Robin] said. 'We shall have to wait for you to get thin again.'
> 'How long does getting thin take?' asked Pooh anxiously.
> 'About a week, I should think.'
> 'But I can't stay here for a *week*!'
> 'You can *stay* here all right, silly old Bear. It's getting you out which is so difficult.' (Milne 1926: 26)

Noticeably, in the prose book *Winnie-the-Pooh* (1926) Milne's attitude towards overeating has changed from the 1924 collection of rhymes *When We Were Very Young*, where Edward Bear met the King of France. This evolution proceeds at the same rate as the development of the ideal reader and recipient of the books, Christopher Robin. He was born in 1920 and consequently he is still very young in 1924, while two years later his father starts setting a few rules and giving him advice.

Even in nursery rhymes the animal world plays a crucial role. Not only is the Hundred Acre Wood inhabited by Pooh and his friends. A number of other animals are also present in the two collections of verse: cows, fish, chickens and mice. They are a fundamental part of the characters' daily routine and children consider them as friends who once in a while provide eggs and milk but absolutely not meat!

In the lines of 'The Little Black Hen', in *Now We Are Six*, for example, five men are running after a hen: their aim is certainly not to cook it but to convince it to lay an egg for tea time. Just like the cow mentioned earlier, the hen refuses to obey the men and only the little protagonist manages to persuade it; only for him will she lay the so much desired egg. Another rhyme in the same collection revolves around an old sailor on a desert island: he isn't worried about being hungry, on the contrary he would like to find 'a goat, or some chickens and sheep' only to have some friends to talk to! (Milne 1926: 37).

Judging by his profound respect toward animals, which characterises all four Pooh books, Milne seems almost to have a vegetarian attitude.

If the exaltation of domestic life, traditional values and social order remain unchanged in the four volumes, the complexity of the stories evolves and it follows Christopher Robin's development and growth. As already noted, in *Winnie-the-Pooh* there are pieces of advice which were not to be found in the first Pooh book. Moreover, Milne includes (almost) literate characters like Owl, who is considered extremely wise because he uses difficult words such as 'customary procedure' (Milne 1926: 45). But then Owl can hardly spell his name and has written the following message on his door: PLES RING IF AN RNSER IS REQIRD (Milne 1926: 43).

In the final chapter Pooh receives a pencil case from his friends:

> It was a Special Pencil Case. [...] There was a knife for sharpening the pencils, an india rubber for rubbing out anything which you had spelt wrong, and a ruler for ruling lines for the words to walk on, and inches marked on the ruler in case you wanted to know how many inches anything was, and Blue Pencils and Red Pencils and Green Pencils for saying special things in blue and red and green. (Milne 1926: 144)

Pooh's universe is more and more frequently characterised by allusions to school and to a world trapped by rules (and not only spelling). This is why in the following Pooh book, the nursery rhymes of 1927 *Now We Are Six*, there are a number of references to mathematics and books. Milne still hints at afternoon tea, the protagonists' meal routine, and to cakes and butter but these cheerful moments are often accompanied by calculations : 'What's twice eleven?' I said to Pooh. [...] 'I think it ought to be twenty-two.' (Milne 1927: 33) – and by serious questions, such as who created God and where the wind comes from.

So here we come to the last Pooh book, *The House at Pooh Corner*, published in 1928. The real Christopher Robin is now eight years old and it is time for him to leave the Hundred Acre Wood. In Chapter 5 his stuffed toys find a notice on the door of the child's house:

> GON OUT
> BACKSON
> BISY
> BACKSON
> C.R. (Milne 1928: 75)

The animals candidly think that Christopher Robin is busy with Backson (an unidentified human or animal being) but the obvious truth is that the young boy has started school. Only Eeyore the donkey realises what is really happening and tries to explain it to the others while showing Piglet how to spell 'A':

> He learns. He becomes Educated. He instigorates – I *think* that is the word he mentioned, but I may be referring to something else – he instigorates Knowledge. In my small way I also, if I have the word right, am – am doing what he does. (Milne 1928: 87)

At the end of the same chapter the notice on the door becomes: 'GONE OUT, BACK SOON, C.R.', so the reader understands that Christopher Robin is ready for his new adult life.

On the final page he withdraws into the Enchanted Forest with his closest friend Pooh and from there they look at the outer world: 'Still with his eyes on the world Christopher Robin put out a hand and felt for Pooh's paw.' (Milne 1928: 176). As to pluck up courage, Christopher Robin nostalgically looks for Pooh's paw but at the same time he doesn't look away from the world waiting for him. His future will include starting school and then definitely leaving the nursery.

Sadly, the world Christopher Robin is observing is also developing into the turbulence of World War II in the 1930s and 1940s.

Our characters are now leaving their little literary world marked by carefree, regular meals but we will meet them again in a cinematic guise: the Disney feature films will present Pooh as fond of honey and food as in the Pooh books but this transformation will necessarily imply 'commercialism, imperialism, and dumbing down' (Ross 2005: 350).

This however is another story.

Works cited

Hunt, P. 1992. Winnie-the-Pooh and Domestic Fantasy. in D. Butts (ed.) *Stories and Society. Children's Literature in Its Social Context*: 112-124. London, Macmillan.
Hunt, P. 1994. *An Introduction to Children's Literature*. Oxford, Oxford University Press.
Milne, A. A. 2004 [1924]. *When We Were Very Young*. London, Egmont.
Milne, A. A. 2004 [1926]. *Winnie-the-Pooh*. London, Egmont.
Milne, A. A. 2004 [1927]. *Now We Are Six*. London, Egmont.
Milne, A. A. 2004 [1928]. *The House at Pooh Corner*. London, Egmont.
Ross, D. 2005. Pooh in America: In Which the Bear Goes on a Long Explore and Becomes Altogether Different. In N. Moody and C. Horrocks (eds) *Children's Fantasy Fiction: Debates for the Twenty First Century*: 349-361. Liverpool, JMU.

Thwaite, A. 1992. *The Brilliant Career of Winnie-the-Pooh. The Story of A. A. Milne and His Writing for Children*. London, Methuen.

Malt biscuits

Ingredients (for 20 biscuits)
110 g butter
200 g sugar
1 dessert spoon milk
1 dessert spoon malt
1 teaspoon bicarbonate of soda
125 g plain flour

Method
Preheat the oven to 140°C. In a bowl, cream together the butter and sugar until light and fluffy. Warm the milk and mix in the malt and the bicarbonate of soda. Beat this mixture into the butter and sugar and finally sift in the flour. Mix well and transfer in teaspoon sized dollops onto a greased baking tray (or on baking paper).

Bake the biscuits in the preheated oven for 45 minutes until firm. Leave to cool before serving.

Angela Anna Iuliucci

Roald Dahl's revolting food fantasies

Some months before his death in 1990, Roald Dahl began work on a new project with the help of his wife Felicity. She remembers that Dahl was rather sceptical about the project. Writing a collection for children that had to include all the dishes described in his novels seemed to be a tough challenge. Dahl thought it would be a flop, but in 1994, Felicity Dahl started work again on the first idea, and the result was *Revolting Recipes*, a cookery book for children that Mrs Dahl describes as 'an interpretation of some of the scrumptious and wonderfully disgusting dishes which appear in Roald's books' (Dahl 1994: 7).

The text is structured like an ordinary cookery book. The recipes, in fact, are divided into six categories: starters, snacks, main courses, cakes and desserts, drinks and confectionery.

Recipe list

STARTERS
Green Pea Soup
George's Marvellous Medicine Chicken Soup
Stink Bugs' Eggs
Scrambled Dregs

SNACKS
Snozzcumbers
Onion Rings
Mosquitoes' Toes and Wampfish Roes Most Delicately Fried
The Enormous Crocodile
Crispy Wasp Stings on a Piece of Buttered Toast

MAIN COURSES
Wormy Spaghetti
Fresh Mudburgers
Bird Pie
Mr Twit's Beard
Hansel and Gretel Spare Ribs
Boggis's Chicken

CAKES AND DESSERTS
Bunce's Doughnuts
Krokan Ice-Cream
Hot Frogs
Lickable Wallpaper for Nurseries
Bruce Bogtrotter's Cake
Hot Ice-Cream for Cold Days

DRINKS
Butterscotch
Peach Juice
Frobscottle

CONFECTIONERY
Strawberry Flavoured Chocolate Coated Fudge
Toffee Apples
Candy-Coated Pencils for Sucking in Class
Eatable Marshmallows Pillows
Stickjaw for Talkative Parents
Willie Wonka's Nutty Crunch Surprise
Hair Toffee to Make Hair Grow on Bald Men

The special feature of the book is that each recipe explains how to cook the dishes already described in some of the most famous works written by Dahl: *James and the Giant Peach* (1961), *Charlie and the Chocolate Factory* (1964), *Fantastic Mr Fox* (1970), *The Twits* (1980), *The BFG* (1982), *The Witches* (1983), *Boy* (1984), *Matilda* (1988) and *Rhyme Stew* (1989). Each recipe is accompanied by a photograph of the dish and an illustration by Quentin Blake, Dahl's regular illustrator, who once again succeeds in representing to perfection the grotesque and irreverent universe of the writer. Another original feature of the text is the way in which the photographs and the illustrations are made to interact.

In the introduction to the book, Felicity Dahl recalls that food had always had a particular meaning in her husband's life:

> Treats were an essential part of Roald's life – never too many, never too few and always perfectly timed. He made you feel like a king receiving the finest gift in the land.
>
> A treat could be a wine gum lifted silently in the middle of the night out of a large sweet jar kept permanently by his bedside. It could be a lobster and oyster feast placed on the table after a secret visit to the fishmonger,

his favourite shop. It could be the first new potato, broad bean or lettuce
from the garden, a basket of field mushrooms or a superb conker. (Dahl
1994: 7)

In addition to this, the recipes included in *Revolting Recipes* show that food also played a relevant role in Dahl's literary production. Perhaps, among all his novels, *Charlie and the Chocolate Factory* is the one that most easily connects with the theme of food. It is no coincidence, therefore, that the greater part of the recipes in the collection relate to the dishes described in this famous book. But apart from *Charlie and the Chocolate Factory* (1964) there is another book in which Dahl uses the theme of food in a very original way.

'Revolting Rhymes': food in irreverent verses

Roald Dahl published *Revolting Rhymes* in 1982. This book includes the retellings of six well-known fairy tales: 'Cinderella', 'Jack and the Beanstalk', 'Snow White and the Seven Dwarfs', 'Goldilocks and the Three Bears', 'Little Red Riding Hood and the Wolf' and 'The Three Little Pigs'. As remarked by the editors of *The Norton Anthology of Children's Literature*,

> The fairy tale distinguished itself as a genre few centuries ago when storytellers began appropriating different kinds of magical folktales and transforming them and conventionalizing them, for it became necessary in the modern world to adapt the oral tales to the moral, literary, and aesthetic standards of a particular society and to make them acceptable for diffusion in the public sphere. (Zipes et al. 2005: 175)

The title *Revolting Rhymes* is actually a pun. The adjective revolting, in fact, has several different meanings, including disgusting and subversive. Dahl's rhymes carry both concepts: the rhymes are disgusting because they are characterised by gruesome and grotesque elements; and they are subversive, insofar as they represent a rebellion against the traditional fairy tale. Christina Murdoch considers Dahl's rewritings as an example of *anti-tale*, which is the natural evolution of the fairy tale, and as an attempt of getting back to 'the original fairy tale with all its gruesome punishments' (Murdoch 2011: 164).

> The poems in Dahl's collection reveal the anti-tale as a strange and contradictory genre which moves in and out of the narrative confines that we have come to associate with the archetypal characters of his poems, sometimes claiming authenticity against a falsified tradition, sometimes deliberately mocking the idea of tradition. By positioning itself in opposition to, or proclaiming itself as a return to an authentic version, the anti-tale strengthens the idea of an original narrative. (Murdoch 2011: 165)

Dahl's retellings are full of mocking references to the fairy tales that often refer to the sphere of food and its consumption. Sometimes Dahl speaks directly to his readers, making them suspect that the fairy tale they know so well is not the true story, as in the opening lines of 'Cinderella':

> I guess you think you know this story.
> You don't. The real one's much more gory.
> The phoney one, the one you know,
> Was cooked up years and years ago,
> And made to sound all soft and sappy
> Just to keep the children happy. (Dahl 1982: 5)

These references to the original fairy tales create an intertextuality between them and Dahl's rewritings. It is thanks to this intertextuality that the idea which is at the basis of Dahl's *Revolting Rhymes* can work. The writer's version of the anti-tale is playful, 'a literary joke which pokes fun at the idea of an impenetrable canon or solid tradition, yet the joke is only funny if the reader has some familiarity with the narrative that is being mocked' (Murdoch 2011: 171). We find a similar device adopted in the recipes included in *Revolting Recipes*.

Through his subversive and irreverent rhymes, Dahl completely twists the fairy tales we all know so well. Remarkably, this distortion is realised by using and twisting the theme of food. The six retellings, in fact, have two elements in common:

1. The presence of a vocabulary strongly connected with the semantic field of food;
2. In each rhyme there is always someone who wants to eat someone else.

In 'Jack and the Beanstalk', for instance, Dahl describes in a really realistic and gruesome way the moment in which Jack's mother is devoured by the giant:

> From somewhere high above the ground
> There came a frightful crunching sound.
> He heard the Giant mutter twice,
> 'By gosh, that tasted very nice.
> 'Although' (and this in grumpy tones)
> 'I wish there weren't so many bones.' (Dahl 1982: 19)

In 'Snow-White and the Seven Dwarfs' the witch wants to eat Snow White's heart, but eventually she just eats the heart of an ox:

> Then (this is the disgusting part)
> The Queen sat down and ate the heart!

(I only hope she cooked it well.
Boiled heart can be as tough as hell). (Dahl 1982: 24)

In 'Goldilocks and the Three Bears' the young protagonist sneaks furtively into the house of the three bears and eats the wonderful breakfast cooked by Mother Bear, a breakfast made of porridge, hot coffee, bread and marmalade. Following a sort of retaliation law, at the end of the story young Goldilocks is eaten by Baby Bear.

The presence of food in Dahl's rewritings bears evidence to a remark offered by Keeling and Pollard in *Critical Approaches to Food in Children's Literature*:

> If food is fundamental to life and a substance upon which civilizations and cultures have built themselves, then food is also fundamental to the imagination and the imaginary arts. Food is fundamental to the imagination because food is fundamental to culture. (Keeling and Pollard 2009: 5)

'Food is never just something to eat' (Daniel 2006: 1), but it always brings with itself some meanings both in real life and in fictional lives. If in *Revolting Rhymes* Dahl explores the meanings that food can acquire in the fantastic atmosphere of the fairy tale, in *Revolting Recipes* he reverts to food as it appears and is enjoyed in real life.

'Revolting Recipes': having fun while cooking

Revolting Recipes (1994) is a book addressed to English children of the 1990s. Following the instructions included in the text, children can use real ingredients to realise recipes with revolting names and with a fanciful *mise en place*. The funny and playful aspect of the book, in fact, is that the names of the recipes, as well as the aspect of some of them, do not make the readers' mouths water. Without doubt, the adult reader is not tempted by the idea of eating worms or beetles. But these shapes are very common in children's sweets. In any case, going beyond the first impression, it is apparent that the dishes conceived by Dahl's imagination are related to the English gastronomic tradition and offer popular recipes, easy to cook and tasty. The wormy spaghetti of *The Twits* (1980) is a perfect example of this. The recipe requires a large saucepan and a food processor, plus the usual ingredients such as tomato sauce, oil, parsley, salt and pepper. The worms are obtained using vermicelli and tricolour spaghetti. Despite its name and its revolting appearance, the dish is part of a well-known culinary culture of the 1990s in England ... and it is really tasty.

Apart from the wormy spaghetti, we also read about fresh mudburgers, stink bugs' eggs, mosquitoes' toes and wampfish roes most delicately fried, all taken from *James and the Giant Peach*. There is a bird pie from *The Twits*, toffee apples and edible marshmallow pillows from *Charlie and the Chocolate Factory*, and finally Hansel and Gretel's spare ribs, from *Rhyme Stew*. All the recipes included in *Revolting Recipes* offer a variety of dishes belonging to the traditional cuisine (as shown by the ingredients used) and rooted in the gastronomic culture tailored to the needs of the child, who must, at once, eat, taste and have fun.

In *Revolting Recipes* Dahl uses these dishes to subvert the universally known canon of children's gastronomy, adding to it some gruesome and grotesque elements, because 'children need darkness, grotesquery and gore, and the sense of being trusted with 'the real story' that Dahl has always given them. Even if (perhaps especially if) that makes grown-ups uncomfortable' (Williams 2014). When we grow up it is hard to appreciate the recipes included in Dahl's book because, as adults, we tend to prefer traditional dishes, typical of our culinary culture and cooked following the original recipes. As a consequence, we perhaps lose the inclination to experiment and to reinvent our gastronomic tradition by employing fantasy and imagination.

Works cited

Dahl, R. 1982. *Revolting Rhymes.* London, Puffin Books.
Dahl, R. 1994. *Revolting Recipes.* London, Red Fox.
Daniel, C. 2006. *Voracious Children: Who Eats Whom in Children's Literature.* New York, Routledge.
Keeling, K. and Pollard, S. T. (eds) 2009. *Critical Approaches to Food in Children's Literature.* New York, Routledge.
Murdoch, C. 2011. The Phoney and the Real: Roald Dahl's *Revolting Rhymes* as Anti-Tales. In C. McAra and D. Calvin (eds), *Anti-Tales: The Uses of Disenchantment*: 164-172. Newcastle upon Tyne, Cambridge Scholars Publishing.
Russell Williams, I. Roald Dahl's children rhymes really are revolting, but that is no bad thing. In *The Guardian*, Thursday 28 August 2014
http://www.theguardian.com/books/booksblog/2014/aug/28/roald-dahl-childrens-rhymes-revolting-aldi-australia (accessed 30 / 07/ 2015)
Zipes, J., Paul, L., Vallone, L., Hunt, P., Avery, G., (eds) 2005. *The Norton Anthology of Children's Literature: The Traditions in English.* New York, W.W. Norton & Company.

Fresh mudmurgers

Makes 10 mudburgers
Ingredients
1 ½ lb (700 g) minced beef
1 medium onion, chopped
3 tbsp (45 ml) tomato puree
2 tbsp (30 ml) mild French mustard
1 tbsp (15 ml) Worcestershire sauce
2-3 tbsp (30-45 ml) capers, drained
4 tbsp (60 ml) fresh parsley, chopped
salt and pepper
1 egg, beaten

In a mixing bowl, break up the minced beef.
Add all the ingredients, *except* the egg, and gently mix together.
Add the egg, binding all the ingredients together and pat into mudburgers.
Preheat the grill and grill for 4-5 minutes on both sides or fry in a non-stick frying pan.
Serve in a bun with a 'revolting' relish. Cucumber relish is ideal!

Onion rings

You will need: large polythene bag

Ingredients
1 onion
seasoned flour
vegetable oil

Peel the onion and cut into ⅛ inch (2-3mm) thick slices, against the grain. Separate the rings. Put them in a large polythene bag, containing seasoned flour, and shake until the rings are lightly coated with the flour, shake off any excess.
Deep fry in hot oil until crispy and golden.

Ilaria Parini

Bridget Jones and the temptations of *junk food*

About Bridget Jones

Bridget Jones's Diary is a novel by the English writer Helen Fielding published in 1996. It is regarded as one of the most popular examples of 'chick lit' (Ferriss 206: 71; Harzewski 2011), the literary genre born in the 1990s and which consists of books mainly by women for women. The name of the genre itself refers to this: *chick*, being an American English term referring to young women, and *lit* the abbreviation of *literature*. The expression was first used by college students to refer informally to a course in the Female Literary Tradition at Princeton in the 1980s. In 1995 Cris Mazza and Jeffrey DeShell used it as an ironic title for their anthology of 22 short fiction pieces, *Chick Lit. Postfeminist Fiction*. The stories were all written by unknown female writers, the protagonists were all female, and they all dealt with issues of modern women and were characterized by a humorous and light-hearted tone (Mazza 2006: 4; Harzewski 2011).

Several scholars who have studied the *chick lit* genre ((Ferriss and Young 2006; Mazza and DeShell 1995) agree in stating that it originated in the nineteenth-century novels written by women, in particular those of Jane Austen and Emily Brontë. The influence is particularly evident in the plot formulas and in the female perspective of the stories. However, *chick lit* heroines often differ from those of nineteenth-century women's novels in various ways.

Firstly, the majority of *chick lit* novels are set in the contemporary world and the main characters are embedded in pop culture. They are usually single women in their twenties or thirties, who mostly work in the publishing or advertising sectors, and have an obsession with their appearance and especially with their weight.

Since *chick lit* often includes romantic elements, it has sometimes been considered as a subcategory of the romantic novel. The two genres differ, however, mainly because the sentimental relationships of the *chick lit* protagonists are not the only important issue in the plot. Indeed, their friends (who are usually either female or gay) are very important in their lives, just as is their career. Moreover, *chick lit* novels are distinguished especially by their tone, which is very personal and confidential and where humour is always present. The language used is usually informal and colloquial, as it is rich in slang words and expressions, and occasionally in obscene terms (Baratz-Logsted 2005; Ferriss and Young 2006; Harzewski 2011; Montoro 2012).

As already mentioned, *Bridget Jones's Diary* is considered to be one of the best-known examples of the genre. It is written in the form of a personal diary and narrates the life of the protagonist – Bridget Jones – throughout a whole year. Bridget is a single woman in her early thirties who lives in London and, as the book begins, works in the advertising sector of a book publishing company, although she later resigns and finds a new job with a television channel. She is the quintessential goofball who never fails to make a fool of herself. She is obsessed with her love life, she is constantly looking for a stable relationship, not least because she feels that this is what is expected by her family, friends and society in general. She leads a most unhealthy lifestyle as she overindulges in smoking and drinking. Furthermore, anyone who is familiar with the character of Bridget Jones knows that one of her most characteristic peculiarities is her particular relationship with food. This peculiarity will be thoroughly analysed in the following pages.

Bridget and food

Bridget is obsessed with her weight. She is rather overweight (actress Renée Zellweger, who plays the role of Bridget Jones in the cinematic adaptation, had to put on about 30 pounds for the part) and is constantly on a diet. In spite of this, she stuffs herself with whatever she finds. Whenever she starts a new entry of the diary, she writes down a detailed account of her weight and of the previous day's intake of calories (as well as the quantity of alcohol units consumed and the number of cigarettes smoked).

The diary starts on the 1st of January and (after the first two pages where Bridget lists her good resolutions for the New Year) we can get a clear idea about her relationship with food from the very beginning:

> *Sunday 1 January*
> 9st 3 (but post-Christmas), alcohol units 14 (but effectively covers 2 days as 4 hours of party was on New Year's Day),cigarettes 22, calories 5424.
> *Food consumed today:*
> 2 pkts Emmenthal cheese slices
> 14 cold new potatoes
> 2 Bloody Marys (count as food as contain Worcester sauce and tomatoes)
> ⅓ Ciabatta loaf with Brie
> Coriander leaves ½ packet

> 12 Milk Tray (best to get rid of all Christmas confectionery in one go and make fresh start tomorrow)
> 13 cocktail sticks securing cheese and pineapple
> Portion Una Alconbury's turkey curry, peas and bananas
> Portion Una Alconbury's Raspberry Surprise made with Bourbon biscuits, tinned raspberries, eight gallons of whipped cream, decorated with glacé cherries and angelica (Fielding 1996: 7)

It is possible to note that Bridget's diet in a single day ranges among the most varied foods, from cheese (Emmenthal and Brie) to potatoes, from Bloody Marys (which she considers food as they contain Worcester sauce and tomatoes) to coriander leaves, chocolate bars, turkey curry and raspberry surprise. Indeed, quite often Bridget combines the most curious culinary elements, and this does not so much depend on her tastes, but rather on the food that happens to be available.

In the book there are other examples of similarly detailed accounts, where Bridget gorges herself with the most varied foods in a single day:

> [...] This morning I definitely felt the beginnings of morning sickness, but that could be because I was so hungover after Daniel finally left yesterday that I ate the following things to try to make myself feel better:
> 2 packets Emmenthal cheese slices.
> 1 litre freshly squeezed orange juice.
> 1 cold jacket potato.
> 2 pieces unbaked lemon cheesecake (very light; also possibly eating for two).
> 1 Milky Way (125 calories only. Body's enthusiastic response to cheesecake suggested baby needed sugar).
> 1 chocolate Viennoise dessert thing with cream on top (greedy baby incredibly demanding)
> Steamed broccoli (attempt to nourish baby and stop it growing up spoilt).
> 4 cold Frankfurter sausages, (only available tin in cupboard - too exhausted by pregnancy to go out to shop again). (Fielding 1996: 115)

In the passage above, Bridget believes she is pregnant and, in spite of this, she keeps eating anything she finds, with no concerns at all about the health of the baby, ranging from Emmenthal cheese to potatoes, from lemon cheesecake to chocolate bars, from chocolate dessert to steamed broccoli and (cold) sausages.

Bridget is so obsessed with her weight that she knows the exact number of calories contained in any food element. During a conversation with her friend Tom she displays such ability. When he, astonished, asks her how she can possibly know all that, Bridget replies that it is just natural for her, just like everybody knows the alphabet or times tables... only to show one moment later that she does not know either the former or the latter.

> 'How many calories are you supposed to eat if you're on a diet?' he said.
> 'About a thousand. Well, I usually aim for a thousand and come in at about fifteen hundred,' I said, realizing as I said it that the last bit wasn't strictly true.
> 'A thousand?' said Tom, incredulously. 'But I thought you needed two thousand just to survive.'
> I looked at him nonplussed. I realized that I have spent so many years being on a diet that the idea that you might actually need calories to survive has been completely wiped out of my consciousness. Have reached point where believe nutritional ideal is to eat nothing at all and that the only reason people eat is because they are so greedy they cannot stop themselves from breaking out and ruining their diets.
> 'How many calories in a boiled egg?' said Tom.
> 'Seventy-five.'
> 'Banana?'
> 'Large or small?'
> 'Small.'
> 'Peeled?'
> 'Yes.'
> 'Eighty,' I said, confidently.
> 'Olive?'
> 'Black or green?'
> 'Black.'
> 'Nine.'
> 'Hobnob?'
> 'A hundred and twenty-one.'
> 'Box of Milk Tray?'
> 'Ten thousand eight hundred and ninety-six.'
> 'How do you know all this?'
>   I thought about it. 'I just do, as one knows one's alphabet or times tables.'
> 'OK. Nine eights,' said Tom.
> 'Sixty-four. No, fifty-six. Seventy-two.'
> 'What letter comes before J? Quick.'
> 'P. L, I mean.' (Fielding 1996: 257-58)

Bridget's obsession for her weight sometimes leads her to strive seriously to diet, but to no avail. In the following passage, we can see that she brings some significant changes to the Scarsdale Diet and guzzles wine, fried food and desserts:

> *Breakfast*: hot-cross bun (Scarsdale Diet — slight variation on specified piece of wholemeal toast); Mars Bar (Scarsdale Diet — slight variation on specified half grapefruit)

Snack: two bananas, two pears (switched to F-plan as starving and cannot face Scarsdale carrot snacks). Carton orange juice (Anti-Cellulite Raw-Food Diet)

Lunch: jacket potato (Scarsdale Vegetarian Diet) and hummus (Hay Diet — fine with jacket spuds as all starch, and breakfast and snack were all alkaline-forming with exception of hot-cross bun and Mars: minor aberration)

Dinner: four glasses of wine, fish and chips (Scarsdale Diet and also Hay Diet — protein forming); portion tiramisu; peppermint Aero (pissed). (Fielding 1996: 74)

Moreover, sometimes she works out some cranky and bizarre nutritional theories. For example, when she wakes up one morning and discovers that she put on three pounds during the night while she was asleep, Bridget wonders whether some food can possibly chemically react with other food, double its density and volume, and then solidify into denser fat. On another occasion, she compares the relationship between food and weight to that between garlic and bad breath, so that if you eat several bulbs then your breath does not smell and, similarly, if you eat industrial quantities of food you may not put on any weight at all:

> *9 a.m.* Aargh. How can I have put on 3lb since the middle of the night? I was 9st 4 when I went to bed, 9st 2 at 4 a.m. and 9st 5 when I got up. I can understand weight coming off — it could have evaporated or passed out of the body into the toilet — but how could it be put on? Could food react chemically with other food, double its density and volume, and solidify into every heavier and denser hard fat? (Fielding 1996:74)

> How come have put on only 8oz after last night's over-consumption orgy? Maybe food and weight are the same as garlic and stenchful breath: if you eat several entire bulbs your breath doesn't smell at all, similarly if you eat huge amount does not cause weight gain: strangely cheering theory but creates v. bad situation in head. (Fielding 1996: 124-25)

The quality of food that recurs the most in Bridget's culinary accounts is without any doubt junk food. Chocolate bars, in particular, are extremely recurrent in the diary entries, where Bridget mentions in a very detailed way both the brand names and the companies that produce them. In the passages reported earlier, she mentions Milk Tray, Milky Way and Areo. There are yet more references to chocolate snacks:

> Anyway, have got giant tray-sized bar of *Cadbury's Dairy Milk* left over from Christmas on dressing table, also amusing joke gin and tonic miniature. Am going to consume them and have fag. (Fielding 1996: 17)

Milky Way

> Obviously, it is like eating the last *Milk Tray* or taking the last slice of a cake. (51)

> He was holding three boxes of *Milk Tray*. (127)

> I started eating all the nut, praline, fudge or caramel-based chocolates out of my box of *Milk Tray*. (128)

> You bring me *Dairy Box*, please, instead of *Quality Street*? [...] Get us a *Twix* and a *Lion* bar. (242)

It is clear that Bridget is not exactly a marvellous cook and feeds herself with pre-packed food products that do not require much preparation (and, as we have seen, she sometimes eats them as they are, without even heating them). On some occasions, however, she tries to show off her culinary skills to impress other people. After pondering various options, she decides to give a dinner party for her birthday in her flat for 19 guests. She immediately comes up with the idea of cooking a typically Anglo-Saxon dish, namely shepherd's pie. She then gets carried away with enthusiasm and decides to serve it with other dishes whose preparation is rather complicated:

> Have decided to serve the shepherd's pie with Chargrilled Belgian Endive Salad, Roquefort Lardons and Frizzled Chorizo, to add a fashionable touch (have not tried before but sure it will be easy), followed by individual Grand Marnier soufflés. (Fielding 1996: 82)

The results are catastrophic. Bridget sets up for failure the very moment she starts cooking. She is all fingers and thumbs, she does not have the ingredients she needs, she does thousands of things at once and does not manage to complete a single dish of all the ones she had planned. Eventually, she is saved by her friends, who take her to a restaurant. The description of the events is extremely funny:

> *6.30 p.m.* Cannot go on. Have just stepped in a pan of mashed potato in new kitten-heel black suede shoes from Pied à terre (Pied-à-pomine-de-terre, more like), forgetting that kitchen floor and surfaces were covered in pans of mince and mashed potato. It is already 6.30 and have to go out to Cullens for Grand Marnier soufflé ingredients and other forgotten items. [...]
> *Schedule:*
> *6.30.* Go to shop.
> *6.45.* Return with forgotten groceries.
> *6.45-7.* Assemble shepherd's pie and place in oven (oh God, hope will all fit).
> *7-7.05.* Prepare Grand Marnier soufflés. (Actually think will have a little taste of Grand Marnier now. It is my birthday, after all.)
> *7.05-7.10.* Mmm. Grand Marnier delicious. [...]
> *7.10-7.20.* Tidy up and move furniture to sides of room.
> *7.20-7.30.* Make frisse lardon frizzled chorizo thing. All of which leaves a clear half-hour to get ready so no need to panic. Must have a fag. Aargh. It's quarter to seven. How did that happen? Aargh.
> *7.15 p.m.* Just, got back from shop and realize have forgotten butter,
> *7.35 p.m.* Shit, shit shit. The shepherd's pie is still in pans all over the kitchen floor and have not yet washed hair.
> *7.40 p.m.* Oh my God. Just looked for milk and realized have left the carrier bag behind in the shop. Also had the eggs in it. That means... Oh God, and the olive oil... so cannot do frizzy salad thing.
> *7.40 p.m.* Hmm. Best plan, surely, is to get into the bath with a glass of champagne then get ready. At least if I look nice I can carry on cooking when everyone is here and maybe can get Tom to go out for the missing ingredients.
> *7.55 p.m.* Aargh. Doorbell. Am in bra and pants with wet hair. Pie is all over floor. Suddenly hate the guests. [...]
> *2 a.m.* Feeling v. emotional. At door were Magda, Tom, Shazzer and Jude with bottle of champagne. They said to hurry up and get ready and when I had dried hair and dressed they had cleaned up all the kitchen and thrown away the shepherd's pie. It turned out Magda had booked a big table at 192 and told everyone to go there instead of my flat, and there they all were waiting with presents, planning to buy me dinner. Magda said they had had a weird, almost spooky sixth sense that the Grand Marnier soufflé and frizzled lardon thing were not going to work out. (Fielding 1996: 82-84)

The book presents another episode when Bridget decides to cook a meal, and once more the aim is to impress somebody, specifically Mark Darcy, a rich barrister for whom she develops a sentimental interest. Despite her poor cooking skills, awkward and clumsy Bridget aims high. On this occasion she even comes up with the idea of cooking Michelin style. In order to make it, she buys a book written by the well-known chef Marco Pierre White, working out a menu which is decidedly ambitious, which, however, seems absolutely easy to her: velouté of celery, grilled tuna on velouté of cherry tomatoes coulis with confit of garlic and potatoes, and confit of oranges with Grand Marnier creme-anglaise for dessert:

> V. excited about dinner party. Have bought marvellous new recipe book by Marco Pierre White. At last understand the simple difference between home cooking and restaurant food. As Marco says, it is all to do with concentration of taste. The secret of sauces, of course, apart from taste concentration, lies in real stock. One must boil up large pans of fish bones, chicken carcasses, etc., then freeze them in form of ice-stockcubes. Then cooking to Michelin star standard becomes as easy as making shepherd's pie: easier, in fact, as do not need to peel potatoes, merely confit them in goose fat. Cannot believe have not realized this before.
> This will be the menu:
> Velouté of Celery (v. simple and cheap when have made stock).
> Char-grilled Tuna on Velouté of Cherry Tomatoes Coulis with Confit of Garlic and Fondant Potatoes.
> Confit of Oranges. Grand Marnier Creme Anglaise. (Fielding 1996: 255-56)

Also in this case, as could be easily foreseen, the results are not the ones she hoped for and, after various amusing events, Bridget ends up serving blue soup, omelette and marmalade. At least she finally realizes that she is not a Michelin-star cook person...

> Have to start preparations tonight as working tomorrow.
> *8 p.m.* Ugh, do not feel like cooking. Especially dealing with grotesque bag of chicken carcasses: completely disgusting.
> *10 p.m.* Have got chicken carcasses in pan now. Trouble is, Marco says am supposed to tie flavour-enhancing leek and celery together with string but only string have got is blue. Oh well, expect it will be OK.
> *11 p.m.* God, stock took bloody ages to do but worth it as will end up with over 2 gallons, frozen in ice-cube form and only cost £1.70. Mmm, confit of oranges will be delicious also. Now all have got to do is finely slice thirty-six oranges and grate zest. Shouldn't take too long.
> *1 a.m.* Too tired to stay awake now but stock is supposed to cook for another two hours and oranges need another hour in oven. I know. Will leave the stock on v. low heat overnight, also oranges on lowest oven setting, so will become v. tender in manner of a stew.
> *9.30 a.m.* Just opened pan. Hoped-for 2-gallon stock taste-explosion has turned into burnt chicken carcasses coated in jelly. Orange confit looks fantastic, though, just like in picture only darker. Must go to work. [...]

7 p.m. Just got home. Right. Calm, calm. Inner poise. Soup will be absolutely fine. Will simply cook and purée vegetables as instructed and then - to give concentration of flavour - rinse blue jelly off chicken carcases and boil them up with cream in the soup.

8.30 p.m. All going marvellously. Guests are all in living room. Mark Darcy is being v. nice and brought champagne and a box of Belgian chocolates. Have not done main course yet apart from fondant potatoes but sure will be v. quick. Anyway, soup is first.

8.35 p.m. Oh my God. Just took lid off casserole to remove carcasses. Soup is bright blue.

9 p.m. Love the lovely friends. Were more than sporting about the blue soup, Mark Darcy and Tom even making lengthy argument for less colour prejudice in the world of food. [...] Never mind, anyway. Main course will be v. tasty. Right, will start on velouté of cherry tomatoes.

9.15 p.m. Oh dear. Think there must have been something in the blender, e.g. Fairy Liquid, as cherry tomato purée seems to be foaming and three times original volume. Also fondant potatoes were meant to be ready ten minutes ago and are hard as rock. Maybe should put in microwave. Aargh aargh. Just looked in fridge and tuna is not there. What has become of tuna? What? What?

9.30 p.m. Thank God. Jude and Mark Darcy came in kitchen and helped me make big omelette and mashed up half-done fondant potatoes and fried them in the frying pan in manner of hash browns [...]. At least orange confit will be good. Looks fantastic. Tom said not to bother with Grand Marnier Crème Anglaise but merely drink Grand Marnier.

10 p.m. V. sad. Looked expectantly round table as everyone took first mouthful of confit. There was an embarrassed silence. 'What's this, hon?' said Tom eventually. 'Is it marmalade?' Horror-struck, took mouthful myself. It was, as he said, marmalade. Realize after all effort and expense have served my guests:
Blue soup
Omelette
Marmalade

Am disastrous failure. Michelin-star cookery? Kwik-fit, more like. (Fielding 1996: 266-271)

Bridget, one of us

Bridget Jones is a woman with many flaws, an awkward and clumsy woman, a woman who is the opposite of the perfect epitome represented by the many female characters portrayed in books, in the cinema and on television. Maybe this is the reason why she has been so successful with female readers, because so many women have identified with her. Her relationship with food is no doubt an element of paramount importance in the portrayal of her identity.

All women have been on a diet at some point in their lives. How often have we vented our frustrations and stress by binging on sweets or junk food? How often have we said 'I'll start my diet on Monday!'? This is why it is easy and natural to sympathize with her. Bridget Jones is not a woman on a glossy cover of a fashion magazine. 'We are all Bridget' (Giovanetti 2009: 98). Bridget Jones is one of us.

Works cited

Baratz-Logsted, L. (ed.) 2005. *This is Chick-Lit*. Dallas, BenBella Books.
Ferriss, S. 2006. Narrative and Cinematic Doubleness: *Pride and Prejudice* and *Bridget Jones's Diary*. In S. Ferriss and M. Young (eds), *Chick Lit: the New Woman's Fiction*: 71-86. New York, Routledge.
Ferriss, S. and Young, M. (eds) 2006. *Chick-Lit: the New Woman's Fiction*. New York, Routledge.
Fielding, H. 2006, *Bridget Jones's Diary* [1996]. London, Picador.
Giovanetti, S. 2009. Chick Lit: una letteratura rosa shopping. In L. Del Grosso Destrieri, A. Brodesco, S. Giovanetti, S. Zanatta (eds), *Una galassia rosa. Ricerche sulla letteratura femminile di consumo*: 85-136. Milano, Franco Angeli.
Harzewski, S. 2011. *Chick-Lit and Post Feminism (Cultural Frames, Framing Culture)*. Charlottesville VA, University of Virginia Press.
Mazza, C. and DeShell, J. 1995. *Chick-Lit: Postfeminist Fiction*. Tallahassee, FC2.
Mazza, C. 2006. Who's laughing now? A short history of chick-lit and the perversion of a genre. In S. Ferriss and M. Young, (eds), *Chick-Lit: The New Woman's Fiction*: 17-28. New York, Routledge.
Montoro, R. 2012. *Chick Lit: The Stylistics of Cappuccino Fiction*. London, Continuum.

Shepherd's pie

Ingredients for 6 servings
1lb Beef or Lamb; minced (ground)
1 large Onion; sliced
1lb Carrots; grated (coarsely)
½ lb Peas; frozen or fresh
2lb Potatoes; peeled and chopped for boiling
Gravy Browning or Liquid Bovril
Cheese, (to your liking) grated
1 tablespoon Cooking oil

Preparation
Peel potatoes and add to pan of cold water.
Grate carrots coarsely.

Peel and chop the onion finely, add it to a medium saucepan with the cooking oil, saute gently until it turns a golden colour.

Add the minced beef to the onions and cook until browned, drain excess liquid into a jug.

Place the meat and onion mixture into a pyrex or enamel dish large enough to take the pie, mix in the frozen peas or fresh peas and carrots.

Using the liquid left over from the meat return it to the pan, and add gravy browning or Liquid Bovril to your own taste, thicken with a little cornstarch (cornflour) and add to the meat mixture.

Boil the potatoes until done, then drain and mash well with a little butter or margarine (a walnut sized piece or more if you like the buttery flavour)

Turn the potatoes out onto the top of the meat mixture and spread well, making sure it touches the sides of the dish.

Fluff the top well with a fork so that there are little peaks in it.

Bake in the oven on the middle shelf at about 350 degrees Fahrenheit until golden brown and crispy on top (approximately 30 minutes).

Remove from the oven and scatter the grated cheese all over the potato topping and place back in the oven for 5 more minutes or until melted.

Ready in 1 hour.

Dalila Forni

Coraline: frozen food vs a warm-hearted family?

Philip Pullman defined it 'a marvellously strange and scary book' (Pullman 2002: 1) and Neil Gaiman's *Coraline* (2002) is indeed a strange and scary book that harks back to traditional themes in children's literature, reinterpreting them in a modern context. For example, the author makes use of gothic elements derived from the Brothers Grimm's tales; he creates an absurd and dreamlike atmosphere, like that of *Alice in Wonderland*, but he also provides the story with a moral firmly rooted in the present age.

The main character of the novel is Coraline Jones, an eleven-year-old girl who has to move to a strange flat with her parents, who are usually too busy with their work to take care of her properly. The girl's attention is immediately caught by a door that opens on a wall of bricks. Coraline loves to explore, and she manages to cross this threshold and enter a parallel universe where she is welcomed by her lovely 'other mother' and 'other father', two distorted copies of her real parents that have two inexpressive black buttons instead of eyes. The house is identical to Coraline's real flat, but in this new world the protagonist finds all the attentions her real family cannot give her. However, she soon discovers that the other mother is a witch who has kidnapped her real parents in order to trap the girl in the world behind the door. The book is enriched with illustrations by David McKean, who artfully depicts the fantastic and partially gothic atmosphere imagined by Gaiman.

Dining with the Joneses

One of the key elements in *Coraline* is food, which has many different meanings. Firstly, it represents the bond – or the lack of it – between two people who are usually part of the same family or, in some cases, are simply friends. Secondly, cooking is a feature used to show that the female figure has undergone some changes, and that nowadays it is more realistic to tell fairy tales and stories about working mothers, and not about women always struggling in the kitchen. Finally, food represents a temptation, a bait to trap Coraline in the other world, in addition to being an element that creates a distant and fabulous atmosphere.

The protagonist of the novel has a particular relationship with her parents: the reader does not know what they do for a living, but they both spend a lot of time at home, working in front of their laptops, and at times they seem quite annoyed by their daughter's presence in the room. Coraline feels lonely, gets easily bored and spends her days exploring the house and the garden. Gaiman depicts a modern family where children are not taken care of by their parents, but are left alone because adults are too busy with their occupations. In particular, lunch or dinner are the moments that show the reader the difference between the Joneses and the stereotyped and ideal family of fairy tales: the meal does not bring together parents and children as used to happen in older tales, but once again sets them apart. Coraline's mother does not like to cook, while her father usually conducts strange experiments in the kitchen, cooking dishes that are not really appreciated by the girl since they are too complex. To quote Gaiman:

> Coraline's father stopped working and made them all dinner.
> Coraline was disgusted. 'Daddy,' she said, 'You've made a *recipe* again.' 'It's leek and potato stew, with a tarragon garnish and melted Gruyère cheese,' he admitted.
> Coraline sighed. Then she went to the freezer and got out some microwave chips and a microwave mini-pizza.
> 'You know I don't like recipes,' she told her father, while her dinner went round and round and the little red numbers on the microwave oven counted down to zero.
> 'If you tried it, maybe you'd like it,' said Coraline's father, but she shook her head. (Gaiman 2002: 18)

The narrator describes this scene only once, but the reader understands that this is a common habit among the Joneses. The protagonist's parents are not particularly interested in her nutrition, which is quite a common characteristic in modern families. Coraline's mother does not encourage her daughter to eat healthy food, but simply warms up precooked products, and Coraline is satisfied with them since she has no other choice. Moreover, Mrs Jones does not even appreciate her husband's recipes, which are certainly bizarre, but healthy and nourishing (Stephens 2013: 51). As a consequence the Joneses' fridge is often empty or full of frozen and precooked food, easy and fast to prepare, as we can see in this passage:

> They got home around lunchtime. [...] Coraline's mother looked in the fridge, and found a sad little tomato and a piece of cheese with green stuff growing on it. There was only a crust in the bread bin. 'I'd better dash down to the shops and get some fishfingers or something,' said her mother. (Gaiman 2002: 35)

In Ann Alston's opinion, food – but also where and how you eat it – might represent the wellbeing – or the malaise – of a family. Indeed, food is not just nourishment, just as the house is not simply a building where you live. Cooking in children's literature is often linked to the idea of a united and lovely family.

Actually, a good family, from any social class, would probably eat homemade food prepared by the mother, with dishes varying depending on their economic status; by contrast, a family which is not united would probably eat ready-made dishes in different rooms and at different times. A significant example is to be found in *Charlie and the Chocolate Factory* by Roald Dahl: the Buckets are extremely poor and can only afford cabbages. Dinner, however, is an important moment since they share what they have with love: the mother cooks the simple meal with care, and they are presented as a strong and united family even in times of trouble. Similarly, Coraline wishes her parents to be more attentive to her needs and to be more thoughtful, especially at dinnertime. As Ann Alston puts it: 'The sharing of food acts as a metaphor for family relationships; to eat the same food emphasizes a sense of belonging, it is an act of union, for the word 'companion' literally means to 'break bread with', and the good family as it shares blood, should share the same food' (2008: 109).

However, Alston highlights that lunch and dinner are also moments of control: to nourish someone means not just to take care of, but also to dominate him or her. A teenager who refuses to eat food cooked by her parents – as Coraline does, since she does not want to taste her father's recipes – probably intends to rebel against adult authority (Alston 2008: 105). The conflicting relationship between Coraline and her family is not entirely caused by the absence of her parents, but it is also due to Coraline's behaviour towards her mother and her father: she is not willing to compromise with them, most of all for what concerns food. For instance, when her mother asks Coraline to go to the supermarket with her, so that they can buy something she likes, the protagonist prefers to stay home alone. The same happens with her father's recipes: Coraline does not want to taste them 'on principle' (Gaiman 2002: 40).

Despite the strong contrast between parents and daughter, Keeling notices that Coraline and her father like the same food. Mr Jones uses potatoes and leeks as principal ingredients, two vegetables typical of England that he re-imagines with creativity, while Coraline prefers precooked French fries warmed up in the microwave (Keeling 2012: 6). The two dishes have the same origin, but are prepared following different methods: as a consequence, it is not food itself that divides the girl and her parents, but the way in which food is cooked. On the one hand, the father loves to be creative and invents strange and complex recipes linked to Britain's tradition; on the other, Coraline prefers simple meals easy to prepare, such as frozen food. Ready-made products became very popular in the UK in the 1950s: working families appreciated precooked food, which was – and still is – very convenient if you want to dine without spending much time in the kitchen after a long day at work. Consequently, the fact that Coraline mainly eats microwaved potatoes or frozen fish fingers places her within the English tradition, but also in a specific social class and in a specific period of time: the working class of the second half of the 20th century, when precooked products became more and more popular (Keeling 2012: 8).

In Gaiman's novel food is also used to deconstruct transformations occurring in female identity. On the one hand, Coraline's father has fun in the kitchen, mixing new ingredients with older flavours; on the other hand, the girl's mother allows her to eat ready-made food and she only cooks – or better, warms up – frozen products. Thus, the Joneses are a contemporary family in which the male figure is the one interested in housekeeping, while the female character differs from the traditional stereotype, which sees her as sheltered in the house as the 'natural place' of the mother and the wife.

As a consequence, the fact that Coraline eats exclusively precooked meals may suggest to conservative readers that her mother is unable to cook and therefore she is not doing her 'job' properly (Keeling 2012: 8). While hardly able to cook, Mrs Jones is not particularly attentive to Coraline's needs and she is presented as a negligent mother: she forgets to go shopping, she cannot remember when her daughter's school starts, she has no time to spend with her and, when Coraline cuts her knee, she does not bandage the wound (Russel 2012: 170). Despite all this, Mrs Jones has a complex personality characterized by different attitudes, and for this reason she cannot be defined as a totally negative figure. Gaiman shows some positive aspects of the woman too: for example, she encourages her daughter to explore the house and the garden, telling her to be careful; she warns her that the weather is cold and she should wear some warm clothes; she stops working, even if just for a few minutes, to answer her questions about the strange door. Mrs Jones is not the typical mother tied to her home, to kitchen and housework, but she is still a key figure for Coraline. Indeed, when her parents are kidnapped by the witch, Coraline immediately misses them, feeling even more lonely.

The mother's identity in children's literature is often shaped by the food she gives – or does not give – to her children: in a simplified vision of this feature, a mother who prepares food for her children is a good mother, while a mother who does not take care of their diet is a bad one (Alston 2008: 111). An example is the case of the typical stepmother of fairy tales who does not provide food to her stepchildren in order to get rid of them, as in Brothers Grimm's *Hansel and Gretel*.

However, Gaiman does not attack the figure of the modern mother who is not interested in her children's nutrition and leaves her husband working in the kitchen: the author simply criticizes a general carelessness. The girl simply wants someone to take care of her, to spend some time with her and give her more attention, especially at dinnertime, a moment when the family should be united (Russell 2012: 172). Even the policeman who answers the phone when Coraline calls the police to report her parents' kidnapping indirectly highlights the link between food and the love of a family:

> 'You ask your mother to make you a big old mug of hot chocolate, and then give you a great big old hug. There's nothing like hot chocolate and a hug for making the nightmares go away. And if she starts to tell you off for waking her up at this time of night, why you tell her that that's what the policeman said.' He had a deep, reassuring voice. Coraline was not reassured. (Gaiman 2002: 67)

Coraline cannot have a cup of hot chocolate since her mother has been kidnapped. And, even when at home, she has no time to prepare hot chocolate for her daughter. When Coraline's parents are trapped in the other world, by the other mother, Coraline is able to take care of herself without any problem: as usual, she eats ready-made food that can be prepared without her parents' help.

> Coraline went to the freezer and took out the spare loaf of frozen bread in the bottom compartment. She made herself some toast, with jam and peanut butter. She drank a glass of water. She waited for her parents to come back. When it began to get dark, Coraline microwaved herself a frozen pizza. [...] She ate tinned spaghetti for breakfast. For lunch she had a block of cooking chocolate and an apple. The apple was yellow and slightly shrivelled, but it tasted sweet and good. (Gaiman 2002: 61)

Despite eating the food she likes, Coraline is not very happy about her meals. The girl eats just to survive, and not because she finds pleasure in food, a pleasure that she does not know since in her family the choice is between the complex – and in some cases unsuccessful – recipes of the father or the tasteless frozen food warmed up by the mother. Moreover, when Coraline goes to the supermarket to buy something to eat, lunchtime has lost all value for her since she cannot share it with her family.

Behind the magic door

Once she has discovered the world behind the door, the situation is completely different. The other mother welcomes Coraline, emphasizing that she and the 'other father' had been waiting for her for a long time in order to become a real family: 'It wasn't the same here without you. But we knew you'd arrive one day, and then we could be a proper family' (Gaiman 2002: 39). Now at last Coraline is the most desired and necessary member of the family.

The first meeting between the girl and the other mother takes place in the kitchen. In order to make the protagonist stay in the world on the other side of the door, the two parents offer her a meal that satisfies Coraline's wishes entirely: it is not too complex, like her real father's recipes, but at the same time it is cooked and served with love by the other mother.

> They [Coraline and the other father] sat at the kitchen table and Coraline's other mother brought them lunch. A huge, golden-brown roasted chicken, fried potatoes, tiny green peas. Coraline shovelled the food into her mouth. It tasted wonderful. [...] It was the best chicken that Coraline had ever eaten. Her mother sometimes made chicken, but it was always out of packets, or frozen, and was very dry, and it never tasted of anything. When Coraline's father cooked chicken he bought real chicken, but he did strange things to it, like stewing it in wine, or stuffing it with prunes, or baking it in pastry, and Coraline would always refuse to touch it on principle. (Gaiman 2002: 40)

The food prepared by the other mother is simple, tasty and genuine. Hers are the traditional common dishes that can recreate the stereotype of the family dinner, making the girl trust her new parents. Coraline can finally enjoy lunch and dinner feeling serene and comfortable: in the other world she does not find three people sitting at the table, but a family which is happy to share a moment of union and sharing. Furthermore, the fact that the two other parents relish their meal makes the group even more united by common feelings usually absent from Coraline's real life, since her real parents eat dinner just to survive, and not because they like what they are tasting. In addition, the food eaten in the other family is defined by Stephens as 'comfort food' (Stephens 2013: 53). Such traditional food carries with it positive memories about pleasant meetings, such as being with the family and sharing some good moments. (Stephens 2013 53). Thus, the real mother and the other mother represent two different models of English womanhood: one is a female figure coming from the working class who prefers the comfort of ready-made food; the other a traditional woman, who prefers to cook homemade dishes with fresh produce.

Moreover, in Stephens' opinion the meal apparently prepared with love by the other mother represents a very recurring feature in children's literature: temptation through food. In children's novels and fairy tales food is nourishing, but also entails potential danger: to eat a dish offered by a stranger means to betray the family and, at the same time, to fall into otherness, into a different and unknown world (Alston 2008: 109). In literature – from any place and written at any time – we can find many examples in which food is presented as an element of temptation. Persephone tastes the pomegranate seeds in the underworld and is forced to stay there forever; Adam and Eve are sent away from Eden because of the apple offered them by the serpent; Snow White is poisoned by the apple prepared by her stepmother; Hansel and Gretel are trapped by the witch who attracts them with the gingerbread house; Alice, moved mainly by curiosity, like Coraline, is tempted by food that makes her larger and smaller in Wonderland; finally, Beatrix Potter's Peter Rabbit is attracted by the vegetables cultivated in Mr McGregor's garden. Moreover, Alston notes that in *Coraline* there are no direct consequences after tasting the forbidden food of the other mother: the girl is not punished and she still has the possibility to save her parents and bring them back to her real house (Alston 2008: 111). Food is not a dangerous element in itself, but is the bait used by the other mother to keep Coraline in her world.

The episode of the meal as a temptation can be compared with *The Chronicles of Narnia* by C. S. Lewis. The White Witch – compare Coraline's other mother – tempts little Edmund with a Turkish Delight, a sweetmeat from Turkey brought to Europe by the English. Both the other mother and the White Witch have a white skin. Coraline is welcomed in the other world with such a tasty dinner that she completely ignores various creepy details that characterize the other mother, who is different from the real one in some physical aspects, namely her white skin and long fingers. We can deduce from this that temptation through food is effective: Coraline does not notice the other mother's real nature; this is only discovered in the second part of the book (Stephens 2013: 55).

When Coraline meets the ghosts of three children in a dark space behind a mirror, they warn her: the woman has evil intentions and Coraline is in danger of ending up like them. The children define her as a 'beldam', an archaic word meaning an old woman with supernatural powers, a kind of witch. Stephens interprets this term as an abbreviation of Belle Dame Sans Merci, a figure that shows her (false) love to conquer her prey (Stephen 2012: 59). Moreover, the talking cat who accompanies Coraline in her adventures behind the door supposes that the woman wants to eat the children she traps to consume their energies and their love. Consequently, food reveals the true identity of the other mother. While the woman at the beginning, in order to deceive Coraline, eats with her the roast chicken with potatoes she has prepared, she later gobbles some black beetles before the girl:

> Expecting it to be a toffee or a butterscotch ball, Coraline looked down. The bag was half-filled with large shiny black beetles, crawling over each other in their efforts to get out of the bag.
> 'No,' said Coraline. 'I don't want one.'
> 'Suit yourself,' said her other mother. She carefully picked out a particularly large and black beetle, pulled off its legs (which she dropped, neatly, into a big glass ashtray on the small table beside the

> sofa), and popped the beetle into her mouth. She crunched it happily. 'Yum,' she said, and took another.
> 'You're sick,' said Coraline. 'Sick and evil and weird.' (Gaiman 2002: 93)

If you really are what you eat, by eating black beetles the other mother is manifestly a weird and cruel person, seen as such by the protagonist, who from now on will mistrust her completely. The girl realizes the real nature of the other mother and refuses to surrender to the temptation of food, so as not to fall into her trap:

> 'I'll make us a midnight snack. And you'll want something to drink—hot chocolate, perhaps?' [...] 'I don't need a snack,' she said. 'I have an apple. See?' And she took an apple from her dressing-gown pocket, then bit into it with relish and an enthusiasm that she did not really feel. (Gaiman 2002: 74)

Coraline is a smart girl who manages to unveil the witch's plans and to save herself and her family without any help (Stephens, 2013: 56). When the following morning the other mother prepares her a full breakfast made of 'eggs and cheeses, butter and a slab of sliced pink bacon [...] along with a glass of freshly squeezed orange juice and a mug of frothy hot chocolate' (Gaiman 2002: 108), Coraline eats to comply, but not with the pleasure she felt before. She does not touch the chocolate, so that she does not altogether meet her other mother's expectations, thus showing herself not to be completely in her power.

After experiencing the strong contrast between the dishes eaten with her real family and those prepared by the other mother, Coraline realizes that food is not just nourishing and tasty, but a token of love and attention, fundamental to her. Once she gets home, she also realizes how important it is to take the first step to have a better relation with her parents. Despite her father's pizza, not to her liking, Coraline eats it without complaining, learning to be more compliant with her family.

> Dinner that night was pizza, and even though it was home-made by her father (so the crust was alternately thick and doughy and raw, or too thin and burnt), and even though he had put slices of green pepper on it, along with little meatballs and, of all things, pineapple chunks, Coraline ate the entire slice she had been given. (Gaiman 2002: 162)

Another indication of the importance of the food element in the novel is the fact that food is used to characterize many secondary characters. There are for instance two old actresses living in the flat below Coraline's. When the girl visits them, Mrs Spink and Mrs Forcible create a kind of parody of the family Coraline would not want. At lunchtime they read tea leaves to predict the future: in their house one can feel a Victorian atmosphere, completely different from the context in which the novel takes place, as if it were a fairy tale within the fairy tale. This particular atmosphere is created not just by the habits of the two women, but most of all by the food they eat: they are used to drinking tea 'in a little pink bone-china cup with a saucer', with 'dry Garibaldi biscuits' (Gaiman 2002: 28), a sweet which was very popular in the second half of the nineteenth century.

Victorian strategies for a modern girl

The same 'antique' atmosphere is recreated in Coraline's dream once she is back home. The protagonist meets the three children she has saved from the other mother and plays with them in the garden, where they have a Victorian picnic:

> There was a white-linen cloth laid on the grass, with bowls piled high with food—she could see salads and sandwiches, nuts and fruit, jugs of lemonade and water and thick chocolate milk. Coraline sat on one side of the tablecloth while three other children took a side each. They were dressed in the oddest cloche. (Gaiman 2002: 163)

Food is not just the element that unites parents and children, but it may also unite a group of friends, even from different ages. The picnic appears again in the last pages of the book, when Coraline uses it as a bait to trap and defeat the other mother once for all. The girl recreates an apparently safe domestic scene near the old well in the garden: a tablecloth, some cups of tea and dolls to play with. In this way, the other mother's hand – the last piece which is left of the witch – comes forward and falls in the well. Coraline uses the same strategy chosen by the other mother, but in the opposite way: this time the girl uses food, to defeat and capture the witch. This choice of the Victorian tea party signals a subversive use of the patriarchal model that the other mother had tried to impose on Coraline (Stephens 2013: 62).

To conclude, Gaiman creates a story for children mixing together traditional and contemporary features. Food in particular is used for very different goals: it is an element of temptation and union of the family, as it was in traditional children's literature, but it is also the element that shows the reader the changes that have occurred in society, especially in the context of gender roles and family habits. Gaiman does not endorse conservative families, nor contemporary ones: as the moral of the tale goes, he simply notices the importance of good habits, such as family dinner. Whatever food is served, modern or traditional, the important thing is that it should be cooked and shared with love.

Works cited

Alston, A. 2004. There's No Place Like Home: The Ideological and Mythological Construction of House and Home in Children's Literature. In S. Chapleau (ed.), *New Voices in Children's Literature Criticism*: 55-62. London, Bookchase.

Alston, A. 2008. *The Family in English Children's Literature.* New York, Routledge.

Gaiman, N. 2002. *Coraline.* London, Bloomsbury Publishing.

Keeling, K. K. and Sprague, M. 2012. T*he Key is in the Mouth: Food and Orality in Coraline. Children's Literature* 40: 1-27.

Pullman, P. 2002. The Other Mother. *The Guardian* http://www.theguardian.com/books/2002/aug/31/booksforchildrenandteenagers.neilgaiman (accessed 30 June 2016).

Russell, D. 2012. Unmasking M(other)hood: Third-Wave Mothering in Gaiman's *Coraline* and *Mirror Mask*. In Prescott, T. and A. Drucker (eds), *Feminism in the Worlds of Neil Gaiman: Essays on the Comics, Poetry and Prose*: 161-176. Jefferson, McFarland.

Stephens, M. 2013. *Nothing More Delicious: Food as Temptation in Children's Literature,* Georgia Southern University, Electronic Theses & Dissertations, Paper 50, http://digitalcommons.georgiasouthern.edu/cgi/viewcontent.cgi?article=1050&context=etd

Garibaldi biscuits

In 1854 Giuseppe Garibaldi visited Tynemouth, in the North-East of England, where he received a warm welcome. But it was not until his successful campaigns in uniting Italy in 1860 that a new kind of biscuit was invented in his honour in England by John Carr. Garibaldi biscuits were made by Peek Freans (now United Biscuits) from 1861. They were much appreciated, and soon became a typically British accompaniment to a cup of tea.

Ingredients
9.5oz flour
2.5oz butter
2.5oz caster sugar
2.5 tsp yeast powder
4 tbsp milk
7oz currants
1 beaten egg white
1 pinch of salt
1 tsp granulated sugar

Directions
Put flour, yeast, salt and butter into a bowl, mix with your fingers until no lumps remain. Add caster sugar, 2oz currants and milk to make a stiff dough. Let stand in a cool place for half an hour. Divide the dough in two parts and roll them out onto the baking sheet to 0.2 inches thick. Sprinkle one half with currants, cover with the other piece of dough and roll the mixture again. Cut it into squares or rectangles, brush with beaten egg white and sprinkle with granulated sugar. Bake at 400° F for 15 minutes.

Garibaldi biscuits

Notes on the authors

CHIARA BISCELLA holds a PhD in English Literature from the University of Milan. She has published articles on William Shakespeare, on contemporary British drama and on women's writing. Her research interests include drama, gender studies and visual studies.

MARCO CANANI is a post-doctoral research fellow at the University of Milan, where he is working on the Italian reception of the works of John Keats and Percy Bysshe Shelley. He earned a PhD in English Literature in 2015 with a dissertation on *Vernon Lee and the Italian Renaissance: Plasticity, Gender, Genre*. He is the author of *Ellenismi britannici. L'ellenismo nella poesia, nelle arti e nella cultura britannica dagli augustei al Romanticismo* (2014), and has written essays and articles on John Keats, Percy Bysshe Shelley, and A.J. Cronin. In 2014 he co-edited the collection *Parallaxes: Virginia Woolf Meets James Joyce*. His research interests include Romantic poetry, Anglo-Italian relations, and gender studies.

CLAUDIA CREMONESI holds a PhD in Anglistics from the University of Milan. Her research interests include *life-writing* and the interaction between literature and visual studies. She has written on Charles Dickens and Virginia Woolf. For Aracne, she has published the volume: *'The proper writing of lives': Biography and the Art of Virginia Woolf* (2013).

DALILA FORNI received her BA from the University of Milan and subsequently her MA with a thesis on Roald Dahl's *Charlie and the Chocolate Factory* and its adaptations. At the moment she writes for an online magazine, and is interested in children's literature and the gothic.

FRANCESCA GORINI obtained a PhD in English Studies from the University of Milan in 2012 with a thesis on Kenneth Branagh's Shakespearean adaptations. Her interests include: adaptation studies, children's literature, and audiovisual translation.

GIOVANNI IAMARTINO is Professor of the History of English at the University of Milan, where he also teaches Middle English Literature. His major research interests include the history of English lexicography (and linguistic codification in general), historical translation studies, and the history of linguistic, literary and cultural relations between Italy and the English-speaking countries. Most recently, he co-edited (with Joan C. Beal) a monograph issue of *Language and History* (59:1, 2016) entitled *Towards a History of the English Normative Tradition*. Dictionary Johnson being his hero, Iamartino has long been a member of The

Samuel Johnson Society of North America; currently, he is also the President of the Italian Association for English Studies.

ANGELA ANNA IULIUCCI obtained a PhD in English Literature from the University of Milan, with a thesis on 'Grotesque and gothic children's literature: from XIX c. picturebooks up to Tim Burton.' Her BA thesis dealt with adaptations of Dickens's *Carol*; her MA thesis, 'Abbecedari, sillabari e grammatiche: i libri didattici per bambini nel Fondo P.A. Wick', explored didactic children's books. Among her publications: '*Home to Mother*: The Long Journey to not Lose One's Own Identity'; '*In Flanders Fields*: The Western Front for (and through) the Eyes of a Child'; '*Tales from Shakespeare* e *The Animated Shakespeare*: reinventare il Bardo per giovani lettori e spettatori' and 'Do not Simply Call Them Alphabet Books'. She is interested in children's literature and in the connection between literature and visual studies.

MARIA CRISTINA MANCINI graduated in Modern Languages with a dissertation on Gertrude Stein, and was awarded a grant to study 20th century American poetry at the Centro di Studi Americani in Rome. She teaches English and French in secondary and vocational schools in the province of Monza and Brianza. In her free time, she plays the violin in the amateur Orchestra Carisch.

BEATRICE MOJA is a PhD student at the State University of Milan. Her project is dedicated to it-narratives and toys in Anglophone children's literature and contemporary culture. She has written on Victorian food, Mrs Beeton (the theme of her MA thesis), and racism in children's literature. She is also interested in history of English drama and creative writing.

KARIN MOSCA obtained her MA in Foreign Languages and Literatures in 2015, from the University of Milan. Among her main interests is biography as a literary genre, as indicated by the title of her BA dissertation, on 'Elizabeth Gaskell and the Writing of Women Lives: from the Novel to the Biography' as well as that of her MA dissertation, on 'Lytton Strachey and the biographies of two queens: *Queen Victoria* (1921) and *Elizabeth and Essex* (1928)'. She currently works in Barcelona as a journalist for an international medical organisation. She is also editor of the poetry section in the Italian cultural magazine *VivaMag*.

ELENA OGLIARI holds an MA in English and Russian Literature from the University of Milan, where she graduated with a thesis on the literary relationship between Henry James and Ivan Turgenev. She is currently a PhD student in the Department of British Culture at the aforementioned university.

FRANCESCA ORESTANO, Professor of English Literature at the University of Milan, works in the areas of landscape aesthetics (William Gilpin and the picturesque, from the 18th century to present), garden history, Victorian and Dickens studies, art criticism and John Ruskin, the gothic and the baroque, and children's literature. Recent research includes: cultural responses to the Italian Renaissance, chemistry and Victorian taste, the child reader. She has edited the 2014 issue of *Cultural Perspectives* on 'History and Children's Literature', and since 2007 the website http://users.unimi.it/childlit.

CRISTINA PARAVANO is a post-doctoral research fellow at the University of Milan. After her BA in Foreign Languages and Literatures (2005) and MA in European and non-European Languages and Literatures (2007), she completed her PhD in 2011 with a dissertation on the Caroline playwright Richard Brome, under the supervision of Professors Margaret Rose and Richard Allen Cave (Royal Holloway). She is the author of *Shakespeare e Ovidio: due maestri a confronto* (2011). Her research interests lie in the areas of early modern drama, modern-contemporary theatre studies, source studies and young adult fiction.

ILARIA PARINI is a contract lecturer in English at the State University of Milan and at IULM, Milan, Italy. She graduated in Translation Studies and holds a PhD in English Linguistics and Translation. She has published the book *Italian American Gangsterspeak* (LAP 2013) and numerous studies on problems relating to the translation of contemporary language. She has presented papers at numerous international conferences.

MARGARET ROSE teaches British Theatre Studies at Milan State University. She has published widely in the areas of theatre translation studies, contemporary British drama and Shakespeare in performance. She led the EU workshop WWW Venice in partnership with Warwick, Szeged and Venice universities and co-led the three-year seminar 'Intercultural Dialogues', supported by the British Council in collaboration with Warwick University. Guest writers included Hanif Kureishi, Kwame Kwei-Armah and Rani Moorthy. In the context of the Shakespeare 400 anniversary, in 2016 she organized the international conference-festival, 'Will Forever Young' devoted to Shakespeare in popular culture.

ANNA RUDELLI, after a summer spent doing research in the Lake District, obtained her BA in Foreign Languages and Literatures in 2012, with the dissertation *A Portrait of the Artist as a Poet's Sister: Dorothy Wordsworth*. She then earned her MA (Milan University) with a dissertation on John Muir, naturalist. Her current research interests revolve around the culture and poetics of the garden from the point of view of gender and life-writing. She is a dedicated gardener.

MICHAEL VICKERS is Professor Emeritus of Archaeology at the University of Oxford, and Emeritus Senior Research Fellow in Classical Studies at Jesus College. His research interests include the archaeology, history and literature of the Greek and Roman worlds. His latest book, *Aristophanes and Alcibiades: Echoes of Contemporary History in Athenian Comedy* appeared in 2015. He spends much of his time in Georgia, and is often asked to put texts in Georgian English into English English. Co-editing this volume was by way of light relief.